BEEP
The Definitive Guide

BEEP
The Definitive Guide

Marshall T. Rose

O'REILLY®

Beijing · Cambridge · Farnham · Köln · Paris · Sebastopol · Taipei · Tokyo

BEEP: The Definitive Guide
by Marshall T. Rose

Published by O'Reilly & Associates, Inc., 1005 Gravenstein Highway North, Sebastopol, CA 95472.

O'Reilly & Associates books may be purchased for educational, business, or sales promotional use. Online editions are also available for most titles (*safari.oreilly.com*). For more information contact our corporate/institutional sales department: 800-998-9938 or *corporate@oreilly.com*.

Editor:	Mike Loukides
Production Editor:	Jane Ellin
Cover Designer:	Ellie Volckhausen
Interior Designer:	David Futato

Printing History:

March 2002:	First Edition.

ISBN: 0-596-00244-0

[M]

Dedicated to my good friend, Lee.

Table of Contents

Foreword

In 1998, in the middle of what looked like a boom but turned out to be a bubble, I started a company with the modest goal of "mapping the Internet." Our company didn't become the next Yahoo!, but we followed the yellow brick road all the way into the magic kingdom, which unfortunately turned out to be made of sand hills.

Much of the heavy lifting for our company was done by three people. I got all lawyered up and spent 18 months writing financial doodles and honing our pitch. My soon-to-be wife and long-time colleague, Rebecca Malamud, became our creative director. And Marshall Rose wrote (and implemented) a protocol.

Our company did the "dot-com" thing. We built something pretty cool, raised lots of money, and hired professionals who were better at spending money than we were. The professionals proceeded to spend money, Becky and I moved on to co-found *betterdogfood.com*, and Marshall worked on his protocol. When the professionals were done, there was no money left and the company dissolved.

The part that lasted was the protocol. Marshall thought long and hard about the problems we were trying to solve and, as he has always done, decided to solve another problem. He invented BEEP. BEEP helped us solve our metadata management problems, but it's also a core that supports a wide range of applications. BEEP is an application layer framework, a long-missing building block for the Internet.

Once Marshall wrote (and implemented) the protocol, some of the best minds in the Internet were asked to review the work. It was then submitted to the IETF for standardization. This fundamental piece of technology has been a quiet revolution, used by a growing cadre of developers trying to build new kinds of applications without repeating old kinds of mistakes.

Marshall has always been one of the seminal thinkers on the Internet. He helped the Internet vanquish OSI by the then-novel technique of implementing the specs and showing that they tried to solve so many problems that they solved none. His work on network management and messaging helped make those two crucial applications work. He was releasing open source software long before the term was invented. And, with BEEP, Marshall has shown us a better way to write network applications.

—Carl Malamud
San Francisco, California

Preface

BEEP is something like "the missing link between the application layer and TCP."

This statement is a horrific analogy because TCP is a transport *protocol* that provides reliable connections, and it makes no sense to compare a protocol to a layer. TCP is a highly-evolved protocol; many talented engineers have, over the last 20 years, built an impressive theory and practice around TCP. In fact, TCP is so good at what it does that when it came to survival of the fittest, it obliterated the competition. Even today, any serious talk about the transport protocol revolves around minor tweaks to TCP. (Or, if you prefer, the intersection between people talking about doing an "entirely new" transport protocol and people who are clueful is the empty set.)

Unfortunately, most application protocol design has not enjoyed as excellent a history as TCP. Engineers design protocols the way monkeys try to get to the moon—i.e., by climbing a tree, looking around, and finding another tree to climb. Perhaps this is because there are more distractions at the application layer. For example, as far as TCP is concerned, its sole reason for being is to provide a full-duplex octet-aligned pipe in a robust and network-friendly fashion. The natural result is that while TCP's philosophy is built around "reliability through retransmission," there isn't a common mantra at the application layer.

Historically, when different engineers work on application protocols, they come up with different solutions to common problems. Sometimes the solutions reflect differing perspectives on inevitable tradeoffs; sometimes the solutions reflect different skill and experience levels. Regardless, the result is that the wheel is continuously reinvented, but rarely improved.

So, what is BEEP and how does it relate to all this? BEEP integrates the best practices for common, basic mechanisms that are needed when designing an application protocol over TCP. For example, it handles things like peer-to-peer, client/server, and server/client interactions. Depending on how you count, there are about a dozen or so issues that arise time and time again, and BEEP just deals with them. This means that you get to focus on the "interesting stuff."

BEEP has three things going for it:

- It's been standardized by the IETF, the so-called "governing body" for Internet protocols.
- There are open source implementations available in different languages.
- There's a community of developers who are clueful.

The standardization part is important, because BEEP has undergone a lot of technical review. The implementation part is important, because BEEP is probably available on a platform you're familiar with. The community part is important, because BEEP has a lot of resources available for you.

The Intended Audience

This book is not for everyone. It is written with two audiences in mind:

- Designers who want to understand how BEEP works and when to use it
- Developers who want to use one of the open source APIs for BEEP

Please note that there are two market segments excluded from this list:

- Administrators who want to understand what's being used in their networks
- Developers who want to write a BEEP library

This book doesn't focus on administrators because the open source APIs for BEEP don't have much to offer the administrator. In time, that will likely change, but for now, there just isn't much to write about.

For the second audience, if you're going to write an API, this book will help by providing the context for what your customer expects, but you'll probably have a lot of questions that this book won't answer. Why is that?

In brief, it's a lot simpler to use an API for BEEP than to write one. Although most of BEEP's concepts are straightforward, there are a lot of interactions between them that make for some tricky implementation strategies. Considering that there aren't thousands of API developers for BEEP, you can see why it's not a good idea to clutter this book with that kind of detail.

However, assuming that you want to develop an API for BEEP, here's my gift to you—a list of issues that your API should transparently handle:

- Encoding piggyback data during channel creation
- Avoiding race conditions when closing a channel
- Enforcing the bidirectional "at most once" limitation on using a SASL mechanism with an active security layer or a transport security profile

- Enforcing the unidirectional "at most once" limitation on user authentication
- Making sure that stuff sent by the transport mapping doesn't interfere with transport security negotiations

Once you know about stuff like this, developing a robust implementation is a simple matter of coding. However, my point is that this book *does not* talk about those kinds of issues.

In fact, this book is a bit different than most of the books in the O'Reilly series, in that the concepts/software ratio is about 60/40. (I think that the typical O'Reilly ratio is closer to 20/80.) So keep this in mind.

Conventions Used in This Book

The following font conventions are used in this book:

Italic is used to introduce new terms and for URLs and filenames.

`Constant Width` is used to indicate code sections and for methods, objects, interfaces, class names, and package names.

 This icon indicates a tip, suggestion, or general note.

 This icon indicates a warning or caution.

We'd Like to Hear from You

Please address comments and questions concerning this book to the publisher:

O'Reilly & Associates, Inc.
1005 Gravenstein Highway North
Sebastopol, CA 95472
(800) 998-9938 (in the United States or Canada)
(707) 829-0515 (international or local)
(707) 829-0104 (fax)

We have a web page for this book, where we list errata, examples, or any additional information. You can access this page at:

http://www.oreilly.com/catalog/beep

To comment or ask technical questions about this book, send email to:

bookquestions@oreilly.com

For more information about our books, conferences, Resource Centers, and the O'Reilly Network, see our web site at:

http://www.oreilly.com

Acknowledgments

There's a long list of people whose work led to this book.

The original work leading up to BEEP was done at Invisible Worlds, a company founded by Carl Malamud. Carl gets credit for providing the initial problem to get solved, and allowing the solution to be presented to the IETF. The early work on BEEP was reviewed by the Invisible Worlds' Protocol Advisory Board, who, at that time, consisted of David Clark, David Crocker, Steve Deering, Danny Goodman, Paul Mockapetris, and Paul Vixie. Also during that time Brad Burdick and Frank Morton implemented the two initial prototypes of BEEP's predecessor.

In the standards world, Keith McCloghrie, one of my long-time collaborators on network management, was kind enough to chair the IETF working group for BEEP. David Crocker, Graham Klyne, and Darren New provided most of the heavy lifting in the working group and in many BEEP-related activities. Pete Resnick now chairs the follow-on working group for BEEP.

Back in the real world, Huston Franklin led the group (consisting of Eric Dixon, Jay Kint, Bill Mills, Scott Pead, and Mark Richardson) that produced two different implementations of BEEP. Darren New, as Free Radical at Invisible Worlds, was responsible for design and implementation of the "core" of beepcore-c, while Kris Magnusson developed and managed the *http://beepcore.org* community web site. Huston was also kind enough to rework a lot of the beepcore-c API in response to my first draft of this book. The resulting API is a lot cleaner. (Of course, I then had to rewrite the chapter, thereby proving the old adage, "In the hell that is the Internet, sinners get exactly what they ask for.")

Finally, David Crocker, Huston Franklin, Bruce Mitchener, Darren New, Chris Newman, and Pete Resnick were gracious in their comments as reviewers.

Personal Notes

This is the ninth book I've written, and the first for O'Reilly & Associates. If you're familiar with my earlier works, you may find the following of interest:

- There are no soapboxes or insider index entries in this book, so don't bother looking—I decided not to renew my liability coverage.
- Cheetah, the alley cat, is now 17 years old and still doing well.
- He is joined by a 3-year-old, 220-pound Mastiff named Oatman.

Or not, as the case may be. Perhaps the more interesting question is, why did I stop writing books in 1998?

The short answer is that nothing much has happened in the Internet since then—well, nothing interesting of a technical nature anyway. Although the Internet got a lot of press, and small fortunes were made and large ones were lost, none of this was due to technology. T.A. Edison was a brilliant businessman and engineer, yet he never once applied for a patent on a business process. The things he did patent were advances in technology. And this, perhaps, provides a concise explanation of the Internet boom and bust. For myself, I'll confess to having "done" a few start-ups, and having modestly reduced the performance of several venture funds. While few of these experiences were good ones, meeting a whole new class of gentry was certainly educational.

Finally, if you've gotten this far, you've noticed that my writing style is different from what you find in most of the books in O'Reilly's excellent series. (Perhaps the pet update was a tip-off.) While this causes a lot of grief to some, I think it makes my writing more readable. At the very least, it makes it more writable. Enjoy.

—Marshall T. Rose
Sacramento, California
November, 2001

## CHAPTER 1

Introduction

An application protocol is a set of rules that says how your application talks to the network. Over the last few years, HTTP has been pressed into service as a general-purpose application protocol for many different kinds of applications, ranging from the Internet Printing Protocol (IPP) to SOAP. This is great for application designers: it saves them the trouble of having to design a new protocol and allows them to reuse a lot of ideas and code.

HTTP has become the reuse platform of choice, largely because:

- It is familiar.
- It is ubiquitous.
- It has a simple request/response model.
- It usually works through firewalls.

These are all good reasons, and—if HTTP meets your communications requirements—you should use it. The problem is that the widespread availability of HTTP has become an excuse for not bothering to understand what the requirements really are. It's easier to use HTTP, even if it's not a good fit, than to understand your requirements and design a protocol that does what you really need.

That's where BEEP comes in. It's a toolkit that you can use for building application protocols. It works well in a wide range of application domains, many of which weren't of interest when HTTP was being designed.

BEEP's goal is simple: you, the protocol designer, focus on the protocol details for your problem domain, and BEEP takes care of the other details. It turns out that the vast majority of application protocols have more similarities than differences. The similarities primarily deal with "administrative overhead"—things you need for a working system, but aren't specific to the problem at hand. BEEP mechanizes the similar parts, and lets you focus on the interesting stuff.

Application Protocol Design

Let's assume, for the moment, that you don't see a good fit between the protocol functions you need and either the email or the Web infrastructures. (We'll talk more about this later on in the section "The Problem Space.") It's time to make something new.

First, you decide that your protocol needs ordered, reliable delivery. This is a common requirement for most application protocols, including HTTP and SMTP. The easiest way to get this is to layer the protocol over TCP.*

So, you decide to use TCP as the underlying transport for your protocol. Of course, TCP sends data as an octet stream—there aren't any delimiters that TCP uses to indicate where one of your application's messages ends and another one begins. This means you have to design a framing mechanism that your application uses with TCP. That's pretty simple to do—HTTP uses an octet count and SMTP uses a delimiter with quoting.

Since TCP is just sending bytes for you, you need to not only frame messages but also have a way of marking what's in each message (e.g., a data structure, an image, some text, and so on). This means you have to design an encoding mechanism that your application uses with the framing mechanism. That's also pretty simple to do— HTTP and SMTP both use something called MIME (which you can find out about in *Programming Internet Email*).

Back in the early 80s, when I was a young (but exceptionally cynical) computer scientist, my advisor told me that protocols have two parts: data and control. It looks like the data part is taken care of with MIME, so it's onto the control part. If you are fortunate enough to know ahead of time every operation and option that your protocol will ever support, there's no need for any kind of capabilities negotiation. In other words, your protocol doesn't need anything that lets the participants tell each other which operations and options are supported. (Of course, if this is the case, you have total recall of future events, and really ought to be making the big money in another, more speculative, field.)

The purpose of negotiation is to find common ground between two different implementations of a protocol (or two different versions of the same implementation). There are lots of different ways of doing this and, unfortunately, most of them don't work very well. SMTP is a really long-lived, well-deployed protocol, and it seems to do a pretty good job of negotiations. The basic idea is for the server to tell the client what capabilities it supports when a connection is established, and then for the client to use a subset of that.

---

* If you're not familiar with these acronyms, you'll need to consult some books on Internet basics, such as *Internet Core Protocols: The Definitive Guide* by Eric Hall for TCP, *HTTP Pocket Reference* by Clinton Wong for HTTP, and *Programming Internet Email* by David Wood for SMTP. (Of course, since you're designing an application protocol, presumably you're already familiar with the protocols behind these acronyms.)

Well, that's just the first control issue. The next deals with when it's time for the connection to be released. Sometimes this is initiated by the protocol, and sometimes it's required by TCP because the network is unresponsive. To further complicate things, if the release is initiated by the protocol, maybe one of the computers hasn't finished working on something, so it doesn't want to release the connection just yet.

Some application protocols don't do any negotiation on connection release, and just rely on TCP to indicate that it's time to go away—even though this is inherently ambiguous. Is ambiguity a good thing in a protocol? Computers lack subtlety and nuance, so in protocols between computers, ambiguity is a bad thing. For example, in HTTP 1.0 (and earlier), you often didn't know whether a response was truncated or not. For a more concrete example, interested readers will be amused by page 2 of RFC 962.

The final control issue deals with what happens between connection establishment and release. Most application protocols tend to be client/server in nature: one computer establishes a connection, sends some requests, gets back responses, and then releases the connection. But, are the requests and responses handled one at a time (in lock-step), or can multiple requests be outstanding, either in transit or being processed, at the same time (asynchronously)?

In the original SMTP, the lock-step model was implicitly assumed by most implementors; later on, SMTP introduced a capability to allow limited pipelining. Regardless, as soon as we move away from lock-stepping, it looks as though we'll need some way of correlating requests and responses.

Although this is a step in the right direction, some application protocols need even more support for asynchrony. The reasoning is a little convoluted, but it all comes down to performance. There's a lot of overhead involved in terms of establishing a connection and getting the right user state, so it makes sense to maximize the number of transactions that get done in a single connection. While this helps in terms of overall efficiency, if the transactions are handled serially, then transactional latency—the time it takes to transit the network, process the transaction, and then transit back—isn't reduced (and may even be increased); a transaction might be blocked while waiting for another to complete. The solution is to be able to handle transactions in parallel.

Earlier I mentioned how, back in the 80s, protocols had two parts, data and control. Today, things have changed. First of all, I'm still cynical, but more comfortable with it, and—perhaps as important—many might argue that protocols now have a third part, security.

The really unfortunate part is that security is a moving target on two fronts:

- When you deploy your protocol in different environments, you may have different security requirements.
- Even in the same environment, security requirements change over time.

This introduces something of a paradox: modern thinking is that security must be tightly integrated with your protocol, but at the same time, you have to take a modular approach to the actual technology to allow for easy upgrades. Worse, it's very easy to get security very wrong. (Just ask any major computer vendor!) Few applications folks are also expert in protocol security, and obtaining that expertise is a time-consuming, thankless task, so there's a lot of benefit in having a security mechanism menu, developed by security experts, that applications folk can pick from.

Now the good news: there's already something around designed to meet just those requirements. It's called SASL, and a lot of existing application protocols have been retrofitted over the last four years to make use of it.

Well, let's see what all this means. Without ever having talked about what your application protocol is going to do to earn a living, we have to develop solutions for:

- Framing messages
- Encoding data
- Negotiating capabilities (versions and options)
- Negotiating connection release
- Correlating requests and responses
- Handling multiple outstanding requests (pipelining)
- Handling multiple asynchronous requests (multiplexing)
- Providing integrated and modular security
- Integrating all these things together into a single, coherent framework

So, going back to the question "Why use BEEP?", the answer is pretty simple: if you use BEEP, you simply don't have to think about any of these things. They automatically get taken care of.

Now maybe you're the kind of hardcore engineer that really wants to solve these problems yourself. Okay, go right ahead! But first, I'll let you in on a little secret: engineers have been solving these problems since 1972. In fact, they keep solving them over and over again. For each problem, there are usually two or three good solutions, and while individual tastes may vary, the sad fact is that you can make any of them work great if you're willing to put in the hours. But why put in the hours if they have nothing to do with the primary reason for writing the application protocol to begin with? Isn't there something more productive that you'd care to do with your life than design yet another framing protocol?

So, what's really *new* about BEEP? The short answer is: not much. The innovative part is that some folks sat down, did an analysis of the problems and solutions, and came up with an integrated framework that put it all together. That's not really innovation, but it's really good news if you're already familiar with the building blocks that BEEP uses.

Doesn't all this stuff add a lot of overhead? The short answer is: nope. The reason is a little more complex. BEEP is fairly minimalistic—it provides a simple mechanism for negotiating things on an à la carte basis. If you don't want privacy, no problem; don't turn it on. If you don't want parallelism, that's easy; just say "no" if the other computer asks for it. The trick here is two-fold:

- BEEP's inner mechanisms (e.g., framing) are pretty lightweight, so you don't incur a lot of overhead using them (even if you don't use all the functionality they provide).
- BEEP's outer mechanisms (e.g., encryption) are all controlled via bilateral negotiation, so you can decide exactly what you want to get and pay for.

There's no free lunch, but if you want to start with something "lean and mean," BEEP doesn't slow you down, and when you want to bulk up (say, by adding privacy), BEEP lets you negotiate it. You incur only the overhead you need. (This overhead *will* show up, regardless of whether you use BEEP or grow your own mechanisms.)

It turns out that this philosophy can yield some interesting results. For example, take a look at this high-level scripting fragment:

```
::init -server example.com -port 10288 -privacy strong
```

This fragment is invoking a procedure to establish a BEEP session. With the exception of the last two terms, it looks pretty conventional.

The last two terms tell the procedure to "tune" the session by looking at the security protocols supported in common, selecting one that supports "strong privacy," and then negotiating its use. What's interesting here is that neither the person who designed the application protocol nor the person who wrote the application making the procedure call has to be a security expert. The choice to use strong privacy, and how it gets transparently used, is all an issue of provisioning. Of course, the application protocol designer may still provide security guidelines to the implementor; naturally, the implementor may bundle a wide range of security protocols with the code. However—and this is key—everyone got to focus on what they do best (even the security guys), and it still comes together into a working system.

The cool part here is how easily this all integrates into an evolving protocol. Back in the good ol' days (say the mid-80s) when the *Post Office Protocol* (POP, RFC 1081) was defined, this kind of flexibility wasn't available. Whenever someone wanted to add a new security mechanism for authentication or privacy, you had to muck with the entire protocol. With BEEP's framework, you just add a module that works seamlessly with the rest of the protocol. This means less work for everyone, and presumably fewer mistakes getting the work done.

Now we've come full circle: the reason for using BEEP is because it makes it a lot easier to specify, develop, maintain, and evolve new application protocols.

The Problem Space

BEEP works for a large class of application protocols.

However, you should always use the right tool for the right job. Before you start using BEEP for a project, you should ask yourself whether your application protocol is a good fit for either the email or Web models.

Dave Crocker, one of the Internet's progenitors, suggests that network applications can be broadly distinguished by five operational characteristics:

- Server push or client pull
- Synchronous (interactive) or asynchronous (batch)
- Time-assured or time-insensitive
- Best-effort or reliable
- Stateful or stateless

For example:

- The World Wide Web is a pull, synchronous, time-insensitive, reliable, stateless service.
- Internet mail is a push, asynchronous, time-insensitive, best-effort, stateless service.

This is a pretty useful taxonomy.

So, your first step is to see whether either of these existing infrastructures meet your requirements. It's easiest to start by asking if your application can reside on top of email. Typically, the unpredictable latency of the Internet mail infrastructure raises the largest issues; however, in some cases it's a non-issue. For example, in the early 90s, some of the earliest business-to-business exchanges were operated over email (e.g., USC/ISI's FAST project). If you can find a good fit between your application and Internet email, use it!

More likely, though, you'll be tempted to use the Web infrastructure, and there are a lot of awfully good reasons to do so. After all, when you use HTTP:

- There's lots of tools (libraries, servers, etc.) to choose from.
- It's easy to prototype stuff.
- There's already a security model.
- You can traverse firewalls pretty easily.

All of this boils down to one simple fact: it is pretty easy to deploy things in the Web infrastructure. The real issue is whether you can make good use of this infrastructure.

HTTP was originally developed for retrieving documents in a LAN environment, so HTTP's interaction model is optimized for that application. Accordingly, in HTTP:

- Each session consists of a single request/response exchange.
- The computer that initiates the session is also the one that initiates the request.

What needs to be emphasized here is that this is a perfectly fine interaction model for HTTP's target application, as well as many other application domains.

The problem arises when the behavior of your application protocol doesn't match this interaction model. In this case, there are two choices: make use of HTTP's extensibility features, or simply make do. Obviously, each choice has some draw-backs. The problem with using HTTP's extensibility features is that it pretty much negates the ability to use the existing HTTP infrastructure; the problem with "just making do" is that you end up crippling your protocol. For example, if your application protocol needs asynchronous notifications, you're out of luck.

A second problem arises due to "the law of codepaths." The HTTP 1.1 specification RFC 2616 is fairly rigorous. Even so, few implementors take the time to think out many of the nuances of the protocol. For example, the typical HTTP transaction consists of a small request, which results in a (much) larger response. Talk to any engineer who's worked on a browser and they'll tell you this is "obvious." So, what happens when the "obvious" doesn't happen?

Some time ago, folks wanted a standardized protocol for talking to networked print-ers. The result was something called the *Internet Printing Protocol* (IPP, RFC 2565). IPP sits on top of HTTP. At this point, the old "obvious" thing (small request, big response) gets replaced with the new "obvious" thing—the request contains an arbi-trarily large file to be printed, and the response contains this tiny little status indica-tion. A surprising amount of HTTP software doesn't handle this situation particularly gracefully (i.e., long requests get silently truncated). The moral is that even though HTTP's interaction model doesn't play favorites with respect to lengthy requests or responses, many HTTP implementors inadvertently make unfortunate assumptions.

A third problem deals with the unitary relationship between sessions and exchanges. If a single transaction needs to consist of more than one exchange, it has to be spread out over multiple sessions. This introduces two issues:

- In terms of stateful behavior, the server computer has to be able to keep track of session state across multiple connections, imposing a significant burden both on the correctness and implementation of the protocol (e.g., to properly handle timeouts).
- In terms of performance, TCP isn't designed for dealing with back-to-back con-nections—there's a fair amount of overhead and latency involved in establishing a connection. This is also true for the security protocols that layer on top of TCP.

HTTP 1.1 begins to address these issues by introducing persistent connections that allow multiple exchanges to occur serially over a single connection, but still the protocol lacks a session concept. In practice, implementors try to bridge this gap by using "cookies" to manage session state, which introduces ad-hoc (in)security models that often result in security breakdowns (as a certain Web-based email service provider found out).

This brings us to a more general fourth problem: although HTTP has a security model, it predates SASL. From a practical perspective, what this means is that it's very difficult to add new security protocols to HTTP. Of course, that may not be an issue for you.

If you can find a good fit between your application and the Web infrastructure, use it! (For those interested in a more architectural perspective on the reuse of the Web infrastructure for new application protocols, consider RFC 3205.)

Okay, so we've talked about both the email and Web infrastructures, and we've talked about what properties your application protocol needs to have in order to work well with them. So, if there isn't a good fit between either of them and your application protocol, what about BEEP?

BEEP's interaction model is pretty simple, with the following three properties:

- Each session consists of one or more request/response exchanges.
- Either computer can initiate requests or notifications.
- It's connection-oriented.

By using BEEP, you get an amortization effect with respect to the cost of connection establishment and state management. This is largely derived from the first property. Similarly, the second property gives BEEP its ability to support either peer-to-peer or client-server interactions. What we really need to explain is the connection-oriented part.

To begin, all three of the interaction models we've looked at (BEEP, email, and the Web) are connection-oriented. (Although email may get delivered out of order, the commands sent over each email "hop" are processed in an ordered, reliable fashion.) The connection-oriented model is the most commonly used for application protocols, but it does introduce some restrictions.

A connection-oriented interaction model means that data is delivered reliably and in the same order as it was sent. If you don't require ordered, reliable delivery, you don't need a connection-oriented interaction model. For example, Internet telephony applications don't fit this model, nor do traditional multicast applications.

So, BEEP is suitable for unicast application protocols (two computers are talking to each other). However, not all unicast applications need a connection-oriented model—for example, the Domain Name System manages name-to-address resolutions just fine without it. In fact, if your protocol is able to limit each session to exactly one request/response exchange with minimalist reliability requirements, and also limit the size of each message to around 65K octets, then it's probably a good candidate for using UDP instead.

The IETF and BEEP

BEEP is an emerging standard from the Internet Engineering Task Force (IETF). The IETF is a voluntary professional organization that develops many of the protocols running in the Internet. (Of course, anyone is free to develop their own protocols to run in their own little part of the Internet, but if you want multi-vendor support, you need an organization like the IETF.) So why does the IETF care about BEEP?

The answer is that the largest area in the IETF deals with application protocols. There are usually over two dozen working groups developing different application protocols. And, the IETF has been doing this for a long, long time. It turns out that even though there are well-engineered solutions to the different overhead issues, BEEP is the first time that the IETF decided to develop a standard approach that integrates the best practices for each issue. Before BEEP, each working group would spend endless hours arguing about different solutions, and then, if any time was remaining, they might sit down and look at the actual problem domain. (Okay, this is an exaggeration... but not by much!)

So, here's the process by which BEEP got designed:

- Identify the common domain-independent problems.
- Determine the best solution for each problem.
- Integrate the solutions into a consistent framework.
- Declare victory.

Now, the obvious question is: how do you determine what's "best?"

The truth is that in some cases, the answer is obvious, and in other cases, the answer is arbitrary. (Protocol experts hate to admit this, but in some cases, there is no clear winner, and it's simply better to pick one and order another drink.) Since most of what BEEP does is hidden from the application designer and implementor, there's really not a lot of mileage in going through it here. If you want to understand the issues, check out the Appendix.

beepcore.org

Where can you find out more about BEEP?

To start, you can always consult the two RFCs: the BEEP core framework (RFC 3080) and the BEEP's mapping onto TCP (RFC 3081). However, it's probably better to start with the BEEP community web site *http://beepcore.org*, where you'll find:

- News about BEEP meetings and events
- Information about BEEP projects, programmers, and consultants
- Information about beepcore (open source) and commercial software
- BEEP-related RFCs, Internet-Drafts, and whitepapers

How This Book Is Organized

Our goal is to explain how to use BEEP to write network applications.

This book is divided into two major parts, one on architecture and the other on implementation. Each of these parts contains three chapters.

The architecture part (Chapters 2–4) introduces the unifying concepts of BEEP and goes into enough detail so you can understand how the concepts are related and how they apply to what you're trying to do. The implementation part (Chapters 5–7) discusses the programmers' interface for the Java, C, and Tcl languages.

Of course, if you already know all about BEEP, you can skip right to the chapter talking about the API of your choice. Regardless, if you are equally comfortable, competent, and interested in the APIs for all three programming languages, you probably have too much time on your hands.

A word of warning though: you're not going to learn *how* to program using this book. For example, before reading Chapter 6, on beepcore-c, you should be comfortable writing (and reading) real-world C programs. Simply speaking, Chapter 5, on beepcore-java is the user-friendliest, because Java is simply more user-friendly than the other two. Chapters 6 and 7 have somewhat higher expectations.

This book is standards-compliant, and therefore satisfies the requirement that books about protocols always include a chapter speculating about the future. (There is, of course, a strict prohibition against anyone ever trying to determine how accurate the speculation actually is.) Finally, in the Appendix, there's a reprint of the initial design document for BEEP.

## CHAPTER 2

Concepts

This chapter introduces the unifying themes of BEEP.

Perhaps the most important aspect of BEEP is integration—there are a lot of different problems being solved, but the "glue" that holds it all together is common throughout. The stuff that makes up the glue consists of:

- Sessions
- Channels
- Exchanges
- Messages

Let's look at each in turn.

To introduce the concepts and relationships throughout the chapters on architecture, some small BEEP "precepts" are scattered throughout. Figure 2-1 is the first.

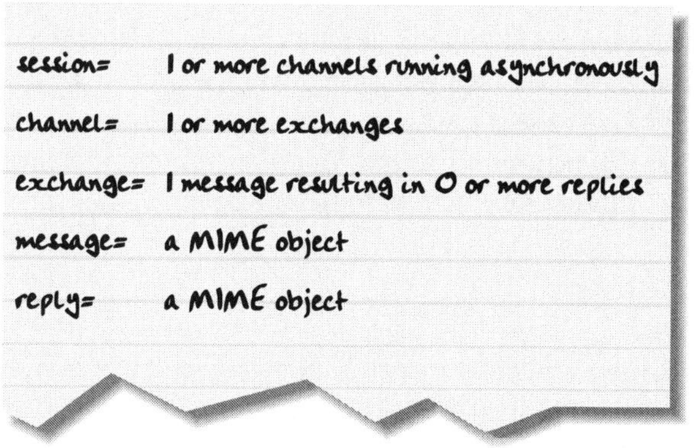

```
session=     1 or more channels running asynchronously

channel=     1 or more exchanges

exchange=    1 message resulting in 0 or more replies

message=     a MIME object

reply=       a MIME object
```

Figure 2-1. The session precept

Sessions

A BEEP session is a peer-wise, full-duplex pipe.

The choice of terms here is intentional:

peer-wise
: Either computer can initiate a message exchange.

full-duplex
: Messages can be exchanged in both directions simultaneously.

pipe
: Messages sent are never duplicated, altered, or re-ordered, and the sender is informed if a message is lost.

Having said that BEEP is peer-wise, it turns out that there are actually two kinds of roles that a peer may engage in:

- Listener or initiator
- Client or server

Before a BEEP session is established, one peer acts as a listener, waiting for the other peer, the initiator, to contact it. If you're familiar with the way TCP works, the listener is the one doing the "passive open" and the initiator is the one doing the "active open." (If you are *really* familiar with the way TCP works, I'll tell you that BEEP doesn't support TCP's "simultaneous open"—which is just fine, because the "simultaneous open" is probably the only part of TCP that's a solution in search of a problem.)

After a BEEP session is established, a peer that initiates a message exchange is the client, and the one that replies is the server. Now, the tricky thing about BEEP is that a listener can act as a server, or a client, or both—even at the same time! In other words, the terms "client" and "server" are meaningful only in the context of a given exchange of messages; they have no meaning with respect to a BEEP session. This is useful because you may have to provision applications in strange environments (e.g., where the initiator sits behind a firewall, but after the session is established the listener is the one that initiates exchanges to the initiator).

Channels

Each BEEP session carries one or more channels simultaneously. A channel is a full-duplex pipe, and the application protocol designer specifies rules indicating who can initiate message exchanges, along with the syntax and semantics of those messages. In other words, a channel is a stream of "typed" messages. But, how do you know what the rules are?

In BEEP, someone writes a document called a "profile" that defines the rules. The profile itself is identified by a URI (Uniform Resource Identifier), such as *http://iana. org/beep/syslog/COOKED*. Note that the URI doesn't have to be on the Web—it just has to authoritatively identify the document. So, in this example, the owner of iana. org is the only one allowed to name profiles with the prefix of *http://iana.org*. The ideas of channels and profiles are illustrated in Figure 2-2.

Figure 2-2. The channel precept

URIs were chosen to identify profiles because this allows *anyone* to define a profile! In the next two chapters, we'll see several examples of profile definitions; for right now, the actual details aren't that important.

Since you can have more than one channel active at the same time, you need a way of identifying them. Whoever asks to create a channel gives the other peer a list of profiles to choose from, along with an unused channel number. If it's all good, the other peer replies with the profile that it wants to use, and from that point on both peers use that integer to refer to the channel, as shown in Figure 2-3. (Of course, it's all up to the API as to what your program uses to refer to the channel, e.g., a pointer, an object, or an int32.) We'll talk about the server name part in this figure in "Virtual hosting" in Chapter 3.

This "suggest many, accept one" philosophy is the cornerstone of negotiation in BEEP. It provides a convenient way to quickly converge on a mutually acceptable choice. Both peers get to decide what's possible, based on the profiles they support and their configurations.

Because profiles and channels are identified by different things, it's possible in BEEP to have more than one channel bound to the same profile. For example, let's say that you have an application that reports events of varying severity. You may want to configure your application to use two channels at the same time, with each using the same event reporting profile, and then divide up the traffic based on urgency. Alternatively, perhaps you want to use one channel to retrieve meta-data about objects,

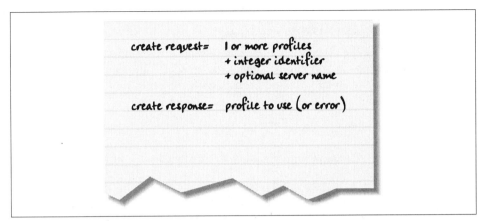

Figure 2-3. The creation precept

and use the second channel to retrieve the actual objects. Depending on the sophistication of the retrieval requirements, you might use the same profile, or different profiles, on the two channels.

This second scenario is attractive because it avoids the problems associated with *Network Address Translators* (NATs, RFC 2663). If you're sitting behind a NAT, it's rewriting the addresses in the IP and TCP headers, which is fine until your data contains an IP address that doesn't get rewritten. When you use BEEP and have two channels running over one session, there's no need to put IP/TCP addressing information in your data, so the NAT doesn't have an opportunity to screw things up.

Of course, using simultaneous channels isn't a necessity. BEEP defines the mechanisms, but it's up to the API developer to provide them, and up to you to decide whether to use them. If you do, do so responsibly. Of course, no matter how many channels you're using on a session, you're still talking to just one remote peer—multiple channels don't get to talk to multiple hosts.

There are two rules about the exchanges that occur on a channel:

- Exchanges are processed serially.
- Exchanges may be pipelined.

What this means is that you can send the message that initiates a new exchange before the previous exchange is completed, but the receiver is working on them one at a time.

So, perhaps the easiest way to think of it is like this: channels are kind of like programming threads. Any given thread is doing at most one thing, and while you can have multiple threads running at the same time, they may be competing for the same resources. This means you probably don't want to have a lot of them running at once. Further, the threads can be running at different "speed," so it's possible that things get processed by the threads in a different order than you'd expect. This covers the basics of the parallelism inherent in BEEP channels.

Finally, you need to appreciate that there are two types of profiles: tuning and exchange. (Chapter 3 talks about tuning profiles, and Chapter 4 talks about exchange profiles.) Think of exchange profiles as the guys who do the "real work," and the tuning profiles as the lawyers and accountants of your session—all companies have this overhead, regardless of the real work that they do.

Exchanges

Each BEEP channel is used to exchange messages between a client and a server. An exchange is how clients and servers talk to each other. A client sends a message, and gets back one of:

- An error (sometimes called a negative reply)
- A reply (sometimes called a positive reply)
- Zero or more answers (each one's a reply), followed by an indication that the exchange is completed

These possibilities are shown in Figure 2-4.

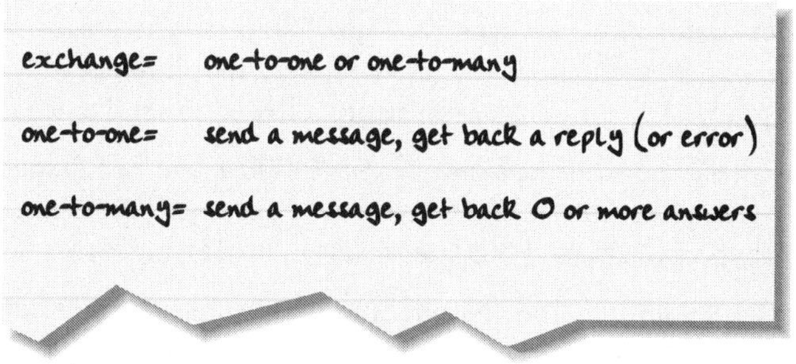

exchange=   one-to-one or one-to-many

one-to-one=   send a message, get back a reply (or error)

one-to-many= send a message, get back 0 or more answers

Figure 2-4. The exchange precept

It's up to the designer who writes the profile to decide what kind of exchanges occur between the client and the server. Most of the time, it's just a few one-to-one exchanges, and normally, the BEEP peer that acted as the initiator (the one that started the session) also acts as the client. That's not mandatory, but it's just the way it usually turns out. (In "Client/Server" in Chapter 4, we'll look at a profile in which the initiators acts as the server for a one-to-many exchange—the listener will wait for the initiator to connect to it, then ask a question and get back as many answers as the initiator is able to provide.)

One part of BEEP that isn't as thought out as it could be is when to issue a negative reply. There are two schools of thought as to who gets to decide when a negative reply is generated. In order to understand the difference, we have to look at how an API for BEEP might be organized, as shown in Figure 2-5.

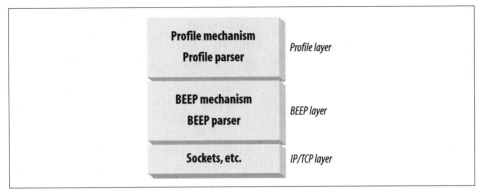

Figure 2-5. The organization of a BEEP API

Both schools of thought agree that if the profile can't parse an incoming message, it should generate a negative response. The question is whether a negative response can ever be generated if the message is successfully parsed.

One school of thought says "no"—a negative response indicates the server never processed the message. The other school of thought says that the profile mechanism can generate a negative response during processing. While you can make valid arguments for either philosophy, perhaps the "no's" have it, the reason being that in a one-to-many response, there are no negative replies. This implies, at least to me, that once you start processing a message, you're not allowed to send a negative reply.

In case you're interested, this ambiguity exists because the BEEP specification talks about negative responses only in the context of malformed messages. It doesn't discuss messages that can be parsed but later result in processing errors.

Regardless, is this such a big deal? No, because the profile designer can specify a status message, returned in a positive reply, that indicates whether good or bad things happened during processing!

Messages

Each BEEP message is encoded using MIME.

BEEP doesn't really care what you put in the messages that get exchanged: binary or textual, structured or unstructured, verbose or compressed—it's just bits to BEEP. However, BEEP does require that you tag the octets you send so that the other peer knows what it's looking at. Modern application protocols use an encoding standard called *Multipurpose Internet Mail Extensions* (MIME, RFC 2045) for this purpose.

In the context of BEEP, all you really need to know about MIME can be summarized by two words: "Content-Type: header." In its simplest form, it's divided into two parts, separated by a solidus (/): a type (e.g., text, image, or application), and a subtype (e.g., html, gif, or pdf). Since the application protocol designer specifies the syntax of the messages exchanged, that's who gets to define the MIME "media type" associated with each message. (If you want to get the full story on MIME, consult Chapter 3 of *Programming Internet Email*.)

BEEP defines a few MIME types itself, and since Chapter 3 talks about those, it's worthwhile for us to introduce one particular media type, called `application/beep+xml`. Since this media type is based on the *Extensible Markup Language* (XML), we have a bit of a digression. If you're already familiar with XML, skip the next section.

XML in Under Two Pages

XML lets you define structured objects using a textual format. You can boil down 90% of XML into two pages. (If you want to know more—and there's lots more to know—take a look at *XML in a Nutshell* by Elliotte Rusty Harold and W. Scott Means.)

There are very few rules when writing in XML, as the syntax is (deceptively) simple. There are five terms you'll need to know:

- An "element" usually refers to a start tag, an end tag, and all the characters in between, e.g., `<example>text and/or nested elements</example>`.

- An "empty element" combines the start tag and the end tag, e.g., `<empty/>`. For readability, I prefer to write this as `<empty />`—both are legal XML. You don't find empty elements in HTML.

- An "attribute" is part of an element. If present, they occur in the start tag, e.g., `<example name='value'>`. Of course, they can also appear in empty elements, e.g., `<empty name='value'/>`.

- An "entity" is a textual macro that starts with &. (Usually, you'll only use one when you want to put a "&" or a "<" in your text.)

- A "token" is a string of characters. The first character is either a letter or an underscore ("_"). Any characters that follow are either letters, numbers, an underscore, or a period (".").

There are four rules to follow when writing XML:

1. Always make sure that all elements are properly matched and nested. A properly matched element that starts with `<example>` is eventually followed with `</example>`. (Empty elements are always matched.) Elements are properly nested when they don't overlap.

   For example:

```
<outer>
    ...
    <inner>
        ...
    </inner>
    ...
</outer>
```

is properly nested. However,

```
<outer>
    ...
    <inner>
        ...
    </outer>
    ...
</inner>
```

overlaps, so the elements aren't properly nested.

2. Never use "<" or "&" in your text. Instead, use either < or &, respectively.

3. There are two quoting characters in XML: apostrophe (') and quotation (").
   Make sure that all attributes values are quoted, e.g., `<example name='value'>`. If
   the value contains one of the quoting characters, then use the other to quote the
   value, e.g., `<example name='"'>`. If the value contains both quoting characters,
   then use one of them to quote the value, and replace occurrences of that character in the attribute value with either ' (apostrophe) or " (quotation),
   e.g., `<example name='"&apos;"'>`.

4. XML is case sensitive, which means that `<foo>` is different from `<Foo>`.

The application/beep+xml Content-Type

Okay, with that out of the way, what is the application/beep+xml content type?

The short answer is that it makes two restrictions to XML:

- The only entities allowed are XML's five predefined general entity references
  (&, <, >, ', and ") and numeric entity references (e.g.,
  —).

- Two of the more complex XML declarations (<?xml ...> and <!DOCTYPE ...>)
  may not be present, so you're limited to encoding the data using UTF-8.

These restrictions are made for simplicity: an XML parser that doesn't have to
account for a lot of optional extras can be a lot smaller. Here's a small example of the
application/beep+xml media type:

```
<greeting>
    <profile uri='http://iana.org/beep/syslog/COOKED' />
    <profile uri='http://iana.org/beep/SASL/DIGEST-MD5' />
    <profile uri='http://iana.org/beep/SASL/OTP' />
    <profile uri='http://iana.org/beep/TLS' />
</greeting>
```

Packet Formats and Traces

We're not going to look at any. Seriously. Here's why:

- If you're reading this book to learn how to use BEEP, then BEEP's framing
  mechanism is provided for you automatically by whatever API you're using.

- If you're reading this book to understand what BEEP traffic looks like, there are numerous examples in the BEEP core framework (RFC 3080); just pull it up in an editor and search for "L:" or "C:".

- If you're reading this book because you want to implement an API for BEEP, then you are reading the wrong book—go back and re-read the Preface.

It turns out that all this pontificating is a bit misleading. There's actually one case where it's useful to know about BEEP's framing mechanism: BEEP takes messages and fragments them into one or more frames; some APIs for BEEP provide both a "cooked" and a "raw" interface. In the cooked interface, you deal in messages; in the raw interface, you deal in frames. If you're using the raw interface, then when the API hands you a frame, it will tell you whether you're looking at the last frame of a message. If so, go ahead and process the message; if not, you'll have to decide what you want to do with the frame until you get the final frame.

Obviously, it's your choice as to whether you use a cooked or a raw interface. You'll probably make that choice depending upon the kind of messages you're sending and receiving and how you plan on handling them.

CHAPTER 3

Tuning

This chapter talks about how BEEP sessions get *lawyered-up*. The term "lawyered-up" is just an expression that some of us use for adding security to a plain vanilla BEEP session. When a BEEP session starts out, you get whatever security properties are provided by the underlying transport service. In most cases, this means that your traffic is unencrypted and unauthenticated. Now, maybe that's okay for your environment, and if that's the case, make sure that you're dosing properly with your meds. If not, then BEEP gives you a way of fixing that. It's called "tuning," which is the official term for the process of giving a newly-created BEEP session the security properties you want, as shown in Figure 3-1.

Figure 3-1. The tuning precept

In BEEP, sessions are tuned for two things:

- Transport privacy
- User authentication

Sometimes you can accomplish both of these simultaneously; in other cases, you have to take care of privacy before authentication. It's all a function of the security technologies you have available. Don't worry, we'll explain the details later on. The one thing you must understand is that BEEP's view of security is entirely protocol-centric—you're still responsible for what happens to the data before and after it gets sent. (In other words, tuning doesn't help with sloppy coding such as buffer over-flows.)

Before we talk about the details of tuning, we have to talk a little bit about two related topics:

- How BEEP peers greet each other at the start of a session
- How channels are managed

The Greeting

In BEEP, as soon as a session is started, both peers send a *greeting*, as shown in Figure 3-2.

```
greeting=           profiles + language + features
profiles=           client-only
                    or privacy-first
                    or privacy-optional
client-only=        no profiles
privacy-first=      only tuning profiles for security
privacy-optional=   profiles for "real work" and,
                    optionally, tuning profiles
```

Figure 3-2. The greeting precept

The purpose of the greeting is three-fold. It allows each peer to:

- Advertise the profiles it supports
- Specify the preferred languages for diagnostics
- Indicate which optional features it supports

We're not going to talk about BEEP's optional features (there haven't been any stan-dardized); instead, let's look at the other two in turn.

Supported Profiles

If you recall from "Channels" in Chapter 2, the way a channel gets created is:

- One peer makes a request with one or more possible profiles.
- The other peer responds by saying which profile it's going to use for the channel.

So, one of the things that a greeting is good for is to let the other peer know what the possible choices are, right?

It turns out that, depending on the kind of peer you're talking to, the greeting you see is going to have a different kind of "feel." If you're using a sophisticated API for BEEP, you probably don't need to appreciate the different feel for the greeting, but it's still worthwhile to explain it.

Let's start with the simplest case. If you're looking at a traditional client/server scenario, then—independent of what's in the server's greeting—the client's greeting is probably going to look like this:

```
<greeting />
```

It doesn't get any simpler than this—the greeting is empty.

When you see this, it's telling you not to bother trying to start any profiles—the peer who sent the empty greeting will be the one who decides what gets started and when. If you're just a server, this is just the way you want it. However, as a server, what's *your* greeting going to look like?

The first choice is whether you *require* that the session be tuned prior to doing any real work. If so, then you send a greeting that contains only tuning profiles, such as:

```
<greeting>
    <profile uri='http://iana.org/beep/TLS' />
</greeting>
```

Think of this as saying "I'm not saying anything more until I lawyer-up."

If you've been paying attention, you should have a very important question at this point: if only tuning profiles are in the greeting, how does any real work get done? The answer is that after a tuning profile makes a session "secure" (i.e., it starts encrypting traffic so third parties can't see what's going on), both peers send another greeting. We'll explain why later, in the section "The TLS Profile," but for now, just keep in mind that tuning a session may result in another greeting.

Of course, the third kind of greeting you might see has both types of profiles:

```
<greeting>
    <profile uri='http://iana.org/beep/TLS' />
    <profile uri='http://iana.org/beep/syslog/COOKED' />
</greeting>
```

This leaves the choice of tuning up to the client.

Hopefully, your API will handle all of these details for you, letting you specify the tuning policy you want (e.g., "privacy first"), and then transparently handling the greeting mechanics for you. If not, you hopefully now understand the way it works.

Localization (L10N)

Sending diagnostic information in English isn't universally helpful. In the golden age of application protocol design, error messages contained two parts:

- A three-digit reply code
- A textual diagnostic

History has shown the combination of a machine-readable reply code with human-readable text to be a good choice. (See the section "Reporting" in the Appendix.) A reply code consists of three digits:

Completion (the first digit)
Explains whether the request succeeded, failed, or didn't complete, and is one of:

Positive preliminary (1)
The request is ready to be performed, pending further confirmation or rejection.

Positive completion (2)
The request has succeeded.

Positive intermediate (3)
The request is ready to be performed, pending further data.

Transient negative (4)
The request wasn't performed, but if retried later, it may very well succeed.

Permanent negative (5)
The request wasn't performed, and some explicit action must be taken before it could ever succeed.

Category (the second digit)
Explains why the request succeeded, failed, or didn't complete, and is one of:

Syntax (0)
The reply deals with syntax issues, such as errors in syntax, or unrecognized commands.

Informational (1)
The reply contains useful information.

Connection (2)
The reply deals with the session or transport connection.

Security (3)
The reply deals with the security subsystem.

Application-specific (5)
The reply deals with the application itself, e.g., something specific to the BEEP profile that generated the reply code.

Instance (the third digit)
Distinguishes between different situations having the same completion and category values.

Although the application protocol designer is responsible for indicating what reply code gets used in each situation, most programs need to be able to make decisions based on the first digit only.

BEEP uses the code/diagnostic pair whenever it needs to convey an error. For example, in Chapter 2 when we talked about creating a channel, you might recall that the server peer either replies with the identity of the profile that is going to be used on the channel, or it refuses and signals an error.

Here's an example:

```
<error code='500'>none of the profiles are supported</error>
```

However, there is this little matter of picking the natural language to use for the text. Historically, the choice has been English (or rather, "geeklish"). More recently, it has been growing more common to allow each peer to advertise its preferences, e.g.:

```
<greeting localize='en-US fr-CA'>
    ...
</greeting>
```

which asks for the U.S. variant of English, and, if that's not possible, Canadian French.

The only real question is where "language tags" such as en-US come from. The answer is that BEEP refers the reader to RFC 3066, which in turn refers the reader to ISO standards 639 and 3166. In practice, the rules are pretty simple:

- Start with the two-letter abbreviation for the language from part one of ISO 639.
- Append a hyphen and the two-letter abbreviation for the country from ISO 3166.

There's actually a lot more flexibility than that, and if you use it, I have every confidence that you'll get exactly what you deserve.

Channel Management

In BEEP, as soon as a session is started, both peers send a greeting. But how can a greeting be sent if there aren't any channels to send it on?

The answer is that a newly-created BEEP session always comes with one channel, channel zero, already created. Channel zero's sole role is channel management, which means three things:

- Creating new channels
- Destroying existing channels
- Releasing the entire session

These are shown in Figure 3-3; let's look at each in turn.

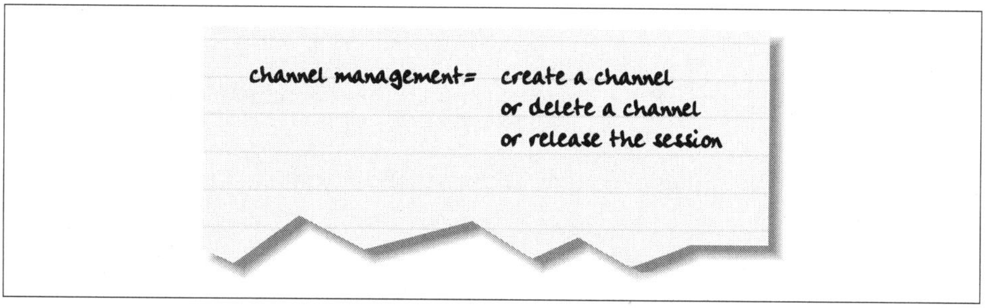

Figure 3-3. The channel zero precept

Channel Creation

Earlier, in the section "Channels" in Chapter 2, we talked about BEEP's "suggest many, accept one" philosophy and how this was used, among other things, for channel creation.

To recap, after they exchange greetings, when one peer wants to open a channel it might suggest:

```
<start number='1'>
    <profile uri='http://iana.org/beep/SASL/DIGEST-MD5' />
    <profile uri='http://iana.org/beep/SASL/OTP' />
</start>
```

and, if the other peer decides to start channel number 1, it will indicate which of these two profiles it selected.

It turns out that there were two nuances that we left out earlier:

- Piggybacking initial data
- Requesting a "virtual host"

The piggyback

BEEP provides a latency-reduction mechanism that lets you create a channel and perform its first exchange at the same time.

The basic idea is to remove one round-trip time from the process. Instead of having to wait a round-trip to find out if the channel creation is successful before performing the first exchange, the exchange gets "piggybacked" on the messages that perform the channel creation.

Here's how it works: when a channel is started, both peers can include a string of octets intended for the channel. When you try to start channel, you can include your first message; if the channel is created, your peer processes the message and includes the corresponding reply when you're told that the channel is successfully created.

Virtual hosting

It's fairly common in today's Internet for a physical server to be known by several logical host names. In HTTP 1.1, the client signals this by including the Host: header in its request.

In BEEP, this is done using the serverName attribute for the first successful channel creation, e.g.:

```
<start number='1' serverName='mosquiton.example.com'>
    <profile uri='http://iana.org/beep/TLS' />
</start>
```

If the channel isn't created, then a different serverName value may be used on the next request. Once a channel with a serverName is created, any serverName attributes used to create future channels are ignored.

The use of the serverName attribute is particularly important in tuning, not only because of the "first success" rule, but because the peer you're talking to may have different certificate and authorization databases for each of its virtual hosts. How do you know what value to use?

The answer depends on context. If your program is dereferencing a URL that maps onto a service that uses BEEP, the answer is self-evident (e.g., *soap.beep://mosquiton. example.com/*). If your program isn't URL-driven, but you started with a fully qualified domain name, just use that. If not, then—in the absence of some other information—don't include a serverName attribute at all.

Channel Destruction

After you create and presumably use a channel, BEEP lets you close it.

Most BEEP usage is of the form:

1. Start a session by establishing the underlying transport connection.
2. Perhaps tune the session (using one channel).
3. Create and use one, or maybe two, channels for exchange.
4. Release the session (which implicitly closes all channels).

This makes it hard to understand why anyone would bother closing channels explicitly.

The reasoning is rather subtle—in some usage scenarios, you may have very long-lived sessions where you want to close a channel prior to a period of inactivity. By doing so, you free whatever application-specific resources are being used by that channel. Of course, only certain kind of applications need this kind of behavior; for those that don't, simply releasing the session does the trick. (In other words, this is an example of BEEP letting you decide exactly what you want to get and pay for.)

Session Release

You release the session by explicitly closing channel zero.

This brings up the one fun part about closing a channel: it involves a round-trip negotiation. What this means is that if one peer is still busy working on something, it can come back and say "no." Of course, the peer that wants the session to go away now can always just drop the underlying transport connection. In this way, BEEP gives you the tools you need to avoid any ambiguity as to whether both sides are ready to close, but in an emergency, you can just blow the bolts.

Now that we've talked about greetings and channel management, we can get to the actual tuning. Let's first talk about transport security and user authentication.

The TLS Profile

TLS is the IETF's version of version 3 of SSL. For our purposes, *Transport Layer Security* (TLS, RFC 2246) provides:

- Certificate-based authentication of one or both peers
- Cryptographic protection against passive eavesdropping
- Cryptographic detection of alteration, duplication, and reordering of traffic

The way TLS does this is outside the scope of this book. If you really want to know how it all works, get a copy of Eric Rescorla's seminal reference *SSL and TLS: Designing and Building Secure Systems*.

However, the key thing to understand about TLS is that the cryptographic certificates and algorithms that it uses are both configurable. Security people delight in unseemly and incomprehensible fights as to what kind of algorithms and key lengths should be used; as a BEEP person, you just don't care—look at the documentation for the API for BEEP that you're using, and it should tell you how to find out what's available in the TLS tuning profile it uses.

To use TLS with BEEP, you start a channel with the profile identified as *http://iana. org/beep/TLS*. Once you've started the channel, the TLS negotiation process begins when you send a message to the other peer.

Recall from an earlier example that you can use the serverName attribute to signal the other peer as to the credentials you're looking for:

```
<start number='1' serverName='mosquiton.example.com'>
    <profile uri='http://iana.org/beep/TLS' />
</start>
```

The only tricky thing to understand about using the TLS profile (or any tuning profile that does transport security) is what happens immediately before and after the underlying negotiation process.

Before:

Channel zero is reset and all other channels are closed.

After:

Both peers send a greeting, regardless of whether the negotiation was success-fully completed or not.

This is called a "tuning reset."

There are two reasons why BEEP has the concept of a tuning reset: the first is for practicality; the second is for correctness.

First, using a transport security profile inserts a new layer immediately between BEEP and the underlying transport service. You don't want any other BEEP messages unex-pectedly showing up; it would be a nightmare trying to straighten it all out. So, just before the TLS engine is invoked to do its voodoo, all channels are closed.

Second, until the session is made tamper-evident, it's possible for someone to alter BEEP's messages in transit. When a tuning reset occurs, both peers reset all state from the session; this means that the first thing that both sides do is send a new greeting.

The SASL Family of Profiles

SASL is the best thing to happen to application protocols since the reply code.

Unlike TLS, the *Simple Authentication and Security Layer* (SASL, RFC 2222) isn't a protocol. Instead, SASL is a framework like BEEP. SASL's goal is to provide a set of rules that allow application protocols to support multiple security mechanisms.

Earlier, back in "Application Protocol Design" in Chapter 1, we saw why SASL came about. Basically, an application's security requirements may be different, depending on where it's provisioned, and may change over time, even in the same environment. Further, security technologies have different price-points for strength, scalability, and ease of deployment.

The practical upshot of this is that we need a flexible way to accommodate different security technologies. SASL defines a set of rules for how security technologies have their data carried by an application protocol. If you're a security engineer, and you follow SASL's rules, your technology is called a SASL *mechanism* and it plugs into any SASL-capable application protocol. This is the genius of SASL: it defines one generic hook that accommodates a wide range of different mechanisms.

At a minimum, each SASL mechanism provides user authentication. Of course, the "strength" of that authentication is dependent on the algorithms used by the mecha-nism. Most SASL mechanisms allow you to convey two identities:

- An authentication identity, which tells who you are
- An authorization identity, which tells who you're acting on behalf of (if you're a proxy)

Some of the mechanisms and their attributes are shown in Figure 3-4.

mechanism	authentication	integrity	privacy
ANONYMOUS	trace	no	no
PLAIN	yes	n/a	n/a
CRAM-MD5	yes	no	no
DIGEST-MD5	yes	optional	optional
OTP	yes	no	no
EXTERNAL	n/a	n/a	n/a

mechanism	requires privacy	server stores	client sends
ANONYMOUS	no	n/a	trace information
PLAIN	yes	hashed value	plaintext password
CRAM-MD5	no	plaintext	challenge/response
DIGEST-MD5	no	hashed value	challenge/response
OTP	no	hashed value	one-time response
EXTERNAL	yes	n/a	n/a

Figure 3-4. Some SASL mechanism precepts

The *Internet Assigned Numbers Authority* (IANA) maintains a registry of SASL mechanisms. You can find the list at the IANA's web site (*http://www.iana.org*). Although there are a lot of choices, there are really only six of interest:

ANONYMOUS

This logs so-called "trace" information. It's not authenticated, just informational—like when you provide your email address to an anonymous FTP server. If you're interested in the details, see RFC 2245.

PLAIN

This is used when you've already encrypted at the transport layer, and you want to send the traditional username and password. This mechanism provides an upgrade path for systems that use a one-way function to store their passwords. For more information, see RFC 2595.

CRAM-MD5

This is the dual of the PLAIN mechanism—it uses a lightweight challenge/response over a plaintext session to a server that stores passwords in plaintext form. This mechanism provides an upgrade path for systems that store their passwords in the clear. See RFC 2195 for more details.

DIGEST-MD5

A replacement for the CRAM-MD5 mechanism, which avoids a serious security weakness. This mechanism also provides mutual authentication and is highly scalable for busy servers. If you want to know more, see RFC 2831.

OTP

This uses a one-time password (suitable for use at untrusted devices such as kiosks), in which the server can one-time authenticate the user without knowing the user's password. Further, at the outcome of a successful authentication, the client can incrementally modify (i.e., update) its passphrase. RFC 2444, RFC 2289, and RFC 2243 have all the details.

EXTERNAL

This is used when you've already authenticated at the network or transport layer, and you just want to tell the server what authorization identity you'd like to use.

Of course, there are many other SASL mechanisms, and some may be available to you. For example, there's a SASL mechanism for version 4 of Kerberos (see RFC 2222). Similarly, if your organization uses SecurID®, there's a SASL mechanism for it too (see RFC 2808). To put this into greater context, Chris Newman has developed an informal taxonomy of SASL mechanisms, which, with his permission, I've condensed into Figure 3-5.*

mechanism	basic idea	speed	ease	secure
ANONYMOUS	anonymous FTP	fastest	simplest	n/a
PLAIN	leverage legacy passwords	fastest	simplest	weakest
CRAM-MD5 DIGEST-MD5	basic challenge/response	fast	simple	good
OTP SECURED	one-time password	good	hard	good
KERBEROS_V4 GSSAPI	trusted third-party	fast	harder	stronger
TLS+EXTERNAL	public-key infrastructure	slow	hardest	best

Figure 3-5. A SASL taxonomy

So, it should now be clear why we always say "the SASL family of profiles"—every time someone registers a SASL mechanism (e.g., XXX) a corresponding tuning profile is *automatically* defined, e.g., *http://iana.org/beep/SASL/XXX*.

---

* Note to security gurus: apologies in advance if you start twitching uncontrollably when I place the terms "secure" and "best" in close proximity. Note to everyone else: any security guru will tell you that a table with a single column labeled "Secure" is vastly oversimplified.

In addition, some SASL mechanisms also provide a security layer, which makes the session tamper-evident, and may also provide privacy. In the latter case, the SASL mechanism provides the same kind of functionality that TLS does. DIGEST-MD5 is an example of a mechanism that does both the "SA" part of SASL (simple authentication) and (optionally) the "SL" part (security layer) too.

Finally, it's likely that the SASL specification (RFC 2222) will be revised in calendar year 2002. If so, although some of the details may change, no changes should be necessary from the application designer/programmer's perspective.

Tuning in Practice

Tuning is a lot simpler in practice than in theory. Let's go straight to "ideal" practice:

1. See if the underlying transport or network service is already authenticated and encrypted; if so, tune using the SASL EXTERNAL profile, and you're done.
2. Otherwise, decide whether you want encryption. If you do, tune using a profile that does transport privacy.
3. Then, decide whether you want authentication. If you do:
   - If you already tuned for transport privacy, and if authentication took place, then tune using the SASL EXTERNAL profile.
   - Otherwise, tune using a profile that does user authentication.

Note that you don't have to tune at all. If your application doesn't need to be provisioned for security, then the first channel you start is an exchange profile to do useful work.

BEEP defines a lot of different tuning profiles, and they each have their own sweet spot. So, what tuning profiles should you use? It depends, of course, on what your requirements are. Having said that, here's what the reliable *syslog* specification (RFC 3195) says:

- If you want user authentication, tune with the SASL DIGEST-MD5 profile for authentication only.
- If you also want tamper-detection, tune with the SASL DIGEST-MD5 profile for both authentication and integrity protection.
- Otherwise, if you want privacy, tune with the TLS profile.

The reason comes down to scaling: tuning with DIGEST-MD5 has a lot less overhead than using TLS, but TLS supports stronger encryption algorithms.

This policy is probably a pretty good middle ground. Of course, a security maven will tell you that there's no such thing. They're right that an application operating in a given environment has its own set of unique requirements, but, in practice, this level of granularity is largely irrelevant (unless you have the term "sigint" in your job description).

But, what if your server is sitting on top of a legacy password database? In that case, you can't use the SASL DIGEST-MD5 profile, and you're not going to get your users to install client-side certificates, so you can't tune using the TLS and EXTERNAL profiles.

This isn't a problem; here's the "legacy" practice: tune using the TLS profile (only the server need authenticate itself), and then tune using the SASL PLAIN profile.

The only trick here is to make sure that your server advertises the SASL PLAIN profile only after transport privacy is in effect.

Tuning Profiles Versus Exchange Profiles

Finally, what's the real difference between a profile used for tuning and one used for exchange? There are two differences: one of which is a rule, the other a convention.

First, as a rule, BEEP demands that once you create a channel with a tuning profile, you can't create another tuning channel until you finish with the first one. This is because tuning channels muck around with the global properties of a BEEP session, and it's too confusing for most implementations to keep track of more than one. Actually, the rules are even stricter—BEEP allows you to authenticate at most once during a session; similarly, once you turn on transport privacy, there's no turning it off or negotiating something else. In contrast, you can have more than one channel created with an exchange profile running at the same time. In fact, you can even have multiple channels bound to the same exchange profile.

Second, as a convention, first you tune, then you exchange. It doesn't make a lot of sense to intermix the activities of the two. (If you can think of a scenario in which it would make sense, drop me a note!)

Beyond these two differences, there aren't any more: anyone is free to define as many profiles as they want, and they can be profiles used for tuning or data exchange. Of course, between TLS and the SASL family of mechanisms, the BEEP folks think the bases are covered, but there are other things you can do with tuning. (For an example, take a look at "Tunneling" in Chapter 8.)

The Lifecycle of a Session

To sum all of this up, let's take a look at a "typical" session as shown in Figure 3-6.

Consider the typical session shown here:

- It begins when a transport connection is established, which creates an untuned BEEP session along with channel zero.
- The first thing that happens on the session is the exchange of greetings between the peers on channel zero.

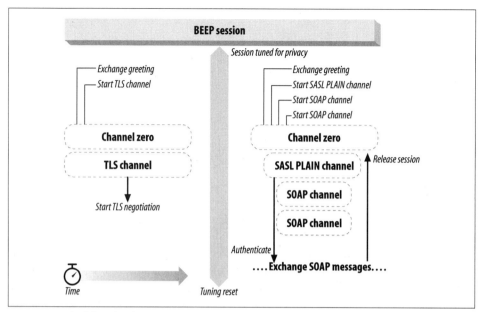

Figure 3-6. The lifecycle of a "typical" session

- After this, a channel bound to the TLS profile is started, which ultimately results in a tuning reset, implicitly closing both channels.

- Assuming the underlying TLS negotiation is successful, the session is now tuned for privacy. Regardless, we have a new channel zero, and the usual exchange of greetings.

- Next, one of the peers starts a channel bound to the SASL PLAIN profile, and authenticates itself. Assuming the authentication is successful, the session is now tuned for authentication (in one direction). Further, once the authentication is complete, this channel could be closed, but it's not necessary.

- Next, a channel bound to the SOAP profile is started, and a SOAP message exchange is begun.

- This exchange seems to be taking a while, so another channel is started, and, for the rest of the session, SOAP messages are exchanged over both of them. Note that although the messages exchanged on each channel are processed serially, the two channels are running independently of each other.

- Finally, when we're ready to wind things up, channel zero is used to release the session, implicitly closing all channels.

CHAPTER 4

Exchanges

This chapter explains the different ways that messages are exchanged in BEEP.

In the section "Channels" in Chapter 2, we saw that the application protocol designer defines a profile that specifies the rules for exchanging messages. Experience shows that these fall into three categories, with each appropriate to a particular set of interaction requirements. It's up to the application protocol designer to decide which one to use. The three exchange styles are:

- Client/server
- Server/client
- Peer-to-peer

Client/Server

The client/server exchange consists of the client sending a message, and the server sending a reply. With the traditional client/server exchange, the peer that acted as the initiator always acts as a client. BEEP doesn't require this, however—it's perfectly fine for the peer that's listening for incoming connections to act as a client once a connection is established.

Because the client/server exchange is so commonplace, we don't have to look too hard to find a good example to use for the basis of a profile. Perhaps you're familiar with XML-RPC, a technology that uses XML to encode remote procedure calls (RPCs) that are transmitted over HTTP. The idea is straightforward, and while XML-RPC won't win any awards for elegance or performance, it gets the job done.* The client/server precept is shown in Figure 4-1.

---

* If you'd like more information on XML-RPC, check out *Programming Web Services with XML-RPC* by Simon St.Laurent, Joe Johnston, and Edd Dumbill.

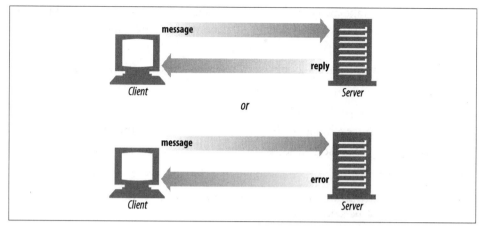

Figure 4-1. The client/server precept

Since no good deed goes unpunished, XML-RPC has evolved into a more generalized messaging protocol called the *Simple Object Access Protocol* (SOAP). Although a purist might quibble, there are only two architectural differences between XML-RPC and SOAP:

- XML-RPC requires the use of HTTP as a transport, while SOAP isn't HTTP-only.
- XML-RPC provides only for request/response remote procedure calls, while SOAP doesn't explicitly require any particular messaging model.

Oddly enough, SOAP doesn't have an object model, and still spends a lot of time on marshaling (encoding low-level data structures to a network representation), so it still looks more like RPC than not.[*]

For example, here's a SOAP message:

```
<SOAP-ENV:Envelope
   xmlns:SOAP-ENV='http://schemas.xmlsoap.org/soap/envelope/'
   SOAP-ENV:encodingStyle='http://schemas.xmlsoap.org/soap/encoding/'>
    <SOAP-ENV:Body>
       <m:GetLastTradePrice xmlns:m='Some-URI'>
           <symbol>DIS</symbol>
       </m:GetLastTradePrice>
    </SOAP-ENV:Body>
</SOAP-ENV:Envelope>
```

If you're an XML aficionado, this makes perfect sense, obviously! If not, the key take-away is the stuff nested in the SOAP-Env:Body element. The m:GetLastTradePrice element looks like a remote procedure call, with one argument, symbol, having the

---

[*] If you'd like more information on SOAP, check out *Programming Web Services with SOAP* by Doug Tidwell, James Snell, and Pavel Kulchenko.

value DIS. Another take-away is that the envelope doesn't contain any addressing information—it doesn't explicitly identify the network service that will process the call.

The precept shown in Figure 4-2 concisely describes the three things you need to do to define a profile:

- Assign a unique identifier for the profile.
- Indicate what gets exchanged when a channel is bound to the profile.
- Indicate what gets passed back and forth in a client/server exchange.

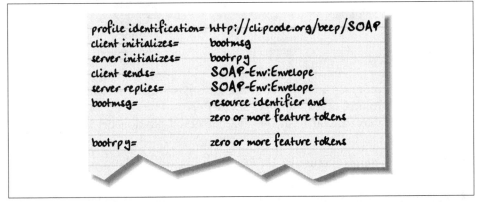

Figure 4-2. The SOAP over BEEP precept

In BEEP, there's actually a formal "registration template" that gets filled out when you define a profile. We'll look at one in a bit, but for now, let's avoid the formalities and concentrate on the concepts.

The URI part is easy enough; whoever is responsible for *http://clipcode.org/* assigned it. (Anyone who can assign a URI can define a profile.) Note that if a URI starts with *http://iana.org/*, this indicates that the profile has had some review by the IETF. In some cases, this URI-prefix indicates that the profile has been approved for the Internet standards-track.

Similarly, the client/server exchange part is pretty easy too. The request sent by the client is a SOAP message, as is the server's reply. That's all BEEP really cares about. But what about the initialization exchange?

When a channel is created, it may require some additional parameters before it can begin normal processing. Many profiles don't have initialization requirements, but the SOAP profile for BEEP does. In particular, it needs to know:

- The identity of the network service that will be processing the SOAP messages
- Optionally, whether any special SOAP "features" might be used

Each of these serves a different purpose.

When SOAP runs over HTTP, the network service that consumes the message is identified by two parameters, e.g.:

```
POST /StockQuote HTTP/1.1
Host: example.com
```

When SOAP runs over BEEP, you need to convey the same information, but it's carried a little differently. Recall from "Channel Creation" in Chapter 3 that BEEP uses the serverName attribute to identify the virtual host, e.g.:

```
<start number='1' serverName='example.com'>
    <profile uri='http://clipcode.org/beep/SOAP' />
</start>
```

So, what about the part that got sent as HTTP's Request-URI parameter?

That's what the bootmsg used for channel initialization is for. As soon as the channel is started, the client sends a bootmsg, e.g.:

```
<bootmsg resource='/StockQuote' />
```

Actually, using BEEP's piggybacking feature (see the section "The piggyback" in Chapter 3), the bootmsg probably gets included in the request to start the channel.

If the server likes the resource, then a bootrpy is sent back; otherwise an error is sent. Once a bootrpy is received, the client is free to start using the channel to exchange SOAP messages. (Of course, after a bootrpy is received, if another bootmsg is sent, an error is returned.)

BEEP URIs

One of the reasons I like to use SOAP as an example is because it raises an interesting question: what does a BEEP URI look like?

The short answer is that since BEEP isn't an application protocol, there's no such thing. A better answer is that when you design a profile, you should ask yourself whether it makes sense to define a URL scheme for the resulting protocol. In the case of the SOAP over BEEP profile, this makes a lot of sense.

Here's some examples, all of which should be self-explanatory:

```
soap.beep://example.com/StockQuote
soap.beep://example.com
soap.beep://example.com:1026
soap.beep://10.0.0.2:1026
```

Here are some fun facts about these four examples:

- For the first three examples, example.com will be used as the serverName attribute.
- For the last three examples, "/" will be used as the resource attribute in the bootmsg.
- For the last two examples, the BEEP listener is on TCP port 1026.

But what TCP port is the BEEP listener using in the first two examples? There are two possible choices, depending on whether you prefer using a constant value or you want to let the DNS tell you.

However, the correct answer is always to start by asking the IANA to assign a port number. At this point, ask yourself whether it would be very helpful for the DNS to distribute the load among multiple servers. If not, you're done! Otherwise, there's a new DNS record called SRV (RFC 2782) that associates port numbers with services and provides a weighting mechanism for services available on multiple hosts.

For example, a DNS lookup of:

```
_soap-beep._tcp.example.com
```

will return zero or more SRV records. Each contains an IP address and TCP port number, along with some parameters that let you decide the order in which you should try to use the records.

For example, consider these resource records:

```
$ORIGIN example.com.

_soap-beep._tcp     SRV 0 1 10288 s1.example.com.
                    SRV 0 1 10288 s2.example.com.
                    SRV 1 0 10288 backup.example.com.
```

These records say to try to split the load between hosts s1 and s2; if both are unavailable, they specify the backup host.

The trick is in understanding the first two numbers after the SRV. The first number is the priority (the lower the number, the better the priority), and the second number is the weight relative to all other entries with the same priority. Since s1 and s2 have the same, lowest priority number, we look at those first. They each have equal weight, so they should have an equal chance of being selected first. If a connection can't be made to either, we go to the next highest priority, of which there's only one entry. So, in the worst case scenario, we'll try to make three TCP connections.

 Here's a helpful hint if you decide to use SRV records: although you can use any port number you want, you can save yourself a lot of grief by always using the IANA-assigned port number. The reason is that dynamically assigned ports aren't supported by a lot of infrastructural software, such as packet tracers, firewalls, and the like.

SOAP Extras

That's about it for the client/server exchange, but there's actually a little more to the SOAP over BEEP profile. Because SOAP isn't tied to a particular messaging model, it actually allows two other exchange styles besides request/response:

- One-way
- 1-request/N-responses

Both of these are handled in BEEP by using a one-to-many exchange, as shown in Figure 4-3.

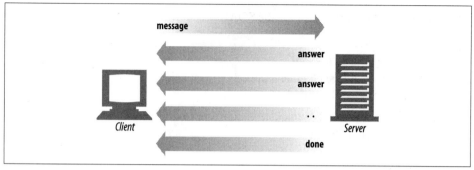

Figure 4-3. A SOAP over BEEP one-to-many exchange

The one thing we didn't discuss about SOAP is the relationship between SOAP and MIME. As we've seen, SOAP is about exchanging envelopes that are encoded using XML. If an envelope needs to contain non-XML information, then the envelope and extra information are sent as a *SOAP package*. This package is nothing more than a MIME multipart/related object (RFC 2387), e.g.:

```
Content-Type: multipart/related; boundary="MIME_boundary";
              type=application/xml;
              start="<claim061400a.xml@example.com>"

--MIME_boundary
Content-Type: application/xml
Content-ID: <claim061400a.xml@example.com>

<?xml version='1.0' ?>
<SOAP-ENV:Envelope
   xmlns:SOAP-ENV='http://schemas.xmlsoap.org/soap/envelope/'>
<SOAP-ENV:Body>
..
<theSignedForm href='cid:claim061400a.tiff@example.com' />
..
</SOAP-ENV:Body>
</SOAP-ENV:Envelope>

--MIME_boundary
Content-Type: image/tiff
Content-Transfer-Encoding: binary
Content-ID: <claim061400a.tiff@example.com>

...binary TIFF image...
--MIME_boundary--
END
```

The Content-ID: header (RFC 2111) is used to identify each component.

The SOAP over BEEP Registration

Earlier, Figure 4-2 showed an informal description of the SOAP over BEEP profile.

Here's a copy of the registration for the SOAP over BEEP profile:

Profile identification
    http://clipcode.org/beep/SOAP

Messages exchanged during channel creation
    `bootmsg, bootrpy`

Messages starting one-to-one exchanges
    `bootmsg, SOAP-Env:Envelope`

Messages in positive replies
    `bootrpy, SOAP-Env:Envelope`

Messages in negative replies
    `error`

Messages in one-to-many exchange
    `SOAP-Env:Envelope`

Message syntax
    `SOAP-Env:Envelope` as defined in Section 4 of *Simple Object Access Protocol (SOAP)* and *SOAP Messages with Attachments*

Message semantics
    See *Simple Object Access Protocol (SOAP)*

Contact information
    See the "Authors' Addresses" section of *Using SOAP in BEEP*

Although not part of the "formal" template, profile designers often find it useful to include a concise summary, termed a *designer doodle*, as a comment, e.g.:

```
SOAP messages, exchanged as application/xml

                client                  server reply
    role        message          positive            negative
    ======      =======          ========            ========
      I         bootmsg          bootrpy             error

    I or L    SOAP-Env:Envelope  SOAP-Env:Envelope   error
```

The way to read this is pretty simple:

- The initiator sends a `bootmsg` and, in reply, gets back either a `bootrpy` or an `error`.
- Then either the initiator or listener sends an `Envelope` and in reply gets back either an `Envelope` or an `error`.

Although brief, this synopsis leaves out some important things, such as the necessity of a successful `bootmsg` before sending a SOAP message. Even so, it does a good job of getting across the ideas behind the exchange.

Server/Client

The server/client exchange consists of the server sending a message, and the initiator sending multiple replies, as shown in Figure 4-4.

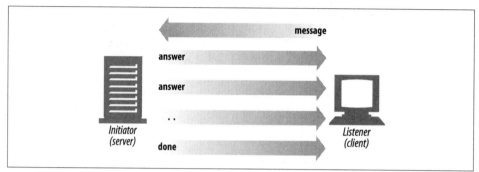

Figure 4-4. The server/client precept

 Note that, unlike the traditional client/server model, with the server/client model the peer that listens for incoming connections is the one that starts an exchange once the session is established.

Although the client/server exchange is useful for many applications, there are still some scenarios in which it doesn't fit. For example, let's say you have a lot of devices that want to "stream" many small pieces of information to a collector (such as access logs from web servers). Since it's not practical for the collector to poll all the devices, each device connects to the collector when it has information to report. After the device starts the desired channel, the collector sends a message indicating that it's ready for the stream. The device then starts sending the information, and then closes the channel and releases the session.

So why is this server/client exchange preferable? The answer is that it allows the client considerable freedom to optimize/customize the communication:

- A device's configuration determines the threshold of information generated before connecting.
- Once connected, the device can stream the previously generated information without waiting on individual acknowledgments.
- If more information is generated during this time, it can be sent as well.
- When all the information is sent, the device can decide how much longer to wait before saying it's "done" with the exchange.

While it's certainly possible to use a series of client/server exchanges to mimic this behavior, it's much more natural to use a single server/client exchange: rather than sending a string of messages carrying a useful piece of information, each being acknowledged by a response with no useful information, this technique sends a message with no useful content, answered by any number of responses each carrying useful information.

For a real-world example of the server/client exchange, let's look at reliably transmitting *syslog* messages.

syslog, or more properly, the BSD *syslog* protocol, is one of those protocols that's been in wide use since the mid-80s, but no one bothered to document it for 15 years. (Check out RFC 3164 for a detailed description.) *syslog* doesn't require either ordered or reliable delivery, so it uses UDP instead of TCP for transport. There are a fair number of tools and processes that "do *syslog*"—you might want to take a look at *Network Troubleshooting Tools* by Joseph D. Sloan to find out more.

A *syslog* message contains four parts:

- A priority, encoding a facility and a severity
- A header, containing a timestamp and sometimes a host identity
- A tag, identifying the process that originated the message
- Some simple text

By convention, the entire *syslog* message should be less than 1024 octets in length.

Section 4.1.1 of RFC 3164 defines the commonly used (but somewhat obscure) values for the facility and severity. The gist is that the facility tells you what part of the system generated the message (e.g., the kernel or a daemon), and the severity tells you how bad things were when the message was generated (e.g., critical or informational).

Why mess around with *syslog*? The short answer is that as long as you don't care about the reliable or secure transmission of *syslog* messages, you shouldn't. However, if you want to provision network auditing in an environment in which messages are sent reliability and possibly securely, then you've got a lot to work to do if you start with UDP-based syslog.

In fact, you start with two choices:

- Keep the existing *syslog* format and use BEEP to move messages around
- Define an equivalent format and use BEEP

The latter approach allows for additional functionality of information carried in the messages (at the cost of having an incompatible format). The working group that defined reliable *syslog* defined two BEEP profiles, since each choice has its uses.

The Syslog Raw Profile

For our purposes, we'll stick to original *syslog* format, and just look at how BEEP can be used to carry those messages. Here's the completed registration for the profile that simply layers syslog messages on top of BEEP:

Profile identification
    http://iana.org/beep/syslog/RAW

Messages exchanged during channel creation
    none

Messages starting one-to-one exchanges
    n/a

Messages in positive replies
    n/a

Messages in negative replies
    n/a

Messages in one-to-many exchanges:
    text

Message syntax
    See Section 4 of RFC 3164

Message semantics
    See RFC 3164

Contact information
    See the "Authors' Addresses" section of RFC 3195

The corresponding designer doodle is:

```
syslog messages, exchanged as application/octet-stream

                client
    role        message                   each server answer
    ======      =======            ==========================
    L           text               1 or more syslog messages
```

The way to read this is pretty simple:

- The listener sends a message containing arbitrary text.
- The initiator sends back one or more answers in reply, each containing one or more *syslog* messages.

The only important detail left out of this doodle is that if more than one *syslog* message is sent in a single answer, each is separated by a CRLF pair, but there is no trailing CRLF allowed on the final message.

So, perhaps a better doodle is one that uses *Augmented BNF* (ABNF, RFC 2234), e.g:

```
syslog messages, exchanged as application/octet-stream

                client
    role        message             each server answer
    ======      =======             =========================
    L           *text               message *(CR LF message)
```

One Packet Trace

Although earlier we said that there weren't any packet traces in this book, here's one from the reliable *syslog* specification:

```
L: MSG 1 0 . 0 50
L:
L: Central Services. This has not been a recording.
L: END
I: ANS 1 0 . 0 119 0
I:
I: <29>Oct 27 13:21:08 ductwork imxpd[141]: Heating emergency.
I: <29>Oct 27 13:21:09 ductwork imxpd[141]: Contact Tuttle.END
I: NUL 1 0 . 119 0
I: END
```

It's provided so you can compare it to the server/client precept presented earlier. (L and I indicate the listener and initiator of the session, respectively.)

So Why Bother?

Since layering *syslog* on top of BEEP is so easy, why bother?

The basic reason is that you "trade up" in session services. UDP is nice and light-weight, and there's a lot of good things to be said about it. Unfortunately, the simplicity comes at a cost which may not be appropriate in all environments. If you must have reliability, then you can either reinvent TCP on top of UDP or just use TCP. I suggest the latter, because the guys who specified TCP and the guys who implemented TCP on your system are probably smarter than "five-niner" (99.999%) of the professional population. Of course, independent of the reliability issue, there's still the security issue, which neither TCP nor UDP was designed to solve. This brings us back full circle because you have to start adding these extra services. If you're going to use TCP, then we're back to that lengthy discussion in "Application Protocol Design" in Chapter 1.

If you remember in the previous chapter, we mentioned the recommendations the reliable *syslog* working group made with respect to security. Let's recap:

- If you want user authentication, tune with the SASL DIGEST-MD5 profile for authentication only.

- If you also want detection of tampering, tune with the SASL DIGEST-MD5 profile for both authentication and integrity protection.
- Otherwise, if you want privacy, tune with the TLS profile.

The reason for this granularity is that it all depends on the amount of security you want. This is a deceptively simple point: the UDP-based *syslog* defines one end of a performance/functionality spectrum. Similarly, reliable *syslog* running with TLS and some bit-fondling/entropy-seeking encryption algorithm is at the other end. Once you move past the vanilla environment, different administrators are going to have different views on what's an acceptable cost-point. One of BEEP's jobs is to make moving along that spectrum as painless as possible.

If layering *syslog* on top of BEEP is so easy, why bother? That's exactly why.

Peer-to-Peer

The peer-to-peer exchange places no restrictions on who acts as a client or a server at any given time. What Figure 4-5 tries to show is that either peer can initiate an exchange at any time, even if it has received and is processing a request. Consequently, there's never any need to block while waiting for something to finish, so completely asynchronous external events can be turned into promptly-delivered messages. Whether you need support for callbacks or unsolicited events, BEEP can handle it.

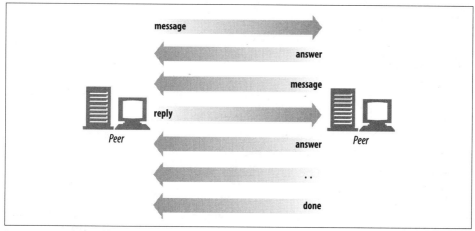

Figure 4-5. The peer-to-peer precept

Since the previous two sections have covered everything in the exchange precept (one-to-one and one-to-many), all that's really left to talk about is a little matter of priorities.

A Digression

If you talk to protocol experts, there's often just "one thing" objectionable about BEEP. The amusing part is that the "thing" that's actually objectionable depends on who you're talking with. For example, some folks really don't like XML, so for them, the fact that BEEP uses XML as the syntax for its channel management is a big problem. Other folks love XML, and, for them, the fact that BEEP doesn't mandate the use of XML—on all channels—is an even bigger problem. (There are some comments on all this in the Appendix, if you're interested.)

Another controversy arises because BEEP allows you to multiplex messages over multiple channels contained in a single transport connection. The reason this is controversial is two-fold:

- Multiplexing is handled more efficiently at the lower layers.
- Multiplexing at adjacent layers may result in deadlock.

These are valid concerns and the BEEP specifications spend a fair amount of time discussing how to maximize efficiency and eliminate deadlock.

From the perspective of someone using an API for BEEP, what you need to know is this: a properly implemented API has a fair amount of code responsible for organizing outgoing traffic. One of the things the API may offer you is the ability to prioritize the traffic you generate for each channel. Obviously, if you have only one open channel on a session, the issue is moot, but if for some reason you're using multiple channels simultaneously, it's worthwhile seeing what knobs and gauges the API makes available to you.

Let's Recap

Even though it wasn't an explicit goal, by now you should understand how to put a profile together. The steps are pretty simple:

1. Decide which exchange style is appropriate.
2. Decide what kind of messages get exchanged.
3. Put together a designer doodle to capture the essence of the profile.
4. Fill out a registration template.

Of course, the hard part happens before any of this—you need to understand enough of the problem you want to solve in order to come up with the syntax and semantics of the exchange. However, the really nice aspect of this hard part is that because BEEP is doing so much work for you, the syntax and semantics you have to come up with are, in fact, your application protocol!

Actually, the hardest part happens after all of this—you need to implement and deploy the solution. The good news is that we're now done with the first part of the book, the part on architecture. Now, it's on to the second part: let's look at the APIs!

## CHAPTER 5

BEEP in Java

Of the three beepcore implementations, beepcore-java has seen the most development. It provides a classic example of solid Java infrastructure, using interfaces and subclassing to provide successive layers of encapsulation. In this chapter, we'll start at the top and work our way down towards the specific (unlike the chapter on beepcore-c, where we'll start at the bottom and work our way up, or the chapter on beepcore-tcl, where we'll start in the middle and stay there!).

As of this writing, beepcore-java requires J2SE 1.2 (or greater). From a licensing perspective, this means that it runs only on a subset of systems that are JVM-capable; fortunately, Linux, Mac OS X, Solaris, and Windows are in that subset.

As with all the versions of beepcore, go to *http://beepcore.org/* to find out where to download the current release of beepcore-java. Inside that release, point your browser to *doc/core/overview-summary.html* and you'll be looking at the index for the class hierarchy.

A Guided Tour

Let's implement an echo profile. Its operation is a simple exercise in client/server:

- One peer connects to the other, starts a channel with the echo profile, and sends zero or more messages.
- Each time a message is received, it's sent back as a reply.
- When the initiator is done sending messages, it closes the channel.

The Echo Initiator

Let's start with the initiating peer.

In order to guide you through this, here's a quick summary of what we're going to do: we'll define a class, Bing, that implements the initiator. The "guts" of that class will:

1. Create a session using `TCPSessionCreator.initiate()`.

2. Tune the session for privacy using `TLSProfile.startTLS()`.

3. Create a channel for the echo profile using `Session.startChannel()`.

4. Iterate a loop that sends a message using `Channel.sendMSG()` and then processes a reply using `Reply.getNextReply()` and `InputStream.read()`.

5. Close the channel using `Channel.close()`.

6. Release the session using `Session.close()`.

Of course, since we're looking at a complete class, there's a lot of detail in between these steps. That's okay—just keep these six points in mind as we go through it.

Example 5-1 shows the beginning of the source file. After the usual package statement, we `import` some packages, two from `java.io` and the rest all under `org.beepcore.beep`:

*core.**
> These are the packages that implement the BEEP mechanisms, including classes for sessions, channels, and the like.

lib.Reply
> This package provides a synchronous interface for dealing with replies to the messages we send.

profile.echo.EchoProfile
> This package implements the server-side of the echo profile.

profile.tls.TLSProfile
> This package implements the profile used to tune for transport privacy as described in "The TLS Profile" in Chapter 3.

*transport.tcp.**
> These packages provide an encapsulation of the BEEP session concept for use over TCP.

Example 5-1. Bing: The beginning

```
package org.beepcore.beep.example;

import java.io.InputStream;
import java.io.IOException;

import org.beepcore.beep.core.*;
import org.beepcore.beep.lib.Reply;
import org.beepcore.beep.profile.echo.EchoProfile;
import org.beepcore.beep.profile.tls.TLSProfile;
import org.beepcore.beep.transport.tcp.*;

public class Bing {

    private static final int PRIVACY_NONE = 0;
```

Example 5-1. Bing: The beginning (continued)

```
private static final int PRIVACY_PREFERRED = 1;
private static final int PRIVACY_REQUIRED = 2;

private static final String usage =
    "usage: bing [options...] host\n\n" +
    "options:\n" +
    "    -port port     Specifies the port number.\n" +
    "    -count count   Number of echo requests to send.\n" +
    "    -size size     Request size.\n" +
    "    -privacy       required = require TLS.\n" +
    "                   preferred = request TLS.\n" +
    "                   none = don't request TLS.\n";

private static String host;
private static int port = 10288;
private static int privacy = PRIVACY_NONE;
private static int count = 4;
private static int size = 1024;
```

With one exception, we'll look at all of these in greater detail later on in the section "Fundamental Classes." In fact, as we're going through this exposition, you may want to occasionally glance ahead at Figure 5-1 to look at the class hierarchy. The one exception is EchoProfile, which we'll detail even earlier, starting with Example 5-8.

Following the import statements, we define a few constants, the most important being usage, which describes the syntax for invoking this class via main( ). After this are the five variables that get set during argument parsing:

- The host to connect to
- The port to connect to
- Our privacy requirements
- The number of exchanges to make
- The number of octets to send in each exchange

The main( ) method is shown in three examples, starting with Example 5-2.

Example 5-2. Bing: Establishing the session and channel

```
public static void main(String[] argv) {

    // Parse command line args

    if (parseArgs(argv) == false) {
        System.out.println(usage);
        return;
    }

    // Initiate a session with the server
```

Example 5-2. Bing: Establishing the session and channel (continued)

```
Session session;
try {
    session = TCPSessionCreator.initiate(host, port);
} catch (BEEPException e) {
    System.err.println("bing: Error connecting to " + host + ":" +
                        port + "\n\t" + e.getMessage());
    return;
}

try {

    // Start TLS if requested

    if (privacy != PRIVACY_NONE) {
        try {
            session =
                TLSProfile.getDefaultInstance()
                        .startTLS((TCPSession) session);
        } catch (BEEPException e) {
            System.err.println("bing: Error unable to start TLS.\n\t" +
                                e.getMessage());
            if (privacy == PRIVACY_REQUIRED)
                return;
        }
    }

    // Start a channel for the echo profile

    Channel channel;
    try {
        channel = session.startChannel(EchoProfile.ECHO_URI);
    } catch (BEEPError e) {
        if (e.getCode() == 550) {
            System.err.println("bing: host does not support echo " +
                                "profile");
        } else {
            System.err.println("bing: Error starting channel - " +
                                e.getCode() + ": " + e.getMessage());
        }
        return;
    } catch (BEEPException e) {
        System.err.println("bing: Error starting channel - " +
                            e.getMessage());
        return;
    }
}
```

First, we parse the argument list. In the interest of brevity, we're not going to look at how this is done, but presumably it's going to involve a loop and an awful lot of calls to equalsIgnoreCase( ).

Next, we try to establish a session by using the initiate( ) method from the TCPSessionCreator class. This class is really just a "convenience class" for

---

establishing BEEP sessions over TCP. With the initiate( ) method, it just creates a Socket object and binds it to a profile registry by calling a constructor for the TCPSession class. In doing so, if it encounters an exception, it maps it to a BEEPException.

Next, we see if we need to tune for transport privacy. This looks a little more complicated, so let's decompose the assignment that's made to session. The TLS profile supports two different implementations of TLS, JSSE and PureTLS. What TLSProfile.getDefaultInstance( ) is doing is returning an instance of a TLSProfile object that's bound to the default TLS implementation provided by your system. At that point, the startTLS( ) method of that TLSProfile object is called to tune the session. The return value is a new session object that's been tuned for privacy. If there's a problem, a BEEPException is raised.

Finally, we use the startChannel( ) method to start up the echo profile. This method is heavily overloaded. In addition to the simple "here's a URI" parameter, we can also supply parameters for:

- Piggybacked data (see the section "The piggyback" in Chapter 3)
- A Collection of profiles to use (recall from Figure 2-3 that a start request can give several choices for the profile to use)
- An object that implements the MessageListener interface

Notice that the startChannel( ) method is different from the session creation and tuning methods we've used in that it can throw a BEEPError in addition to a BEEPException. This corresponds to BEEP's localized diagnostics (see "Localization (L10N)" in Chapter 3), which have a numeric code, a textual diagnostic, and an optional language string.

Now that the channel is created, Example 5-3 shows the loop we use to send messages.

Example 5-3. Bing: Doing work

```
// build a request string

char[] c = new char[size];
c[0] = 'a';
for (int i = 1; i < c.length; ++i) {
    c[i] = (char) (c[i - 1] + 1);

    if (c[i] > 'z') {
        c[i] = 'a';
    }
}
String request = new String(c);

try {
    for (int i=0; i<count; ++i) {
```

Example 5-3. Bing: Doing work (continued)

```java
            long time;
            int replyLength = 0;
            Reply reply = new Reply( );

            time = System.currentTimeMillis( );

            try {
                channel.sendMSG(new StringOutputDataStream(request),
                                reply);
            } catch (BEEPException e) {
                System.err.println("bing: Error sending request - " +
                                    e.getMessage( ));
                return;
            }

            InputDataStream ds = reply.getNextReply().getDataStream( );
            InputStream is = ds.getInputStream( );

            while (is.read ( ) != -1) {
                ++replyLength;
            }

            System.out.println("Reply from " + host + ": bytes=" +
                                replyLength ( ) + " time=" +
                                (System.currentTimeMillis( ) - time) +
                                "ms");
        }
    } catch (BEEPInterruptedException e) {
        System.err.println("bing: Error receiving reply - " +
                            e.getMessage( ));
        return;
    } catch (IOException e) {
        System.err.println("bing: Error receiving reply - " +
                            e.getMessage( ));
        return;
    }
}
```

Before entering the loop, we build a string that we're going to send over and over again. Then, once each time through the loop, we first construct a new Reply object. The exchange is started by using the channel's sendMSG( ) method, which takes two parameters:

- An OutputDataStream object, containing the MIME object to be sent
- An object that implements the ReplyListener interface

The OutputDataStream class is the top-level class used to represent the payload that gets sent. This may be subclassed according to how you want to build the payload. For example, you may find it useful to send using a byte array or a String object, so there's both a ByteOutputDataStream and a StringOutputDataStream class.

When you initiate an exchange on a channel, you indicate how the corresponding reply should be handled. The ReplyListener interface defines this behavior. An object implementing this interface makes available four methods that are invoked, depending on what kind of reply is received.

If you recall from Figure 2-4, we saw how BEEP has two kinds of exchanges: one-to-one and one-to-many. A one-to-one exchange is made up of the client sending a message and the server sending back either a reply or an error. beepcore-java (and BEEP) use three-letter terms to refer to each of these. Therefore, a one-to-one exchange is either:

- Send a MSG, get back a RPY
- Send a MSG, get back an ERR

Similarly, a one-to-many exchange is:

- Send a MSG, get back zero or more ANS, followed by an NUL

When an object implements the ReplyListener interface, it provides a method for each of these possible reply types (receiveRPY( ), receiveERR( ), receiveANS( ), and receiveNUL( )). The current release of beepcore-java provides two convenience classes that implement this interface:

Reply
> Objects of this class provide a convenient mechanism for the caller to block execution of the current thread until a reply is received.

NullReplyListener
> Objects of this class simply ignore whatever reply they're given.

Of course, you're free (actually encouraged) to write your own! Objects implementing the ReplyListener interface will provide other methods. The reason is that ReplyListener specifies the requirements necessary for beepcore-java to deliver replies to the class, but other methods are probably needed for you to process those replies. For example, the Reply class implements a getNextReply( ) method. Alternatively, you might define a class that gets replies and writes them to a file. In order to make things like this happen, the class you define is either going to configure its objects via a constructor method, or the class will provide other methods that implement the behavior you desire. (Of course, the NullReplyListener class is the exception that proves the rule—it exists solely for the purpose of receiving replies from beepcore-java and then discarding them!)

After invoking sendMSG( ), the next step is to wait for a reply, so the getNextReply( ) method is called, which blocks until a reply *starts* to be received. It returns a Message object, which we convert into an InputDataStream object, and then into an java.io. InputStream object. Once we have our InputStream, we just loop through the data, counting the number of octets. The tricky part is that the getNextReply( ) method doesn't wait until the reply has been completely received before it returns. But that's okay—all the complexity is hidden from us! Finally, as you can infer from the catch clause, sendMsg( ) can throw a BEEPException, and getNextReply( ) can throw a BEEPInterruptedException.

The final part of the main( ) method is shown in Example 5-4. There's not really much here. First, we invoke the channel's close( ) method. Then, we reach the finally clause of the try statement that we started right after we created the session. All we do there is invoke the session's close( ) method.

Example 5-4. Bing: Closing the channel and session

```
    // Close the Channel

    try {
        channel.close();
    } catch (BEEPException e) {
        System.err.println("bing: Error closing channel - " +
                        e.getMessage());
        return;
    }

} finally {
    // Close the Session

    try {
        session.close();
    } catch (BEEPException e) {
        System.err.print("bing: Error closing session - " +
                        e.getMessage());
        return;
    }
}
}
```

Obviously, there's a lot of stuff going on behind the scenes here. However, the magic of Java is that the authors of beepcore-java were able to hide it all quite handily.

The Echo Listener

The listening peer is a little more complicated, but only because we spend a lot of time on configuration. In order to guide you through the code, here's a quick summary of what we're going to do. We'll define a class, Beepd, that implements a multi-threaded listener:

- The run( ) method loops forever, creating sessions using TCPSessionCreator. listen( ).

- The Beepd( ) method takes configuration information about what profiles to offer on a given TCP port, and build a ProfileRegistry with pointers to each of these profiles. An instance of the ProfileRegistry class is little more than a

collection of profiles. If you want to allow the remote peer to start channels, this
is the thing that knows what profiles can be bound to those channels. It's also
used to determine what the greeting should look like.

- The main( ) method looks at its parameters to figure out which configuration file
to read, and then start as many threads as appropriate.

- Finally, we'll define a second class, EchoProfile, which implements the server-
side of the echo profile. (This is actually a lot simpler than our driver class, Beepd.)

Because we're parsing a configuration file, there's a lot of administrative overhead, so
just focus on these four points throughout.

Example 5-5 shows the beginning of the source file. After the usual package statement, we import a lot of packages. The ones that don't come from org.beepcore.beep
are all related to the configuration work we're going to do: parsing XML files, building up lists, and so on. (One of these packages, javax.xml.parsers, may not come
with the Java distribution on your system, so check the installation notes that come
with beepcore-java for the relevant pointers.)

Example 5-5. Beepd: The beginning

```
package org.beepcore.beep.example;

import java.io.File;
import java.io.FileInputStream;
import java.io.IOException;

import java.util.Collection;
import java.util.Iterator;
import java.util.LinkedList;
import java.util.Hashtable;
import java.util.StringTokenizer;
import java.util.NoSuchElementException;

import javax.xml.parsers.*;

import org.w3c.dom.*;

import org.xml.sax.SAXException;

import org.beepcore.beep.core.ProfileRegistry;
import org.beepcore.beep.core.SessionTuningProperties;
import org.beepcore.beep.profile.Profile;
import org.beepcore.beep.profile.ProfileConfiguration;
import org.beepcore.beep.transport.tcp.TCPSessionCreator;
import org.beepcore.beep.util.ConsoleLog;
import org.beepcore.beep.util.Log;

public class Beepd extends Thread {

    private static final String usage =
        "usage: beepd [-config <file>]\n\n" +
```

Example 5-5. Beepd: The beginning (continued)

```
        "options:\n" +
        "   -config file  File to read the configuration from.\n";

    private int port;
    ProfileRegistry reg;

    public void run() {
        try {
            // Loop listening for new Sessions

            while (true) {
                TCPSessionCreator.listen(port, reg);
            }
        } catch (Exception e) {
            Log.logEntry(Log.SEV_ERROR, e);
            Log.logEntry(Log.SEV_ERROR, "Listener exiting");
        }
    }
}
```

In terms of the beepcore-java packages, there's a couple of new objects:

profile.Profile
> This interface defines a convenient behavior for initializing a profile module.

profile.ProfileConfiguration
> This class provides mechanisms for passing configuration information to an object that implements the Profile interface.

core.SessionTuningProperties
> This class provides a similar service for how the session was tuned.

util.Log
> This class implements a simple logging facility.

Following the import statements, we define the usage constant that describes the syntax for invoking this class via main( ). Following this are the two variables that configure the behavior of each instances of this class:

- The port number to listen on
- The ProfileRegistry object that contains the profiles known to this instance

Finally, because the Beepd class extends Thread, we define a run( ) method. The idea here is very simple: the listen( ) method from TCPSessionCreator is repeatedly called until an exception is thrown. (We've already seen the initiate( ) method from this class.) Both methods return a TCPSession object. The difference is that the listen( ) method blocks while waiting for incoming connections, each of which it then binds to a profile registry by calling a constructor for the TCPSession class. Of course, any exceptions that are encountered get thrown as a BEEPException. So the real question is, how do we initialize the port number and the ProfileRegistry object?

Let's say we'll do that using a configuration file something like this:

```xml
<?xml version="1.0"?>

<config>
    <beepd port='10288'>
        <profile uri='http://iana.org/beep/TLS'
                 class='org.beepcore.beep.profile.tls.jsse.TLSProfileJSSE' />

        <profile uri='http://xml.resource.org/profiles/NULL/ECHO'
                 class='org.beepcore.beep.profile.echo.EchoProfile' />

        <profile uri='http://xml.resource.org/profiles/SASL/PLAIN'
                 class='org.beepcore.beep.profile.sasl.plain.SASLPlainProfile'
                 tuning='ENCRYPTION=true' />
    </beepd>
</config>
```

XML is used for the syntax. Our job will be to parse it. Fortunately, there are excellent XML parsing libraries available for Java.

Example 5-6 shows the constructor method that will parse each beepd element. (The code in the main method will break the file up into these elements and invoke the constructor method.) The logic is a bit tedious, but straightforward. First, we initialize the port number. Next, we loop through the immediate children of the beepd element that are named profile. After some paranoid checks to make sure we're looking at a profile element, we extract the uri and class attributes.

Example 5-6. Beepd: The constructor

```java
private Beepd(Element serverConfig) throws Exception {
reg = new ProfileRegistry();

if (serverConfig.hasAttribute("port") == false) {
    throw new Exception("Invalid configuration, no port specified");
}

port = Integer.parseInt(serverConfig.getAttribute("port"));

NodeList profiles = serverConfig.getElementsByTagName("profile");
for (int i=0; i<profiles.getLength(); ++i) {
    if (profiles.item(i).getNodeType() != Node.ELEMENT_NODE) {
        continue;
    }

    Element profile = (Element) profiles.item(i);

    if (profile.getNodeName().equalsIgnoreCase("profile") == false) {
        continue;
    }

    String uri;
    String className;
```

Example 5-6. Beepd: The constructor (continued)

```
String requiredProperites;
String tuningProperties;

if (profile.hasAttribute("uri") == false) {
    throw new Exception("Invalid configuration, no uri specified");
}
uri = profile.getAttribute("uri");

if (profile.hasAttribute("class") == false) {
    throw new Exception("Invalid configuration, no class " +
                        "specified for profile " + uri);
}
className = profile.getAttribute("class");

ProfileConfiguration profileConfig =
    parseProfileConfig(profile.getElementsByTagName("parameter"));

SessionTuningProperties tuning = null;
if (profile.hasAttribute("tuning")) {
    String tuningString = profile.getAttribute("tuning");
    Hashtable hash = new Hashtable();
    StringTokenizer tokens = new StringTokenizer(tuningString,
                                                 ":=");

    try {
        while (tokens.hasMoreTokens()) {
            String parameter = tokens.nextToken();
            String value = tokens.nextToken();

            hash.put(parameter, value);
        }
    } catch (NoSuchElementException e) {
        e.printStackTrace();

        throw new Exception("Error parsing tuning property on " +
                            "profile " + uri);
    }

    tuning = new SessionTuningProperties(hash);
}

Profile p;
try {
    p = (Profile) Class.forName(className).newInstance();
} catch (ClassNotFoundException e) {
    throw new Exception("Class " + className + " not found");
} catch (ClassCastException e) {
    throw new Exception("class " + className + " does not " +
                        "implement the " +
                        "org.beepcore.beep.profile.Profile " +
                        "interface");
}
```

Example 5-6. Beepd: The constructor (continued)

```
        reg.addStartChannelListener(uri,
                                p.init(uri, profileConfig),
                                tuning);
    }
}
```

We then call a helper routine to look at the content of the profile element, and parse any parameter elements found into a `ProfileConfiguration` object:

```
private static ProfileConfiguration
    parseProfileConfig(NodeList profileConfig) throws Exception {
    ProfileConfiguration config = new ProfileConfiguration();

    for (int i=0; i<profileConfig.getLength(); ++i) {
        Element parameter = (Element) profileConfig.item(i);

        if (parameter.hasAttribute("name") == false ||
            parameter.hasAttribute("value") == false)
        {
            throw new Exception("Invalid configuration parameter " +
                                "missing name or value attibute");
        }

        config.setProperty(parameter.getAttribute("name"),
                            parameter.getAttribute("value"));
    }

    return config;
}
```

This object will contain any profile-specific initialization settings (e.g., database settings).

Next, we look for a tuning attribute indicating what tuning requirements the profile has. For example, we may not want to advertise the profile until the session is tuned for transport privacy. (Take another look at the sample configuration file we saw earlier.) Now comes the fun part: we try to load the class that implements the profile and create a new object. Assuming our CLASSPATH is set correctly, and there aren't any typos in the configuration file, we now invoke the addStartChannelListener() method to add this profile to the ProfileRegistry object. The method takes three parameters:

- A URI that identifies this particular profile
- An object that implements the StartChannelListener interface
- The tuning requirements for the profile

It's this middle parameter that's of interest to us. In beepcore-java, the Profile interface provides a convenient way of initializing a profile module. It has only one requirement: that objects have an init() method that initializes a profile object (based on two parameters, a URI and a `ProfileConfiguration` object) and returns an object that implements the `StartChannelListener` interface. This second interface is a little more complicated; its behavior requires three methods:

advertiseProfile()
> Prior to sending a greeting, this method is invoked to decide whether the profile should be present in that greeting.

startChannel()
> When the remote peer asks to start a channel bound to this profile, this method decides whether to honor the request.

closeChannel()
> When the remote peer asks to close a channel bound to this profile, this method decides whether to honor the request.

What's important to understand is that the `ProfileRegistry` compares the current `SessionTuningProperties` to the tuning requirements given to `addStartChannelListener()` to determine whether the first two methods should even be invoked. Going back to the sample configuration file, you can see how the `advertiseProfile()` method for `SASLPlainProfile` won't be advertised if the session hasn't been tuned for transport privacy.

Once we dispose of the `main()` method, we'll look at a profile in more detail. Until then, let's compare this to how the initiator started a channel, where it simply invoked the session's `startChannel()` method with a single parameter, a URI. In this case, the initiator is taking all the responsibility for implementing the semantics of the channel—it simply says "create a channel using this URI and I'll take care of the rest." Of course, the `Beepd()` method doesn't start any channels; its job is simply to initialize the port number and the `ProfileRegistry` object.

Example 5-7 shows the method that does all the driving, `main()`. Parsing arguments is simple; if an argument is present, it must be `-config` followed by a filename. Next, we fire up the XML parser on the file to access an XML document.

Example 5-7. Beepd: Main

```
public static void main(String[] argv) {
        File config = new File("config.xml");

        // Parse arguments

        for (int i=0; i < argv.length; ++i) {
            if (argv[i].equalsIgnoreCase("-config")) {
                config = new File(argv[++i]);
                if (config.exists() == false) {
                    System.err.println("Beepd: Error file " +
                                    config.getAbsolutePath() +
                                    " does not exist");

                    return;
```

Example 5-7. Beepd: Main (continued)

```
            }
        } else {
            System.err.println(usage);
            return;
        }
    }

    // Parse configuration file into XML document

    Document doc;
    try {
        DocumentBuilder builder =
            DocumentBuilderFactory.newInstance().newDocumentBuilder();
        doc = builder.parse(new FileInputStream(config));
    } catch (ParserConfigurationException e) {
        System.err.println("Beepd: Error parsing config\n" +
            e.getMessage());
        return;
    } catch (SAXException e) {
        System.err.println("Beepd: Error parsing config\n" +
            e.getMessage());
        return;
    } catch (IOException e) {
        System.err.println("Beepd: Error parsing config\n" +
            e.getMessage());
        return;
    }

    // Extract configuration from XML document

    Collection servers;
    try {
        servers = parseConfig(doc.getDocumentElement());
    } catch (Exception e) {
        System.err.println(e.getMessage());
        return;
    }

    // log to the System.out

    ConsoleLog log = new ConsoleLog(Log.SEV_ERROR);
    Log.setLogService(log);

    // Start the servers listening

    Iterator i = servers.iterator();
    while (i.hasNext()) {
        ((Beepd) i.next()).start();
    }

    System.out.println("Beepd: started");
}
```

We then call a helper routine to look at the XML document, and build a Collection of Beepd objects, one for each beepd element in the configuration file:

```
private static Collection parseConfig(Element doc) throws Exception {
        LinkedList servers = new LinkedList();
        NodeList serverNodes = doc.getChildNodes();

        for (int i=0; i<serverNodes.getLength(); ++i) {
            Node s = serverNodes.item(i);
            if (s.getNodeType() != Node.ELEMENT_NODE) {
                continue;
            }

            if (s.getNodeName().equalsIgnoreCase("beepd") == false) {
                continue;
            }

            servers.add(new Beepd((Element) s));
        }

        return servers;

    }
```

So, that's how the constructor gets invoked, once for each beepd element. After this, we turn on the logging package and simply iterate over the collection we've built, starting a thread for each. Although this example is longer than the initiator example, the concepts are equally simple: build a ProfileRegistry object and invoke the listen() method from TCPSessionCreator. This process leaves us with one thing to discuss. What does a server-side implementation of a profile look like?

Example 5-8 shows the beginning of the source file. After the usual package and import statements, we declare this class as implementing three interfaces. We're already familiar with two of them. The third, MessageListener, we'll look at in a bit. In the body of the class, we see the default URI used for this profile (the EchoProfile. ECHO_URI we used back in Example 5-2), and the one method required for the Profile interface. So far, we haven't seen much—just some Java linkage.

Example 5-8. EchoProfile: The beginning

```
package org.beepcore.beep.profile.echo;

import java.io.ByteArrayOutputStream;
import java.io.IOException;
import java.io.InputStream;

import org.beepcore.beep.core.*;
import org.beepcore.beep.profile.*;
import org.beepcore.beep.util.*;

public class EchoProfile
```

Example 5-8. EchoProfile: The beginning (continued)

```
implements Profile, StartChannelListener, MessageListener {

public static final String ECHO_URI =
    "http://xml.resource.org/profiles/NULL/ECHO";

public StartChannelListener init(String uri, ProfileConfiguration config)
        throws BEEPException {
    return this;
}
```

Things get a little more interesting in Example 5-9, where we see the methods that implement the StartChannelListener interface. The first method, advertiseProfile( ), isn't exactly a model of complexity. startChannel( ) tells the channel which object should receive incoming messages (this). Finally, closeChannel( ) simply forgets about the object listening for incoming data. (Both of these are in the name of aiding garbage collection.)

Example 5-9. EchoProfile: Start channel listener

```
public boolean advertiseProfile(Session session) {
        return true;
    }

    public void startChannel(Channel channel, String encoding, String data)
            throws StartChannelException {
        channel.setMessageListener(this);
    }

    public void closeChannel(Channel channel) throws CloseChannelException {
        channel.setMessageListener(null);
    }
```

The "useful work" in the profile is done by the part that implements the MessageListener interface (shown in Example 5-10). When we called the setMessageListener( ) method for the newly started channel, we used this as the argument. You might recall from "Packet Formats and Traces" in Chapter 2 that BEEP automatically segments large messages into smaller units called *frames*. In many cases, an entire message fits into one frame, but this isn't necessarily the case. The beepcore-java implementation leaves it up to the programmer as to how incoming data should be presented—that's why the InputDataStream class gives you access to the data on a per-frame basis.

Example 5-10. EchoProfile: Message listener

```
public void receiveMSG(Message message) throws BEEPError
    {
        new ReplyThread(message).start( );
    }
```

Example 5-10. EchoProfile: Message listener (continued)

```
private class ReplyThread extends Thread {
    private Message message;

    ReplyThread(Message message) {
        this.message = message;
    }

    public void run() {
        OutputDataStream rs = new OutputDataStream();
        InputDataStream ds = message.getDataStream();

        while (ds.isComplete() == false || ds.availableSegment()) {
            try {
                rs.addSegment(ds.waitForNextSegment());
            } catch (InterruptedException e) {
                message.getChannel().getSession()
                                    .terminate(e.getMessage());
                return;
            }
        }

        rs.setComplete();

        try {
            message.sendRPY(rs);
        } catch (BEEPException e) {
            try {
                message.sendERR(BEEPError.CODE_REQUESTED_ACTION_ABORTED,
                              "Error sending RPY");
            } catch (BEEPException x) {
                message.getChannel().getSession()
                                    .terminate(x.getMessage());
            }
        }
    }
}
```

}

Objects implementing the MessageListener interface need one method, receiveMSG( ), that gets invoked whenever a MSG is received. For the echo profile, we start( ) a newly created ReplyThread object. The run( ) method for this object looks a bit like the code we saw for the initiator back in Example 5-3. Since we're going to echo, we create a new OutputDataStream, and then we invoke the message's getDataStream( ) method to get an InputDataStream object. Now we loop, waiting until we've completely received the MSG (using the isComplete( ) method) and we've completely consumed it (using the availableSegment( )). Until that happens, we invoke the waitForNextSegment( ) method to block until more data is available, which we subsequently add to the OutputDataStream we created. At this point, we mark that object as being complete, and call the message's sendRPY( ) method to send back a RPY reply. After queuing the reply, the thread terminates.

Although this approach gets the job done, we could be a little smarter by overlapping the reading and the writing:

```
public void run( ) {
        OutputDataStream rs = new OutputDataStream( );
        InputDataStream ds = message.getDataStream( );

        try {
            message.sendRPY(rs);
        } catch (BEEPException e) {
            try {
                message.sendERR(BEEPError.CODE_REQUESTED_ACTION_ABORTED,
                                "Error sending RPY");
            } catch (BEEPException x) {
                message.getChannel().getSession( )
                                    .terminate(x.getMessage( ));
            }
        }

        while (ds.isComplete( ) == false || ds.availableSegment( )) {
            try {
                rs.addSegment(ds.waitForNextSegment( ));
            } catch (InterruptedException e) {
                message.getChannel().getSession( )
                                    .terminate(e.getMessage( ));
                return;
            }
        }

        rs.setComplete( );
}
```

All we did was invoke the sendRPY( ) method first. Since the corresponding OutputDataStream isn't complete, nothing gets sent at first; however, every time we wake up after invoking waitForNextSegment( ) (by calling the addSegment( ) method for the OutputDataStream), we give the sendRPY( ) method a chance to do something. In other words, for a large message, we can still be receiving when we start to transmit the reply.

Fundamental Classes

Now let's look at the classes that make up the bulk of beepcore-java. Figure 5-1 shows a comprehensive class hierarchy for the beepcore-java implementation. Unless otherwise noted, all classes and interfaces are named under org.beepcore. beep.core. We've already seen a lot of these in action, so there's only a few details we need to cover in the remaining sections.

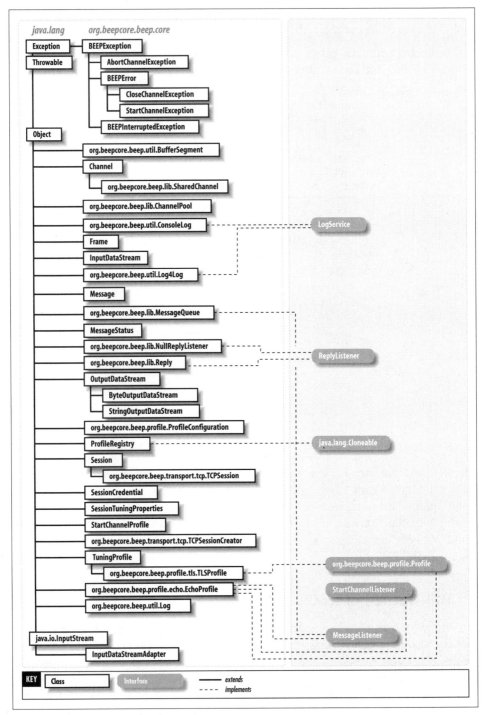

Figure 5-1. beepcore-java class hierarchy

Sessions

Three concepts deal with sessions: session creators, the Session class, and the ProfileRegistry class.

Session creators

When you create a session, you bind the session concept with an underlying transport mapping. The primary class provided for this is TCPSession, though few applications use this class directly. Instead, the TCPSessionCreator class provides two methods, initiate( ) and listen( ), which handle all the TCP socket manipulations and instantiate a TCPSession object. Both of these methods are overloaded, so you can provide the "host" parameter as either a String or InetAddress object, e.g.:

```
String host = "example.com";

session = TCPSessionCreator.initiate(host, 10288);

// or

InetAddress addr = InetAddress.getByName ("example.com");

session = TCPSessionCreator.initiate(addr, 10288);
```

You may want to use the latter form so you can explicitly catch the UnknownHostException, since the initiate( ) method will map this to a BEEPException.

If you do want to use the TCPSession class, the methods you probably want are called createInitiator( ) and createListener( ), e.g.:

```
Socket s = new Socket("example.com", 10288);

session = TCPSession.createInitiator(s, new ProfileRegistry ());
```

Note that neither createInitiator( ) nor createListener( ) is overloaded, so you have to provide an instance of a ProfileRegistry object to the constructor.

Once you've created a session, you may want to tune for transport privacy. In the future, potentially many different tuning profiles may support this. However, in the current implementation, there's only one profile that does—the TLSProfile. As we've seen before, the incantation is:

```
session = TLSProfile.getDefaultInstance( ).startTLS((TCPSession) session);
```

where session is an existing Session object. You may want to use something other than the default values, so let's flesh this out a bit.

After you create a TLSProfile object, you can configure the profile when you invoke the init( ) method. Recall that this method takes two parameters: a URI to identify the profile and a ProfileConfiguration object. The configuration keys you store are dependent on the security provider you're using, either JSSE or PureTLS. So point your browser to *doc/tls/overview-summary.html* and look at the field summary for Strings that are named starting with "PROPERTY_". For example:

```
String provider = "org.beepcore.beep.profile.tls.jsse.TLSProfileJSSE";

// or

String provider = "org.beepcore.beep.profile.tls.ptls.TLSProfilePureTLS";

ProfileConfiguration config = new ProfileConfiguration( );
// use config.setProperty( ) to set desired property values

TLSProfile p = (TLSProfile) TLSProfile.getInstance(provider)
                                    .init(TLSProfile.URI, config);

session = p.startTLS ((TCPSession) session);
```

The only thing new here is the getInstance( ) method, which returns a TLSProfile object implemented by the indicated security provider.

The Session class

The Session class encapsulates the behavior of a BEEP session. As you might expect, this class doesn't know anything about the transport layer. So, if you want to implement BEEP over "something other than TCP," you should be using the TCPSession class as your model.

There are a lot of methods available:

startChannel()
Starts a channel, specifying at a minimum a URI to use. Optionally, specifies a collection of URIs to use, piggybacked data to send, and an object (implementing the MessageListener interface) to handle incoming frames or messages.

close()
Closes the session, using BEEP's graceful release mechanism.

terminate()
Aborts the session, without requiring any further network interaction.

getLocalCredential( )/getPeerCredential()
Returns the SessionCredential object created during the tuning process for either the local or remote peer.

getPeerSupportedProfiles()
Returns a Collection of String objects for URIs that were found in the peer's greeting.

getProfileRegistry()
Returns the ProfileRegistry used in the creation of this session.

getTuningProperties()

Returns a `SessionTuningProperties` object describing the current tuning properties of the session. This class is rather embryonic at present. The only property that is currently supported determines whether transport privacy is in effect—use the method `getEncrypted( )` to find out.

isInitiator()

Returns `true` if the local peer initiated the session.

It turns out that we've already seen all of these supporting classes except for `SessionCredential`. When a tuning profile is successful, it creates an instance of this class so your application (and other profiles) can find out who you're talking to. The methods are:

getAuthenticator()

Returns a `String` identifying the user that was authenticated (e.g., a distinguished name from a certificate or the SASL authentication identity).

getAuthenticatorType()

Returns a `String` indicating what mechanism was used to generate the credential (e.g., `"SASL/OTP"`).

getAlgorithm()

Returns a `String` identifying the cryptographic algorithm that was used by the mechanism (e.g., `"otp-md5"`).

getAuthorized()

Returns a `String` identifying the SASL authorization identity (see the section "The SASL Family of Profiles" in Chapter 3).

getLocalCertificate( )/getRemoteCertificate()

Returns an `Object` containing the actual certificate used to authenticate the local or remote peer.

toString()

Returns what you'd expect.

The thing to keep in mind is that different tuning profiles fill in different subsets of this information. For example, the TLS profile provides information for only the `getAuthenticator( )` and `getRemoteCertificate( )` methods.

The ProfileRegistry class

The `ProfileRegistry` class is the Java equivalent of a BEEP greeting.

Earlier, in Example 5-6, we saw how a listening peer can fill in this object, using the `addStartChannelListener( )` method. Is there anything more? Well, here are the methods:

addStartChannelListener()

Adds a profile to the registry by specifying a URI, an object that implements the `StartChannelListener` interface, and the `SessionTuningProperties` that must be satisfied for the profile to be advertised or started.

removeStartChannelListener()
> Removes a profile from the registry, returning the StartChannelListener object that was provided when it was previously added.

getStartChannelListener()
> Returns a StartChannelListener object, based on URI and SessionTuningProperties.

getProfiles()
> Returns an Enumeration of String URIs registered.

getLocalization()
> Gets the local language to be advertised in the greeting.

setLocalization()
> Sets the local language to be advertised in the greeting.

Finally, note that ProfileRegistry is Cloneable.

Channels

There are three concepts that deal with channels: the Profile interface, the Channel class, and message listeners.

The Profile interface

As we've seen, the Profile interface requires nothing more than the init( ) method.

The purpose of this method is two-fold:

- It initializes an object by providing a URI and a ProfileConfiguration object.
- It returns an object (usually this) that implements the StartChannelListener interface.

In other words, the Profile interface exists for the purpose of providing a generic way to initialize a profile module.

At present, the ProfileConfiguration is similar in functionality to the java.util. Properties class. The StartChannelListener interface is more interesting.

An object that implements this interface is used with the ProfileRegistry class we saw earlier in the section "The ProfileRegistry class." A profile registry expects the object to provide the three methods we saw back in Example 5-9.

The Channel class

The Channel class encapsulates the behavior of a BEEP channel. As with the Session class, there are a lot of methods available:

close()
> Closes the channel.

getBufferSize()
> Returns the size (in octets) of the receive buffer for this channel. (There's also a setReceiveBufferSize( ) method.)

getBufferUsed()
> Returns how much of the receive buffer is in use.

getMessageListener()
> Returns the object (previously set by the setMessageListener( ) method) that implements the MessageListener interface for this channel.

getProfile()
> Returns the String URI associated with this channel.

getSession()
> Returns the Session object associated with this channel.

sendMSG()
> Sends a message (represented as an OutputDataStream object) and remembers the object (implementing the ReplyListener interface) that will handle the associated reply.

All of these are pretty straightforward, with the exception of the sendMSG( ) method. Its return value is a MessageStatus object, which lets us check on the transmission (and reply) status of the message. Its getMessageStatus( ) method returns one of:

- MESSAGE_STATUS_NOT_SENT, if the message is still queued for output
- MESSAGE_STATUS_SENT, if the message has been transmitted
- MESSAGE_STATUS_RECEIVED_REPLY, if a RPY, ANS, or NUL response was received
- MESSAGE_STATUS_RECEIVED_ERROR, if an ERR response was received

Finally, beepcore-java provides a ChannelPool class that can be used to manage multiple channels bound to the same profile module. The upshot here is that event-driven programs don't have to worry about creating or closing channels—the ChannelPool class manages that transparently.

The ChannelPool methods are:

close()
> Closes the session associated with the channel pool.

getSharedChannel()
> Returns a SharedChannel object (bound to a profile module identified by a String URI) from the channel pool; if the pool is empty, a new channel is started, and the associated object is returned.

releaseSharedChannel()
> Puts a SharedChannel object back into the channel pool.

setSharedChannelTTL()
> Sets the number of milliseconds that a SharedChannel object can be in the pool before the underlying channel is closed.

As you might guess, the SharedChannel class simply extends Channel.

Message listeners

Once a channel is started, we need to deal with incoming data. Objects implementing the MessageListener interface deal with each incoming MSG by providing a receiveMSG( ) method. As we saw in Example 5-10, this method is given a Message object to process. A convenience class, MessageQueue, implements this interface. In addition to receiveMSG( ), it provides a getNextMessage interface, which blocks until at least one message is available, and then returns the earliest Message received.

Of course, we also have to be able to deal with incoming replies, which is what objects implementing the ReplyListener interface do. These objects provide four methods—receiveRPY( ), receiveERR( ), receiveANS( ), and receiveNUL( )—for this purpose. beepcore-java provides two convenience classes for you.

The Reply class implements this interface, and a Reply object is typically used as the second parameter to a call to sendMSG( ). Two additional methods are provided: getNextReply( ), which blocks until the reply is first received and returns it as a Message; and hasNext( ), which returns true if additional replies are possible. (This latter method is used to figure out when you're at the end of a one-to-many exchange—each ANS is returned by getNextReply( ), and when hasNext( ) returns false, you're done.)

Alternatively, if you really don't care what reply is returned, then you can use the NullReplyListener class instead. It consumes whatever it's given, with nary a word.

Data

There are two concepts that deal with data: the Message class, and data streams.

The Message class

The Message class encapsulates the behavior of a BEEP message. The use of this class is somewhat asymmetric in beepcore-java. Specifically, a channel's sendMSG( ) method doesn't take a Message as a parameter. It takes an OutputDataStream instead. In the opposite direction, beepcore-java passes a Message as a parameter to objects implementing the MessageListener or ReplyListener interfaces.

There are a fair number methods available:

getChannel()
> Returns the Channel object associated with this message.

getMessageType()
> Returns one of: MESSAGE_TYPE_MSG, MESSAGE_TYPE_RPY, MESSAGE_TYPE_ERR, MESSAGE_TYPE_ANS, or MESSAGE_TYPE_NUL.

getMsgno( )/getAnsno( )

    Returns the message number and answer number associated with this message. (If the message isn't an ANS, getAnsno( ) returns -1.)

getDataStream( )

    Returns the InputDataStream object associated with this message.

sendRPY( )/sendERR( )/sendANS( )

    If the message is a MSG, sends a response (represented as a OutputDataStream object), returning a MessageStatus.

sendNUL( )

    If the message is a MSG, ends a one-to-many exchange, returning a MessageStatus.

Data streams

Input and output data streams are used by beepcore-java to provide a convenient abstraction for message payloads.

When sending a message, an OutputDataStream is used. What you need to concern yourself with is how you construct and initialize the object. There are three possibilities: via BufferSegment, via byte array, or via String. (In the future, additional possibilities—e.g., via InputStream and via FileInputStream—may be available.)

A BufferSegment is little more than a byte array wrapped with some methods:

getData( )

    Returns the byte array.

getOffset( )

    Returns the first offset in the byte array that contains valid data.

getLength( )

    Returns the number of valid bytes in the array, starting from the offset.

So, if you want to construct an OutputDataStream object using a BufferSegment, the constructor takes no parameters, and you use the addSegment( ) method to append as many BufferSegment objects as you want. When you're done, invoke the setComplete method to let beepcore-java know this. Note that you're responsible for starting the payload with MIME headers. (Of course, just putting "\r\n" at the start of the first BufferSegment works too....)

If you want to use a byte array to build a payload, use the ByteOutputDataStream subclass. The constructor method for this class is overloaded—in addition to supplying a byte array, you can also supply an offset and a length, and/or a String containing a MIME Content-Type: header.

Similarly, if you want to use a String to build a payload, use the StringOutputDataStream subclass. Its constructor is also overloaded; in addition to supplying a String, you can supply a String containing a MIME Content-Type: header.

Both of these subclasses provide an additional method, getHeaderNames(), that returns an Enumeration of String objects, one for each MIME header built by the constructor. This is an important point: with these two subclasses, the "data" you supply doesn't contain any MIME headers—those are provided as an additional parameter to the constructor.

When receiving a message, an InputDataStream is used. This class has several methods:

isComplete()
> Returns true if the message is completely received.

availableSegment()
> Returns true if at least one BufferSegment is ready for processing.

getNextSegment()
> Returns the next unprocessed BufferSegment for this message, or null if none are available.

waitForNextSegment()
> Returns the next unprocessed BufferSegment, blocking if need be.

getInputStream()
> Returns a subclass of java.io.InputStream, termed an InputDataStreamAdapter, to be used for reading the payload.

The only abstractions in beepcore-java that aren't closely tied to BEEP are the data streams. Although it may take a "BEEP person" a little while to get used to them, they should seem pretty natural to a "Java person." Let's look at why.

To begin, recall the example in Example 5-3 that showed how easily we move from a Message to the familiar InputStream:

```
InputStream is = reply.getNextReply().getDataStream().getInputStream();

while (is.read () != -1) {
    ++replyLength;
}
```

So, the first advantage is that we leverage Java's ability to encapsulate the same behavior of a well-used class (InputStream) using a radically different implementation.

Next, recall the example in Example 5-10 that showed how easily threads and parallelism are accommodated. In fact, in the follow-up example, we saw how we could start sending a reply even before receiving the complete message, and that we could do this without interfering with other work going on in the process.

An important aspect of this architecture is that beepcore-java doesn't read from the network until you start telling it to. In other words, beepcore-java will "prime the pump" by telling an object implementing the ReplyListener interface that a reply is being received, but it won't keep more than getBufferSize() octets in its receive buffer (see the section "The Channel class" earlier in this chapter). So, you need to keep in mind that it's your application—and not beepcore-java—that is setting the consumption rate of data being received.

Exceptions

beepcore-java defines several subclasses of Exception, and they all do pretty much what you'd think. If you glance back to Figure 5-1, you'll see the class hierarchy under BEEPException. This parent class doesn't add anything (members or methods) to java.lang.Exception.

An AbortChannelException is thrown by objects that implement either the MessageListener or ReplyListener interfaces. It just tells beepcore-java that something really bad has happened, and the BEEP session should be terminated immediately. In contrast, a BEEPInterruptedException is thrown when a beepcore-java thread in a synchronous call gets an InterruptedException. It's up to you to determine what action to take.

The BEEPError class, which corresponds to BEEP's ERR, is the most interesting kind of exception: not only does it indicate a failure of some kind, but it also contains methods that allow you to convey that information to the remote peer. In addition to the usual String diagnostic associated with an Exception, there's also a numeric code and, optionally, a language string. The constructor method is overloaded to allow any combination of these that makes sense (i.e., you can't supply a localization language without also supplying a diagnostic). The methods are:

getCode()
> Returns the numeric code.

getmessage()
> The same as getMessage.

getXMLLang()
> Returns the localization language.

createErrorMessage()
> Returns an error element as a String (see the section "Localization (L10N)" in Chapter 3).

As a convenience, the createErrorMessage( ) method is overloaded, so you can build an error element using:

```
String s = BEEPError.createErrorMessage(code, diagnostic);

// or

String s = BEEPError.createErrorMessage(code, diagnostic, language);
```

without having to instantiate a BEEPError object.

Finally, there are two subclasses of BEEPError used to convey failure in very specific situations:

StartChannelException
> Thrown by objects that implement the startChannel() method of the StartChannelListener interface, this is used to tell beepcore-java that a channel for this profile should not be started.

CloseChannelException
> Thrown by objects that implement the closeChannel() method of the StartChannelListener interface, this is used to tell beepcore-java that this channel is declining the remote peer's request to close it.

Utilities

Finally, what implementation is complete without a logging package? beepcore-java provides a simple logging facility based on the Log class. Each message to be logged has an associated severity:

- SEV_EMERGENCY, for a message explaining that the system is unusable
- SEV_ALERT, for messages describing a condition that must be immediately corrected
- SEV_CRITICAL, for messages describing a critical condition
- SEV_ERROR, for error messages
- SEV_WARNING, for warning messages
- SEV_NOTICE, for significant, but not unexpected, events
- SEV_INFORMATIONAL, for informational messages
- SEV_VERBOSE, for verbose debugging messages

Three methods are available:

isLogged()
> Returns true if a message of the given severity would be logged.

logEntry()
> Logs either a String or a Throwable.

setLogService()
> Associates an object implementing the LogService interface with the logging mechanism.

The behavior of the LogService interface contains two very similar methods:

isLogged()
> Returns true if a message of the given severity would be logged.

logEntry()
> Logs either a String or a Throwable, but also requires a String parameter indicating the service doing the logging.

At present, beepcore-java defines two classes that implement this service:

ConsoleLog:
> Writes to System.out, and provides one other method, setSeverity( ), which is used to indicate the lowest severity for logging (the default is SEV_ERROR).

Log4JLog:
> Maps onto the Apache Log4J library.

## CHAPTER 6

BEEP in C

Of the three beepcore implementations, beepcore-c is the newest. Its design goals are portability and functionality. The heart of the implementation, termed the core, is suitable as the basis for a kernel module, inclusion in a PDA, or as the basis of a multithreaded library for Linux and Windows.

As of this writing, beepcore-c runs on Linux, NetBSD, Solaris, and Windows. (By the time you read this, other platforms may be supported as well.) So, in this chapter, we're going to look at how to write both client/server and server/client profiles on Linux.

As with all the versions of beepcore, go to *http://beepcore.org/* to find out where to download the current release of beepcore-c. When you get to the project's summary page, click on the "Home Page" link to find the documentation hierarchy, which includes the definitions of each call.

A Portable Implementation

Historically, the word *portability* has many meanings. Today, Java is the portability darling. However, for many deployed systems that don't include a JVM, C is considered the "portable" programming language.[*] Coming up with a highly portable implementation of BEEP is something of a challenge, because managing I/O, threads, and memory is inherently non-portable. Fortunately, a lot of time was spent devising the architecture of beepcore-c to get around this problem.

Architecture

The key to understanding beepcore-c is to appreciate the tight integration between these layers and modules:

---

[*] Some might argue that use of the word "deployed" is a euphemism for "legacy," and in many cases that's right; then again, "legacy" is often a euphemism for the terms "stable" or "production quality."

- The *core*, which contains a full BEEP implementation that uses callbacks for resource management
- A *wrapper*, which provides the "glue" to the operating environment.
- One or more *profile modules*

The pictorial representation is shown in Figure 6-1.

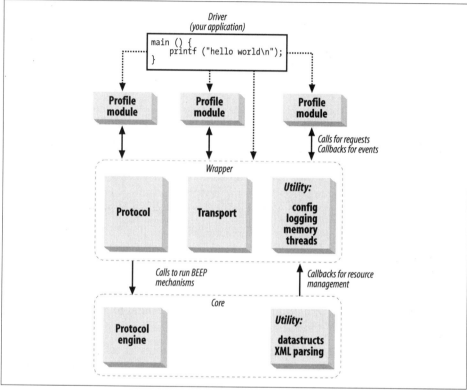

Figure 6-1. The beepcore-c architecture

The architecture isn't as complicated as this figure makes it appear; just think of the wrapper as the thing that talks to the operating system and provides a lot of different APIs for doing resource management. What's important to understand is that your application and the profile modules are written to the APIs provided by a particular wrapper implementation. If you're careful and/or lucky, a profile module that works on one operating system supported by a particular wrapper will also work on all operating systems supported by that one wrapper. However, there is no portability guarantee between wrapper implementations. For example, a profile module written for a wrapper that runs as a Win32 application is unlikely to work with a wrapper that runs inside the Linux kernel.

The bottom line is that you really don't have to write much code if there's already a wrapper written for your operating system—you just write a profile module and call it and the wrapper from your program. For clarity's sake, let's use the term *driver* to refer to the part of your program that calls either the wrapper or a profile module.

The threaded_os Wrapper

The threaded_os wrapper implements beepcore-c on Linux, NetBSD, Solaris, and Windows, using a preemptive threading model.

The tricky part in writing a profile module for this wrapper is understanding its event-driven model. In brief, two different sets of code are going to call your module: the wrapper and your driver. Obviously, you can pretty much control how the profile module and the driver interact; the interesting part is the wrapper/profile interaction.

To kick things off, the driver asks the profile module to create a PROFILE_REGISTRATION structure (or PR for short). This is done independently of any wrapper, session, or channel. The PR contains mostly addresses of routines for the wrapper to call when events happen ("callbacks"). When the driver creates a BP_CONNECTION structure, it registers one or more profile modules with it, passing the PR as a parameter. After all the modules are registered, the driver tells the wrapper to bind the BP_CONNECTION structure to a TCP connection and then the games begin!

In order to understand how often and exactly when these callbacks are made, we need to understand how beepcore-c relates connections, sessions, and channels:

- At any given instant, a session is bound to a connection; however, every time a tuning reset occurs, the current session is destroyed and a new session is created.
- At any given instant, zero or more channels can be bound to a session, and those channels can be bound to the same, or different, profile modules.

In beepcore-c, the BP_CONNECTION structure is what the driver uses to communicate with the wrapper code. Over the lifetime of the wrapper, it makes several callbacks to the profile module:

Connection initialization
> When the driver registers the profile module with the wrapper, the wrapper makes a connection_init( ) callback to the module (using a PR) asking it to initialize; if something goes wrong, the return value tells the wrapper not to register it, and this information is returned to the driver.

Session initialization
> Whenever a session is created, the wrapper makes a session_init( ) callback to the module (using a PR); the return value tells the wrapper if the module is available for this session.

Channel start
> If the remote peer asks to start a channel bound to this module, the wrapper makes a start_indication( ) callback to the module; the callback invokes a

routine to indicate whether the request is accepted or declined. Similarly, if the local peer successfully starts a channel bound to this module, a second callback (start_confirmation( )) is made. In both cases, the callback is passed a PROFILE_ INSTANCE structure (or PI for short).

Data exchange

Whenever data is available from the remote peer for this channel, the wrapper makes either a message_available( ) or frame_available( ) callback to the module (using a PI).

Channel close

Whenever anyone (i.e., either your driver or the remote peer) asks to close a channel bound to this module (or to close the entire session), the wrapper makes a close_indication( ) callback to the module (using a PI); the callback invokes a routine to indicate whether the request is accepted or declined. Regardless, whenever the outcome of the request is known, or if the session is aborted (e.g., due to connectivity problems), the wrapper makes a close_confirmation( ) callback to the module (using a PI).

Session finalization

Whenever a session is destroyed, the wrapper makes a session_fin( ) callback to the module (using a PR) for the purpose of clean-up.

Connection finalization

When a BP_CONNECTION structure is about to be destroyed, it makes its final callback of connection_fin( ) to the module (using a PR).

If you think this is a lot of callbacks, you're right. In fact, these are just the mandatory hooks—there are at least six optional hooks we haven't mentioned! Don't worry though; when we look at the code examples, you'll see that most of these hooks can be written in a dozen or so lines.

So, the lifetime of a wrapper/profile interaction might look like this:

1. Your driver registers PR with the wrapper: connection_init( ).

2. Your driver binds a connection to the wrapper: session_init( ).

3. Your driver starts the TLS profile and a tuning reset occurs: session_fin( ) followed by session_init( ).

4. Your driver asks to start a channel bound to the profile module: start_ confirmation( ).

5. Your driver sends messages and (eventually) receives replies: message_available( ).

6. Your driver asks to start another channel bound to the module: start_ confirmation( ) using a different PI than the one used in Step 4.

7. Your driver asks to close the session: close_indication( ) twice (once with the PI used in Step 4, once with the PI used in Step 6).

8. Assuming both profile instances agree: close_confirmation() twice, then session_fin().

9. Your driver destroys the wrapper: connection_fin().

One thing you'll need to decide when writing a profile module is the functionality split with the driver. For example, we haven't talked about how to ask to start a channel. Should this be done by the driver or the profile module? The threaded_os wrapper leaves the choice up to you. For example, Figure 6-2 shows a timing diagram of what happens when your driver asks to start a channel:

1. If the channel was started, a callback is made to the module (using a PI).

2. Regardless, the wrapper makes a callback indicating whether the channel was started or not.

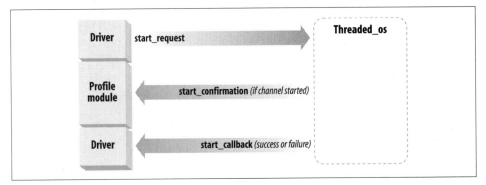

Figure 6-2. Asking to start a channel

Even so, it's recommended that each profile module should provide an entry point to the driver that's used to start a channel—it just makes it easier for the module to keep track of things.

Finally, in addition to the callbacks, there are a couple of configuration settings for a PR:

initiator_modes/listener_modes
> Indicates whether this module should be considered for use on "plaintext" or "encrypted" sessions, or both ("plaintext,encrypted").

full_messages
> Indicates which callback, message_available() or frame_available(), should be used with this module.

Depending on whether transport privacy is present, a profile module may not want to be advertised in the greeting. For example, if you recall from "The SASL Family of Profiles" in Chapter 3, the SASL PLAIN profile should be used only when transport privacy is in effect. Similarly, once transport privacy is running, the TLS profile shouldn't be advertised. So, the initiator_modes setting is consulted by a

BP_CONNECTION structure associated with an initiating connection, and the listener_modes setting is consulted by a BP_CONNECTION structure associated with a listening connection.

Depending on what a profile's messages look like and how lazy a programmer you are, your profile module may want to be notified as soon as data is available, or it may want to wait until a message has been completely received. The drawback to the latter approach is that a message may be larger than the buffer space allocated to the PI by the wrapper. If this happens, the wrapper will make (yet) another callback, window_full( ), and the module can then read some of the message, ask to allocate additional buffer space, close the channel, etc.

Echo and Sink

Let's implement an echo profile and a sink profile. The operation of each is a simple exercise in client/server:

- One peer connects to the other, starts a channel with either the echo or sink profile, and sends zero or more messages.
- Each time a message is received, it's sent back as a reply (echo) or the reply is empty (sink).
- When the initiator is done sending messages, it closes the channel.

Well, that's pretty simple. In order to implement this, we'll need to write three pieces of code:

- The "null" profile module
- A driver for the listener
- A driver for the initiator

The null Profile Module

There are always two parts to a profile module: a header file and a source file. The organization of a profile module usually follows the same structure:

- The header file defines keys for configuring the profile module, along with entry points for use by the driver.
- The source file defines the callbacks invoked by the wrapper, along with the entry points for the driver.

The header file

Example 6-1 shows the first part of the file *null-profiles.h*. It begins by including two header files from the threaded_os wrapper:

bp_config.h:
> This contains definitions for the configuration package provided by the wrapper.

bp_wrapper.h:
> This contains definitions for the threaded_os primary API—it defines things like PRs, PIs, and so on.

Example 6-1. null-profiles.h

```
/* includes */

#include "../threaded_os/utility/bp_config.h"
#include "../threaded_os/wrapper/bp_wrapper.h"

/* keys for configuration package */

#define NULL_ECHO_URI        "beep profiles null_echo uri"
#define NULL_ECHO_IMODES     "beep profiles null_echo initiator_modes"
#define NULL_ECHO_LMODES     "beep profiles null_echo listener_modes"

#define NULL_SINK_URI        "beep profiles null_sink uri"
#define NULL_SINK_IMODES     "beep profiles null_sink initiator_modes"
#define NULL_SINK_LMODES     "beep profiles null_sink listener_modes"
```

Throughout this chapter, we'll look at the various structures and routines that are defined by both of these header files.

Next, some keys for the configuration package are defined. A *key* is a string containing space-separated elements, with the leftmost element (always beep) being the most significant. When a PR wants to query a configuration object for any initialization information, it uses the prefix "beep profiles *XXX*" where "*XXX*" is a unique string. In our case, we're defining two profiles, which we're naming null_echo and null_sink.

As we'll see later on, configuration objects can be initialized from either a file, and/or be manually updated by the driver itself. If you've gotten this far in your reading, you ought to be able to easily guess what kinds of things these keys are referring to. If not:

... uri
> The URI used to identify the profile.

... initiator_modes/listener_modes
> What kind of sessions this profile should be available on.

Example 6-2 shows the remainder of the file *null-profiles.h* by defining the entry points used by the driver

Example 6-2. null-profiles.h, part two

```
/* module entry points */

extern PROFILE_REGISTRATION *
```

Example 6-2. null-profiles.h, part two (continued)

```
null_echo_Init (struct configobj        *appconfig);

extern PROFILE_REGISTRATION *
null_sink_Init (struct configobj        *appconfig);

/* initiator routines */

extern void *
null_start (BP_CONNECTION              *w,
            PROFILE_REGISTRATION       *pr,
            char                       *serverName);

extern int
null_trip (void                        *v,
           char                        *ibuf,
           int                          ilen,
           char                        *obuf,
           int                          omaxlen);

extern int
null_close (void                       *v);

#define NULL_OK        0      /* no problema                */
#define NULL_ERROR     (-1)   /* error performing task      */
#define NULL_BUSY      (-2)   /* still doing null_trip      */
#define NULL_DONE      (-3)   /* channel is closed          */
#define NULL_DENIED    (-4)   /* remote peer refused to close */
```

The first two routines create a PR:

null_echo_Init()
> Creates a PR for the echo profile.

null_sink_Init()
> Creates a PR for the sink profile.

For each, the sole parameter appconfig is a pointer to a configuration object, which the driver has previously filled in.

The remaining entry points are used by an initating driver. Although we'll see all of these in considerable detail, here's a brief synopsis:

1. The driver calls either null_echo_Init() or null_sink_Init(), creates a BP_CONNECTION structure, registers the PR, and binds the structure to a connection.

2. The driver calls null_start() to start a channel. The return value is an opaque handle used with null_trip() and null_close().

3. The driver calls null_trip() as many times as it wants, supplying the address and size (ibuf and ilen) of a buffer containing a message. The return value is the number of octets read into (obuf), which will not exceed (omaxlen), or a negative number to indicate failure.

4. The driver calls `null_close( )` to close the channel.

5. The driver destroys the wrapper and the PR it created in Step 1.

The Source File

Now it's time to look at *null-profiles.c*, the start of which is shown in Example 6-3.

Example 6-3. null-profiles.c: The beginning

```
/*     includes */

#include "null-profiles.h"
#include "../threaded_os/utility/logutil.h"
#include "../threaded_os/utility/semutex.h"

/*     defines and typedefs */

#define PRO_ECHO_URI          "http://xml.resource.org/profiles/NULL/ECHO"
#define PRO_SINK_URI          "http://xml.resource.org/profiles/NULL/SINK"

#define EMPTY_RPY \
        "Content-Type: application/beep+xml\r\n\r\n<null />"

typedef struct pro_localdata {
    int         pl_flags;            /* mode flags                   */
#define PRO_ECHOMODE    (1<<0)       /* doing echo, not sink         */
#define PRO_START       (1<<1)       /* did null_start               */
#define PRO_READY       (1<<2)       /* ready for null_send          */
#define PRO_RSPWAIT     (1<<3)       /* waiting for peer's response  */
#define PRO_CLSWAIT     (1<<4)       /* waiting for close            */
#define PRO_DENIED      (1<<5)       /* close request was denied     */

    PROFILE_INSTANCE
                *pl_pi;              /* return value for null_start  */

    char        *pl_rbuf;            /* out parameters for null_trip */
    int         pl_rlen;             /*   ..                         */

    sem_t       pl_sem;              /* semaphore used for receive   */
} PRO_LOCALDATA;
```

In addition to the header file that we just defined (*null-profiles.h*), it also includes definitions provided by the threaded_os wrapper that pertain to logging (*logutil.h*) and thread management (*semutex.h*). The logging package is uninteresting, so let's look at the threading package instead.

Although the use of threading inside the wrapper is either sophisticated or baroque (depending on whether you wrote or are reading the code), the facilities provided to profile modules are rather basic, and can be split into two types, semaphores and threads.

Semaphores (typedef ... `sem_t`) provide loose synchronization to threads, and are:

`SEM_INIT( )`

> Initializes a semaphore pointer and sets the number of tokens currently available. A mutual exclusion zone is realized as `SEM_INIT (&s, 1)`, while a condition is realized as `SEM_INIT (&s, 0)`.

`SEM_WAIT( )`

> If at least one token is available, claim it; otherwise, execution of the current thread is suspended until a token is available.

`SEM_TRY( )`

> If at least one take is available, claim it and return `TRUE`; otherwise, return `FALSE`. Regardless, don't suspend the current thread.

`SEM_POST( )`

> Make another token available. (Note that I didn't write "Return a token.")

`SEM_DESTROY( )`

> Free any dynamic memory associated with the semaphore.

Threads (typedef ... `THREAD_T`) provide process-level threads, and are:

`THR_CREATE( )`

> Create a thread, have it execute a routine, and terminate it if it returns.

`THR_EXIT( )`

> Terminate the current thread.

`THR_JOIN( )`

> Suspend the current thread until the named thread terminates; then, store the return value and resume the current thread.

`YIELD( )`

> Suspend the current thread and resume the scheduler thread.

Next, we define some handy values (such as the default URIs used to identify the echo and sink profiles), along with the reply (`EMPTY_RPY`) sent by the sink profile. Finally, we define a `PRO_LOCALDATA` structure that contains state information used by the module. Rather than spell out what each field of `PRO_LOCALDATA` does, we'll point this out as each is used.

Module entry points

Example 6-4 shows the entry points for the module. Both `null_echo_Init( )` and `null_sink_Init( )` are pretty simple: they call `pro_init( )` to do the real work.

Example 6-4. null-profiles.c: Module entry points

```
PROFILE_REGISTRATION *
null_echo_Init (struct configobj *appconfig) {
    return pro_init (appconfig, 1);
}
```

Example 6-4. null-profiles.c: Module entry points (continued)

```
PROFILE_REGISTRATION *
null_sink_Init (struct configobj  *appconfig) {
    return pro_init (appconfig, 0);
}

static PROFILE_REGISTRATION *
pro_init (struct configobj  *appconfig,
          int               echoP) {
    char                *cp;
    PRO_LOCALDATA       *pl;
    PROFILE_REGISTRATION *pr;

    if (!(pr = (PROFILE_REGISTRATION *) lib_malloc (sizeof *pr +
                                                    sizeof *pl))) {
        log_line (LOG_PROF, 6, "unable to allocate PR");
        return NULL;
    }
    memset (pr, 0, sizeof *pr);

    cp = echoP ? NULL_ECHO_URI : NULL_SINK_URI;
    if (!(pr -> uri = config_get (appconfig, cp)))
        pr -> uri = echoP ? PRO_ECHO_URI : PRO_SINK_URI;

    cp = echoP ? NULL_ECHO_IMODES : NULL_SINK_IMODES;
    if (!(pr -> initiator_modes = config_get (appconfig, cp)))
        pr -> initiator_modes = "plaintext,encrypted";
    cp = echoP ? NULL_ECHO_LMODES : NULL_SINK_LMODES;
    if (!(pr -> listener_modes = config_get (appconfig, cp)))
        pr -> listener_modes = "plaintext,encrypted";

    pr -> full_messages = 0;

    pr -> proreg_connection_init = pro_connection_init;
    pr -> proreg_connection_fin = pro_connection_fin;
    pr -> proreg_session_init = pro_session_init;
    pr -> proreg_session_fin = pro_session_fin;
    pr -> proreg_start_indication = pro_start_indication;
    pr -> proreg_start_confirmation = pro_start_confirmation;
    pr -> proreg_close_indication = pro_close_indication;
    pr -> proreg_close_confirmation = pro_close_confirmation;
    pr -> proreg_tuning_reset_indication = pro_tuning_reset_indication;
    pr -> proreg_tuning_reset_confirmation = pro_tuning_reset_confirmation;
    pr -> proreg_frame_available = pro_frame_available;

    pr -> user_ptr = pl = (PRO_LOCALDATA *) (((char *) pr) + sizeof *pr);
    memset (pl, 0, sizeof *pl);
    if (echoP)
        pl -> pl_flags |= PRO_ECHOMODE;

    return pr;
}
```

Although kind of long, pro_init( ) is direct. It starts by allocating enough memory to accommodate both a PR structure and a PRO_LOCALDATA structure. The interesting thing is that the routine calls something named lib_free( ) instead of free( ). Why is that? lib_malloc( ) and lib_free( ) are entry points to the memory allocator provided by the threaded_os wrapper. Even though they both probably map directly onto malloc( ) and free( ), as someone writing a profile module, it's important to use the API exposed by the wrapper to increase portability.

If the allocation fails, we write an entry to the log. The threaded_os wrapper provides two routines for making entries. If you have access to a BP_CONNECTION structure, use bp_log; otherwise, use log_line. The only difference between the two is that bp_log takes an extra parameter—its first parameter, which is a pointer to the BP_CONNECTION. Otherwise, the parameters are:

category
> One of LOG_WRAP (for wrapper information), LOG_PROF (for profile module information), LOG_CORE (for protocol information), or LOG_MISC.

severity
> The inverse of a syslog severity code (e.g., to log an information entry, calculate the severity as LOG_DEBUG-LOG_INFO).

format, args...
> A format string, followed by zero or more arguments.

After allocating a PR, the routine fills in a lot of fields. In doing so, it often calls config_get( ) which is provided by the threaded_os wrapper to retrieve a value from a configuration object. (The value retrieved should be viewed as a const—please don't modify or free it!) The pattern is pretty simple:

- See if we're the echo or sink profile (from the parameter echoP).
- Get the corresponding key (defined in *null-profiles.h*).
- Call config_get( ) to see if there's a corresponding value in the configuration object.
- If not, set a hard-coded default.

After this, we indicate that we want the frame-based interface.

Now, there are eleven routines to remember for future callbacks. Finally, we do the pointer-arithmetic to get the cast for the PRO_LOCALDATA that will be used as a template whenever a PI is created from this PR. The pl_flags field is told whether this PR is for echo or sink.

Outer callbacks

The four methods shown in Example 6-5 constitute the "outer" set of methods for the profile module.

Example 6-5. null-profiles.c: PR methods

```
static char *
pro_connection_init (PROFILE_REGISTRATION  *pr,
                     BP_CONNECTION          *w) {
    return NULL;
}

static char *
pro_session_init (PROFILE_REGISTRATION  *pr,
                  BP_CONNECTION          *w) {
    return NULL;
}

static char *
pro_session_fin (PROFILE_REGISTRATION  *pr,
                 BP_CONNECTION          *w) {
    return NULL;
}

static char *
pro_connection_fin (PROFILE_REGISTRATION  *pr,
                    BP_CONNECTION          *w) {
    return NULL;
}
```

Each is called with a pointer to a PR and a BP_CONNECTION structure, and returns a pointer to a character string. If the return isn't NULL, it points to a diagnostic string explaining why the method failed. Although all four methods shown in this example are empty, it's up to you to decide how much machinery goes in each. For example, if channels bound to the same profile in a single session need some way of communicating, these four methods are used to manage that process.

Channel start callbacks

Now, let's look at three methods, starting with the one in Example 6-6, that get called when starting a channel bound to this module. Not all of these methods will get called; it depends on which peer makes the request to start a channel.

Example 6-6. null-profiles.c: pro_start_confirmation

```
static void
pro_start_confirmation (void              *clientData,
                        PROFILE_INSTANCE  *pi,
                        PROFILE           *po) {
    PRO_LOCALDATA     *il = (PRO_LOCALDATA *) clientData;

    il -> pl_pi = pi, pi -> user_ptr1 = il;
}
```

Later on, we'll look at a routine called null_start( ) that's used to start a channel bound to the PR. For now, the important thing to know is that the start request

---

contains some client data that gets passed to the callback. As we'll see in a bit, the client data is a pointer to the PRO_LOCALDATA structure that was built for the new channel. When we ask to start a channel, if the request is accepted, the wrapper calls pro_start_confirmation( ). The parameters are:

clientData
> The client data given to the wrapper when the request to start a channel was made.

pi
> A pointer to a PROFILE_INSTANCE structure (what we've been calling a PI). There are five fields in the structure that are interesting to a module:
>
> channel
> > A pointer to the corresponding CHANNEL_INSTANCE structure.
>
> user_ptr1 *and* user_ptr2
> > Two user-defined pointers, managed exclusively by the module.
>
> user_long1 *and* user_long2
> > Two user-defined scalars, managed exclusively by the module.
>
> The user_* fields are the only ones that are read/write; all other fields should be considered read-only by the module.

po
> A pointer to a PROFILE structure. There are three fields of interest in the structure:
>
> uri
> > The URI of the profile to use.
>
> piggyback *and* piggyback_length
> > If the peer included any piggybacked data in its request, these are pointers to the data and its size in octets.

Because null_start( ) inside the profile module made the request, we'll let the pro_start_confirmation( ) callback handle the success case, and have pro_start_callback( ), shown in Example 6-7, handle the failure case.

So, on success, we cast the client data back to a pointer to a PRO_LOCALDATA structure. Then, we set its pl_pi field to remember the PI associated with the channel; similarly, we use the user-defined pointer (user_ptr1) in the PI to remember the PRO_LOCALDATA.

Example 6-7. null-profiles.c: pro_start_callback

```
static void
pro_start_callback (void              *clientData,
                    CHANNEL_INSTANCE  *ci,
                    DIAGNOSTIC        *error) {
    if (error)
        printf ("unable to start channel: [%d] %s\n",
                error -> code, error -> message);
}
```

To recap, when a request is made to start a channel, that request contains both a callback and some client data. When null_start( ) makes this request, the callback supplied is pro_start_callback and the client data is PRO_LOCALDATA. When the outcome of the request is finally known (regardless of whether the channel got started or not) the wrapper will invoke the callback with these parameters:

clientData
> The client data given to the wrapper when the request to start a channel was made.

ci
> A pointer to a CHANNEL_INSTANCE structure. This is the analogue of the PROFILE_INSTANCE—for each channel it manages (including those channels it's thinking about starting or closing), the wrapper manages a pair of these two structures. There are four fields in the structure that are interesting:

> conn
>> A pointer to the BP_CONNECTION structure for this callback.

> profile_registration
>> A pointer to the associated PR.

> profile
>> A pointer to the associated PI.

error
> A pointer to a DIAGNOSTIC structure. This is used throughout beepcore-c to convey failure. If NULL, the start request is successful; otherwise, it explains why the channel was not started. There are three fields in the structure:

> code
>> An integer containing a reply code.

> message
>> A pointer to a string (or NULL) containing a textual diagnostic.

> lang
>> A pointer to a string (or NULL) identifying the natural language used for the message.

> Sound familiar? It should; we've just described BEEP's localized diagnostics, which were introduced back in "Localization (L10N)" in Chapter 3.

Since pro_start_confirmation handled the successful case, the logic of pro_start_callback( ) is very simple: if error is non-empty, then the channel didn't start, so it prints out the reason why.

If you remember back to Figure 6-2, there was a brief discussion as to whether channels should be started by the profile module or the driver. If a channel is started by the profile module, then pro_start_callback( ) is all that's needed. However, if the driver starts a channel, then the wrapper needs a way of telling the profile module that a new instance has started. That's why there are two callbacks.

So, those are the two callbacks that get made when we ask to start a channel. What about the case where the remote peer requests a channel start? That's when pro_start_indication( ) (shown in Example 6-8) gets called by the wrapper with two parameters:

pi   A pointer to a PROFILE_INSTANCE structure.

po   A pointer to a PROFILE structure.

Example 6-8. null-profile.c: pro_start_indication

```
static void
pro_start_indication (PROFILE_INSTANCE  *pi,
                      PROFILE           *po) {
    DIAGNOSTIC        ds,
                      *d = &ds;
    PRO_LOCALDATA     *pl = pi -> channel -> profile_registration
                               -> user_ptr,
                      *il;
    PROFILE           ps,
                      *p = &ps;

    if (!(il = (PRO_LOCALDATA *) lib_malloc (sizeof *il))) {
        memset (d, 0, sizeof *d);
        d -> code = 421;
        d -> message = "out of memory";
        bpc_start_response (pi -> channel, po, d);
        return;
    }
    memcpy (il, pl, sizeof *il);
    il -> pl_pi = pi, pi -> user_ptr1 = il;

    if (il -> pl_flags & PRO_ECHOMODE)
        p = po;
    else {
        memset (p, 0, sizeof *p);
        p -> uri = po -> uri;
    }

    bpc_start_response (pi -> channel, p, NULL);
}
```

Although there are only two parameters, this callback actually has to do some think-ing because it must tell the wrapper whether or not the channel should be started. Before the callback returns, regardless of the actual decision, it must call bpc_start_response( ) to tell the wrapper. This routine takes three parameters:

ci   A pointer to the CHANNEL_INSTANCE structure for this callback.

po   A pointer to a PROFILE structure for this callback. If we are accepting the request, this contains a pointer to (and the size in octets of) any piggybacked data.

d   If we are declining the request, this contains a pointer to a DIAGNOSTIC structure explaining why (otherwise NULL is used).

Here's the logic we're using in this routine:

- First, we set pl to the PRO_LOCALDATA structure that was created by pro_init( ). We do this by going from the PI we were passed to its corresponding CI, then to its PR, then to its user-defined pointer.
- We want to make a copy of the PRO_LOCALDATA structure, so we call lib_malloc( ). On failure, we decline the start request.
- Next, we see whether we're in echo or sink mode. If it's sink mode, then we forget about any piggybacked data we were passed.
- Finally, we call bpc_start_response( ) to accept the request.

That covers the callbacks dealing with starting a channel.

Channel close callbacks

Now, let's look at three methods, starting with Example 6-9, that get called when closing a channel bound to this module. Not all of these methods will get called; it depends on which peer makes the request to close a channel. Sometimes, however, a callback is made independently of this (for example, when the transport connection fails).

Example 6-9. null-profiles.c: pro_close_indication

```
static void
pro_close_indication (PROFILE_INSTANCE  *pi,
                      DIAGNOSTIC        *request,
                      char              origin,
                      char              scope) {
    BP_CONNECTION    *w = pi -> channel -> conn;
    DIAGNOSTIC       *d;
    PRO_LOCALDATA    *il = (PRO_LOCALDATA *) pi -> user_ptr1;

    d = ((il -> pl_flags & PRO_START) && (origin == PRO_ACTION_REMOTE))
            ? bp_diagnostic_new (w, 500, NULL, "no thanks")
            : NULL;

    bpc_close_response (pi -> channel, d);

    if (d)
        bp_diagnostic_destroy (w, d);
}
```

Whenever it looks like a channel might be closing, regardless of who requested it, pro_close_indication( ) gets called by the wrapper with these parameters:

pi
> A pointer to a PROFILE_INSTANCE structure.

request
> A pointer to a DIAGNOSTIC structure explaining why the channel close is being requested (or demanded).

origin

> Indicates who made the request/demand, either the remote peer (PRO_ACTION_ REMOTE), or a local entity (PRO_ACTION_LOCAL). For the latter case, the wrapper itself could be making the request, e.g., the driver is asking to close the session.

scope

> Indicates why this callback is being made: to close the channel (PRO_ACTION_ CHANNEL), to close the session (PRO_ACTION_SESSION), or because the session is being aborted (PRO_ACTION_ABORT).

We've seen examples of the two structures before, so all that's really new are the final two parameters explaining the who and why of the request. If the scope is PRO_ ACTION_ABORT, then this isn't a request at all—the wrapper is telling us that the connection has gone away. Otherwise, we get to decide whether or not to accept the request.

Regardless of our choice, the wrapper requires that we call bpc_close_response( ) to give our answer. This routine takes two parameters:

- A pointer to CHANNEL_INSTANCE structure for this callback
- A pointer to a DIAGNOSTIC structure explaining why the request is being declined, or NULL

So, what's the logic used by pro_close_indication( )?

1. We look to see if we started this channel and the remote peer is asking to close it.
2. If so:
    - We create a new DIAGNOSTIC structure to decline the request.
    - We call bpc_close_response( ).
    - We free the DIAGNOSTIC structure (because bpc_close_response( ) makes its own copy).
3. If not, we call bpc_close_response( ) with a NULL second parameter.

The final thing to understand about this callback is that even if we accept the request, the close may not actually occur. For example, when the remote peer asks to close the session, the wrapper is going to ask each and every channel what it thinks about the request by making this callback. We may agree, but if another channel doesn't agree, the channel won't be closed. That's why there's a second callback, shown in Example 6-10, that gets made a little while later.

Example 6-10. null-profiles.c: pro_close_confirmation

```
static void
pro_close_confirmation (PROFILE_INSTANCE    *pi,
                        char                status,
                        DIAGNOSTIC          *error,
                        char                origin,
```

Example 6-10. null-profiles.c: pro_close_confirmation (continued)

```
                           char                    scope) {
    PRO_LOCALDATA          *il = (PRO_LOCALDATA *) pi -> user_ptr1;

    if (status != PRO_ACTION_SUCCESS)
        return;

    pi -> user_ptr1 = NULL;

    if (il -> pl_flags & PRO_CLSWAIT)
        il -> pl_flags &= ~PRO_CLSWAIT;
    else if (il -> pl_flags & PRO_START) {
        il -> pl_pi = NULL;
        if (il -> pl_flags & PRO_RSPWAIT) {
            il -> pl_flags &= ~PRO_RSPWAIT;
            SEM_POST (&il -> pl_sem);
        }
    } else
        lib_free (il);
}
```

When the wrapper finally decides whether or not the channel has actually closed, pro_close_confirmation( ) gets called by the wrapper with these parameters:

pi
> A pointer to a PROFILE_INSTANCE structure.

status
> Indicates whether the channel is now closed (PRO_ACTION_SUCCESS) or not (PRO_ACTION_FAILURE).

error
> A pointer to a DIAGNOSTIC structure explaining why the channel close was rejected, or NULL.

origin/scope
> Parameters repeated from pro_close_indication( ).

Here's the logic:

1. If the channel's still open, there's nothing to do, so we're done.

2. Otherwise, remove the reference to the PROLOCAL_DATA structure for this PI from the user-defined pointer.

3. If we asked to close this channel, update the pl_flags field to tell null_close( ) that we're no longer waiting for a callback.

4. Otherwise, if we started this channel, remove the reference to the PI from the PRO_LOCALDATA structure. (This tells null_trip( ) and null_close( ) that the channel was closed out from under them.) Further, if we're in the middle of a round-trip, post to the semaphore.

5. Otherwise, we know that the remote peer started this channel, so we can just free the PROLOCAL_DATA.

Later on, we'll look at a routine called null_close( ) that's used to close a channel bound to the PR. For now, the important thing to know is that the close request contains a pointer to a routine and some client data. (Sound familiar?) The routine is pro_close_callback( ) and the client data is a pointer to the PRO_LOCALDATA structure associated with the channel, shown in Example 6-11.

Example 6-11. null-profiles.c: pro_close_callback

```
static void
pro_close_callback (void              *clientData,
                    CHANNEL_INSTANCE  *ci,
                    DIAGNOSTIC        *error) {
    PRO_LOCALDATA      *il = (PRO_LOCALDATA *) clientData;

    if (error) {
        il -> pl_flags |= PRO_DENIED, il -> pl_flags &= ~PRO_CLSWAIT;

        printf ("unable to close channel: [%d] %s\n",
                error -> code, error -> message);
    }
}
```

After pro_close_callback( ) is invoked, the wrapper makes a final callback passing it these parameters:

clientData

> The client data given to the wrapper when the request to close the channel was made.

ci

> A pointer to a CHANNEL_INSTANCE structure.

error

> A pointer to a DIAGNOSTIC structure. If NULL, then the close request is successful; otherwise, it explains why the channel was not closed.

The logic of pro_close_callback( ) is:

1. See if error is NULL; if so, the channel is going to close, and all the work was already done in pro_close_confirmation( ).

2. Otherwise, update the pl_flags field to note that we had a problem in closing the channel, and tell null_close( ) that we're no longer waiting for a callback.

3. Finally, print the diagnostic to the standard output.

Tuning reset callbacks

Now let's look at the two callbacks that are invoked when a tuning reset occurs:

```
static void
pro_tuning_reset_indication (PROFILE_INSTANCE  *pi) {
}
```

```
static void
pro_tuning_reset_confirmation (PROFILE_INSTANCE       *pi,
                               char                    status) {
    pro_close_confirmation (pi, status, NULL, PRO_ACTION_LOCAL,
                            PRO_ACTION_SESSION);
}
```

There's a lot more bark than bite here.

The first callback gets invoked when a local profile is about to start something that may result in a tuning reset. It's just a "FYI" for the profile—there's no way to decline.

The second callback gets invoked when we know if a tuning reset occurred. If so, all the channels have been closed, so we invoke the callback we just saw for closing a channel.

So, we've dealt with the four callbacks that deal with the profile module, the six callbacks that deal with starting and closing channels, and the two callbacks that deal with tuning resets. Now here's some good news: very few profile modules will require anything more complicated than the design pattern that we've just gone through. And now, here's some even better news: only one more callback to go!

Data exchange callback

The pro_frame_available( ) callback is made whenever a frame is available to be read. Before we dive into the code, let's think about the logic for this. The easiest way to do this is to start by constructing a decision table:

Frame received	Action taken by ECHO	Action taken by SINK
MSG	Send echo RPY	Partial: ignore
		Complete: send empty RPY
RPY	Update out parameters for null_trip	Update out parameters for null_trip
	If complete, leave RSPWAIT	If complete, leave RSPWAIT
ERR	If complete, leave RSPWAIT	If complete, leave RSPWAIT
ANS	Ignore	Ignore
NUL	If complete, leave RSPWAIT	If complete, leave RSPWAIT

Now all we have to do is explain what we mean by MSG, RPY, and so on. These are the components that make up BEEP's one-to-one and one-to-many exchanges.

Way back in Figure 2-4, we saw how BEEP has two kinds of exchanges: one-to-one and one-to-many. A one-to-one exchange is made up of the client sending a message and the server sending back either a reply or an error. beepcore-c (and BEEP) use three-letter terms to refer to each of these, so a one-to-one exchange is either:

- Send a MSG, get back a RPY.
- Send a MSG, get back an ERR.

Similarly, a one-to-many exchange is:

- Send a MSG, get back zero or more ANS, followed by a NUL.

The decision table explains the behavior of the profile module in these terms. For example, if we're doing the echo profile and we receive a MSG, then we send back an identical frame except that it says RPY instead of MSG. Similarly, if we're doing the sink profile and we receive a MSG, we send back an empty RPY, but only when we encounter the final frame of the MSG. The nuance here is using the frame-based interface of beepcore-c (instead of the message interface).

With that out of the way, let's look at the pro_frame_available( ) callback. As shown in Example 6-12, the wrapper calls pro_frame_available( ) with only one parameter, the PI.

Example 6-12. null-profiles.c: pro_frame_available

```
static void
pro_frame_available (PROFILE_INSTANCE   *pi) {
    int                size;
    char               *buffer,
                       *payload;
    FRAME              *f;
    PRO_LOCALDATA      *il = (PRO_LOCALDATA *) pi -> user_ptr1;

    if (!(f = bpc_query_frame (pi -> channel, BLU_QUERY_ANYTYPE,
                          BLU_QUERY_ANYMSG, BLU_QUERY_ANYANS)))
        return;

    switch (f -> msg_type) {
        case BLU_FRAME_TYPE_MSG:
            if (il -> pl_flags & PRO_ECHOMODE)
                payload = f -> payload, size = f -> size;
            else if (f -> more == BLU_FRAME_COMPLETE)
                payload = EMPTY_RPY, size = sizeof EMPTY_RPY - 1;
            else
                break;
            if (buffer = bpc_buffer_allocate (pi -> channel, size)) {
                memcpy (buffer, payload, size);
                bpc_send (pi -> channel, BLU_FRAME_TYPE_RPY,
                        f -> message_number, BLU_FRAME_IGNORE_ANSNO,
                        f -> more, buffer, size);
            } else
                bp_log (pi -> channel -> conn, LOG_PROF, 5,
                        "null frame: out of memory");
            break;

        case BLU_FRAME_TYPE_RPY:
            if (f -> size <= il -> pl_rlen) {
                memcpy (il -> pl_rbuf, f -> payload, f -> size);
                il -> pl_rbuf += f -> size, il -> pl_rlen -= f -> size;
            } else
                il -> pl_rlen = -1;
            /* and fall... */
```

Example 6-12. null-profiles.c: pro_frame_available (continued)

```
        case BLU_FRAME_TYPE_ERR:
        case BLU_FRAME_TYPE_NUL:
            if (f -> more == BLU_FRAME_COMPLETE) {
                il -> pl_flags &= ~PRO_RSPWAIT;
                SEM_POST (&il -> pl_sem);
            }
            break;

        case BLU_FRAME_TYPE_ANS:
        default:
            break;
    }

    bpc_frame_destroy (pi -> channel, f);
}
```

First we get a pointer to the associated PRO_LOCALDATA structure. Then, we call bpc_
query_frame( ) to get the next frame. There are four parameters:

channel
> A pointer to a CHANNEL_INSTANCE structure.

msgtype
> Indicates what kind of frame to look for, one of: BLU_FRAME_TYPE_MSG, BLU_FRAME_
> TYPE_RPY, BLU_FRAME_TYPE_ERR, BLU_FRAME_TYPE_ANS, BLU_FRAME_TYPE_NULL, or, if
> you don't care, then BLU_QUERY_ANYTYPE.

msgno
> The particular message number you want, or, if you don't care, then BLU_QUERY_
> ANYMSG.

ansno
> If looking for an ANS, then the particular answer number that you care about, or,
> if you don't care, then BLU_QUERY_ANYANS.

So, looking at the parameters given to bpc_query_frame( ), we're asking for the first
frame that matches any criteria (i.e., the first frame available). Here's what's in a
FRAME structure:

msg_type
> One of BLU_FRAME_TYPE_MSG, BLU_FRAME_TYPE_RPY, and so on.

message_number
> The associated message number.

answer_number
> If msg_type is BLU_FRAME_TYPE_ANS, then the associated answer number.

more
> Either BLU_FRAME_PARTIAL or BLU_FRAME_COMPLETE.

payload/size
> Pointers to the data carried by the frame and its size in octets.

The logic in pro_frame_available( ) follows the decision table in a "C" sort of way:

1. If we get a MSG then:

    a. If we're doing the echo profile, we going to send back the exact payload we got; if this is the final frame of the MSG and we're doing the sink profile, we're going to send back an empty message. Otherwise, we don't send anything back.

    b. We call bpc_buffer_allocate( ) to create the payload to be included in the frame to be sent back. This routine *must* be used, because what it really does is allocate a new frame for the channel, and return a pointer to the payload portion of it. As a courtesy, it always allocates an extra octet at the end of the payload, so instead of using memcpy( ), we can also use something like strcpy( ) or sprintf( ).

    c. We call bpc_send( ) to send a frame, which, later on, will automatically free the payload created by bpc_buffer_allocate( )—so you mustn't call bpc_buffer_destroy( ).

2. If we get a RPY, we see if we have enough room in a buffer we're maintaining in the associated PRO_LOCALDATA structure. If so, we copy the payload to the buffer and update the buffer state; if not, we set the "octets remaining" counter to "-1" to signal a problem. Regardless, we fall into the code for the next two message types.

3. If we get an ERR or a NUL, we see if this is the last frame of the response. If so, we update the pl_flags field of the PRO_LOCALDATA structure to indicate that we are no longer waiting for a response, and post to the semaphore.

4. If we get an ANS, we don't process it.

Finally, regardless of which branch we took, we destroy the frame by calling bpc_frame_destroy( ).

Driver entry points

Great! We're close to being done with *null-profiles.c*. The only thing left is to talk about the three routines it makes available to the driver:

- After the session is started, the driver calls null_start( ) to start a channel.
- After the channel is started, the driver calls null_trip( ) zero or more times to do a round-trip exchange.
- When the driver is ready to close the channel (or session), it calls null_close( ).

We'll start with null_start, as shown in Example 6-13.

Example 6-13. null-profiles.c: null_start

```
void *
null_start (BP_CONNECTION          *w,
```

Example 6-13. null-profiles.c: null_start (continued)

```
            PROFILE_REGISTRATION        *pr,
            char                        *serverName) {
    DIAGNOSTIC          *d;
    PRO_LOCALDATA       *pl = pr -> user_ptr,
                        *il;
    PROFILE             ps,
                        *p = &ps;

    memset (p, 0, sizeof *p);
    p -> uri = pr -> uri;
    p -> piggyback_length = strlen (p -> piggyback = "");

    if (!(il = (PRO_LOCALDATA *) lib_malloc (sizeof *il)))
        return NULL;
    memcpy (il, pl, sizeof *il);
    il -> pl_flags |= PRO_START;

    /* this blocks! */
    d = bp_start_request (w, BLU_CHANO_CHANO_DEFAULT, BLU_CHANO_MSGNO_DEFAULT,
                        p, serverName, pro_start_callback, (void *) il);

    if (d) {
        printf ("unable to start channel: [%d] %s\n",
                d -> code, d -> message);
        bp_diagnostic_destroy (w, d);
    }

    if (il -> pl_pi) {
        SEM_INIT (&il -> pl_sem);
        il -> pl_flags |= PRO_READY;
    } else
        lib_free (il), il = NULL;

    return ((void *) il);
}
```

null_start begins by following the user-defined pointer (user_ptr) of the PR to get to the PRO_LOCALDATA structure that was created by either null_echo_Init() or null_sink_Init(). Next, we zero a PROFILE structure residing on the stack. This structure is one of the parameters we're going to use to make the request to start a channel. Earlier, when we looked at this structure, we left out one of the fields, next, that's used to make a linked-list of PROFILE structures. (If you want to propose multiple profiles when asking to start a channel, that's how you do it.) Now, we create a copy of the PRO_LOCALDATA structure, and set the pl_flags field to indicate that we're the one who is starting the channel. This leads to the call to bp_start_request(), with these parameters:

connection
    A pointer to the BP_CONNECTION structure.

channel_number

> The desired channel number to use, or, if you don't care, then BLU_CHANO_CHANO_
> DEFAULT to select any unused channel number.

message_number

> The desired message number to use for the start request, or, in the likely case
> that you simply don't care, then BLU_CHANO_MSGNO_DEFAULT to select any unused
> message number.

profile

> A pointer to the profile structure containing the profile's URI and the piggy-
> backed data, if any.

server_name

> A pointer to a character string containing the serverName attribute to use, if any
> (see "Virtual hosting" in Chapter 3).

callback/clientData

> This is the pro_start_callback( ) callback from Example 6-7 that we discussed
> earlier.

This routine is a bit odd in comparison to many of the other protocol-related functions provided by the threaded_os wrapper, because it actually *blocks* execution until
an answer is received from the remote peer and all callbacks have been invoked. This
is a deficiency in the current implementation, with a very serious drawback: you *must
never* call bp_start_request( ) from inside a callback invoked by the wrapper. If you
do, the threaded_os wrapper will wedge. (A future release will fix this limitation.) At
present, there is actually an "exception that proves the rule," but we won't see it until
Example 6-28.

The return value from bp_start_request( ) is a pointer to a DIAGNOSTIC structure:

- If NULL, the channel was successfully created, and both the pro_start_
  confirmation( ) and pro_start_callback( ) callbacks were made (in that order).
  This means that the pro_start_confirmation( ) callback set the pl_pi field for us,
  so we set a flag in the PRO_LOCALDATA structure to indicate that we're ready for
  subsequent calls to null_trip( ) and null_close( ), and return an (opaque)
  pointer to this structure.

- Otherwise, the channel wasn't created, so we'll print the diagnostic to the standard output, free the copy of the PRO_LOCALDATA copy we made, and return NULL.

As shown in Example 6-14, null_trip( ) begins by converting the opaque parameter
v into a pointer to the PRO_LOCALDATA structure created and returned earlier by null_
start( ).

Example 6-14. null-profiles.c: null_trip

```
extern int
null_trip (void *v,
```

Example 6-14. null-profiles.c: null_trip (continued)

```
          char *ibuf,
          int   ilen,
          char *obuf,
          int   omaxlen) {
    char                *buffer;
    PRO_LOCALDATA       *il = (PRO_LOCALDATA *) v;
    PROFILE_INSTANCE    *pi;

    if (!(pi = il -> pl_pi)) {
        SEM_DESTROY (&il -> pl_sem);
        lib_free (il);
        return NULL_DONE;
    }
    if (!(il -> pl_flags & PRO_READY))
        return NULL_BUSY;

    if (!(buffer = bpc_buffer_allocate (pi -> channel, ilen)))
        return NULL_ERROR;
    memcpy (buffer, ibuf, ilen);

    il -> pl_rbuf = obuf, il -> pl_rlen = omaxlen;
    il -> pl_flags |= PRO_RSPWAIT, il -> pl_flags &= ~PRO_READY;

    bpc_send (pi -> channel, BLU_FRAME_TYPE_MSG, BLU_FRAME_MSGNO_UNUSED,
              BLU_FRAME_IGNORE_ANSNO, BLU_FRAME_COMPLETE, buffer, ilen);

    SEM_WAIT (&il -> pl_sem);

    if (!il -> pl_pi) {
        SEM_DESTROY (&il -> pl_sem);
        lib_free (il);
        return NULL_DONE;
    }

    il -> pl_flags |= PRO_READY;

    if (il -> pl_rlen < 0)
        return NULL_ERROR;

    return (omaxlen - il -> pl_rlen);
}
```

First, we look to see if something caused the PI to go away earlier. If so, we free the PRO_LOCALDATA structure and return NULL_DONE. Next we look to see if we're ready to do another round-trip, and if not, we return NULL_BUSY. Otherwise, we allocate and fill in the buffer we're going to send as a payload. We now update several fields in the PRO_LOCALDATA structure:

- We remember the address and size of the driver's output buffer that's going to be used to store the reply.
- We remember that we're now waiting for a response.

- We remember that the driver isn't allowed to invoke either null_trip( ) or null_close( ) until after we get that response.

We call bpc_send( ) to send a message and then yield execution using SEM_WAIT, waiting on either pro_frame_available( ) or pro_close_confirmation( ) to post to the semaphore. (When we look at null_close( ), we'll see how to use a spinlock instead of a semaphore.) Now here's where it gets tricky: if the pl_pi field got set to NULL, then the pro_close_confirmation( ) callback was made, so we free the PRO_LOCALDATA structure and return NULL_DONE. Otherwise, we allow the driver to once again call either null_trip( ) or null_close( ). Then, we see if the response would have overflowed the output buffer. If so, we return NULL_ERROR. Otherwise, we return the number of octets in the response.

In Example 6-15, null_close( ) begins by converting the opaque parameter v into a pointer to the PRO_LOCALDATA structure created and returned earlier by null_start( ).

Example 6-15. null-profiles.c: null_close

```
extern int
null_close (void        *v) {
    BP_CONNECTION       *w;
    DIAGNOSTIC          *d;
    PRO_LOCALDATA       *il = (PRO_LOCALDATA *) v;
    PROFILE_INSTANCE    *pi;

    if (!(pi = il -> pl_pi)) {
        SEM_DESTROY (&il -> pl_sem);
        lib_free (il);
        return NULL_DONE;
    }
    if (!(il -> pl_flags & PRO_READY))
        return NULL_BUSY;

    il -> pl_flags |= PRO_CLSWAIT, il -> pl_flags &= ~PRO_READY;

    w = pi -> channel -> conn;
    if ((d = bpc_close_request (pi -> channel, BLU_CHANO_MSGNO_DEFAULT, 200,
                        NULL, NULL, pro_close_callback,
                        (void *) il) != NULL) {
        printf ("unable to close channel: [%d] %s\n",
                d -> code, d -> message);
        bp_diagnostic_destroy (w, d);

        il -> pl_flags |= PRO_READY, il -> pl_flags &= ~PRO_CLSWAIT;
        return NULL_ERROR;
    }

    while (il -> pl_flags & PRO_CLSWAIT)
        YIELD ( );

    if (il -> pl_flags & PRO_DENIED) {
        il -> pl_flags |= PRO_READY, il -> pl_flags &= ~PRO_DENIED;
```

Example 6-15. null-profiles.c: null_close (continued)

```
        return NULL_DENIED;
    }

    SEM_DESTROY (&il -> pl_sem);
    lib_free (il);
    return NULL_OK;
}
```

We make the usual first two checks, and if everything's good, we remember that we're trying to close the channel and that the driver isn't allowed to call null_trip( ) or null_close( ). Next, we call bpc_close_request( ) with these parameters:

channel
> A pointer to our CHANNEL_INSTANCE structure.

message_number
> The desired message number to use for the close request, or BLU_CHANO_MSGNO_DEFAULT.

code/language/message
> The fields we normally see in a DIAGNOSTIC structure (each passed as a seperate parameter for convenience).

callback/clientData
> This is the pro_close_callback( ) callback from Example 6-11 that we dicussed earlier.

If an error is detected in the call, a pointer to a DIAGNOSTIC structure is returned. In this case, we'll print the diagnostic to the standard output, free it, and revert the pl_flags field back to its value when we were called. Otherwise, we start spinning, yielding execution of the current thread while we wait for the wrapper to make the pro_close_callback( ) and (possibly) pro_close_confirmation( ) callbacks. If the request was denied, we revert the pl_flags field, and return NULL_DENIED. Otherwise, we free the PRO_LOCALDATA structure and return NULL_OK.

The Listening Driver

The driver for the listener is straightforward. Example 6-16 shows the beginning of the source file.

Example 6-16. beepd: The beginning

```
/*    includes */

#include <stdio.h>
#include <stdlib.h>
#include <string.h>
#include <syslog.h>
#include <unistd.h>
```

Example 6-16. beepd: The beginning (continued)

```
#include "../utility/bp_config.h"
#include "../utility/logutil.h"
#include "../wrapper/bp_wrapper.h"
#include "../transport/bp_tcp.h"
#include "../wrapper/profile_loader.h"

/*    static variables */

static
char    *pgmname = "beepd";

static
char    *dataname = "default";

static
struct configobj *appconfig = NULL;
```

In addition to several libc include files, it also includes definitions by the threaded_os wrapper that pertain to:

bp_config.h
>   The configuration package

logutil.h
>   The logging package

bp_wrapper.h
>   The primary API for threaded_os

bp_tcp.h
>   The API for wrappers mapped onto TCP

profile_loader.h
>   Dynamically loading profile modules

Next, three static variables are declared:

pgmname
>   The "tail" of argv[0]

dataname
>   Identifies which configuration dataset to use

appconfig
>   A configuration object

Example 6-17 shows the initialization phase of the listener.

Example 6-17. beepd: Parsing arguments

```
/*    main */

int
main (int        argc,
```

Example 6-17. beepd: Parsing arguments (continued)

```
    char        *argv[]) {
int                 i,
                    optchar;
    char            buffer[BUFSIZ];
    char            *configF,
                    *hostName,
                     logF[BUFSIZ],
                    *portNo;
DIAGNOSTIC          *d;
PROFILE_REGISTRATION
                    *pr;

if (!(pgmname = strrchr (argv[0], '/')) || !(*++pgmname))
    pgmname = argv[0];


/* initialize tcp-based wrapper library */

tcp_bp_library_init ();

/* create a configuration object */

if (!(appconfig = config_new (NULL))) {
    fprintf (stderr, "config_new: failed\n");
    return 1;
}

configF = NULL, logF[0] = '\0', portNo = NULL;
while ((optchar = getopt (argc, argv, "a:f:l:p:")) != -1)
    switch (optchar) {
        case 'a':
            if (!(dataname = optarg))
                goto usage;
            break;

        case 'f':
            if (!optarg)
                goto usage;
            if (configF) {
                fprintf (stderr,
                        "specify \"-f configFile\" at most once\n");
                goto usage;
            }
            if ((i = config_parse_file (appconfig, configF = optarg))
                    != CONFIG_OK) {
                fprintf (stderr, "config_parse_file: failed %d\n", i);
                return 1;
            }
            break;

        case 'l':
            if (!optarg)
```

Example 6-17. beepd: Parsing arguments (continued)

```
                goto usage;
            strcpy (logF, optarg);
            break;

        case 'p':
            if ((!(portNo = optarg)) || (atoi (portNo) <= 0))
                goto usage;
            break;

        default:
            goto usage;
    }

    hostName = (argc == optind + 1) ? argv[optind++] : "";
    if (argc != optind) {
usage: ;

        fprintf (stderr,
                "usage: %s [-a dataname] [-f configFile] [-l logFile]\n\
            [-p portNo]   [hostName]\n",
                pgmname);
        return 1;
    }

    if (!portNo) {
        sprintf (buffer, "beep %s application %s port_number",
                pgmname, dataname);
        if (!(portNo = config_get (appconfig, buffer))) {
            fprintf (stderr, "specify \"-p portNo\"");
            if (configF)
                fprintf (stderr, " if \"-f %s\" doesn't define it", configF);
            else
                fprintf (stderr, " or use \"-f configFile\"");
            fprintf (stderr, "\n");
            goto usage;
        }
        if (atoi (portNo) <= 0) {
            fprintf (stderr, "invalid port_number in \"-f %s\": %s\n",
                    configF, portNo);
            goto usage;
        }
    }
}
```

After setting pgmname, we call tcp_bp_library_init( ) which initializes the threaded_os library and tells it we're going to be creating wrappers using TCP. This *must* be the very first call made to the library. Next, we create a configuration object. The call to appconfig takes one parameter, a pointer to another struct configobj, which, if present, is used to initialize the new object.

Next, we use getopt(3) to crack the command line, placing the value of each argument into the external character pointer optarg. The options are:

-a dataName

    The dataset to use when retrieving values from the configuration object.

-f configFile

    The file to use to initialize the configuration object.

-l logFile

    The file to use for logging.

-p portNo

    The TCP port number to listen on.

To make sense of the routine config_parse_file( ) that gets called by the -f switch, let's take a look at the configuration files used by the threaded_os wrapper. Example 6-18 shows an example; XML is used for the syntax.

Example 6-18. beepd.cfg

```
<beep>
 <profiles>
    <null_echo>
       <uri>http://xml.resource.org/profiles/NULL/ECHO</uri>
       <libfile>libnull-profiles.so</libfile>
       <initname>null_echo_Init</initname>
    </null_echo>
    <null_sink>
       <uri>http://xml.resource.org/profiles/NULL/SINK</uri>
       <libfile>libnull-profiles.so</libfile>
       <initname>null_sink_Init</initname>
    </null_sink>
    <sasl_anon>
       <uri>http://iana.org/beep/SASL/ANONYMOUS</uri>
       <libfile>libsasl-profiles.so</libfile>
       <initname>sasl_profiles_Init</initname>
    </sasl_anon>
    <sasl_otp>
       <uri>http://iana.org/beep/SASL/OTP</uri>
       <libfile>libsasl-profiles.so</libfile>
       <initname>sasl_profiles_Init</initname>
    </sasl_otp>
    <tls>
       <uri>http://iana.org/beep/TLS</uri>
       <libfile>libtls-profile.so</libfile>
       <initname>tls_profile_Init</initname>
       <certfile>/etc/openssl/certs/beepd.pem</certfile>
       <keyfile>/etc/openssl/certs/beepd.pem</keyfile>
    </tls>
 </profiles>
 <beepd>
  <application>
    <default>
       <log_mode>file</log_mode>
       <log_name>beepd.log</log_name>
       <log_ident>beepd</log_ident>
       <log_severity>debug</log_severity>
```

Example 6-18. beepd.cfg (continued)

```
      <log_facility>daemon</log_facility>
      <port_number>10288</port_number>
      <load_profiles>null_echo null_sink sasl_anon sasl_otp tls</load_profiles>
    </default>
  </application>
 </beepd>
</beep>
```

When it's read by config_parse_file( ), each leaf element is stored under a key. The key is named using the containment hierarchy starting at the root element. For example, "beep beepd application default log_name" is the name of the key that contains "beepd.log". Similarly, we now see why *null-profiles.h* chooses its keys (e.g., for NULL_ECHO_URI). Note that there is one weakness to this approach—all sibling elements must be uniquely named.

After we exit the getopt( ) loop (and make sure there weren't any extraneous arguments), we see our first call to config_get( ). This explains what dataname is used for. Each container element under "beep beepd application" is a configuration dataset. You can define one or more of these in a single configuration file, and when beepd is invoked, you use the -a switch to select the dataset you want.

Example 6-19 shows what happens next.

Example 6-19. beepd: Doing work

```
   /* configure logging package, initialize the log */

   if ((d = log_config (appconfig, pgmname, dataname, logF)) != NULL) {
       fprintf (stderr, "unable to configure logging: [%d] %s\n",
                  d -> code, d -> message);
       bp_diagnostic_destroy (NULL, d);
       return 1;
   }

   /* dynamically load and initialize profiles */

   if (!(pr = load_beep_profiles (appconfig, pgmname, dataname))) {
       fprintf (stderr, "no profiles loaded, consult log file\n");
       return 1;
   }


   /* loop forever: accept connections */

   tcp_bp_listen (hostName, atoi (portNo), pr, appconfig);

   /* got a termination signal */

   tcp_bp_library_shutdown ();

   return 0;
}
```

First, we call `log_config()`, which uses the configuration object to initialize the logging package provided by the wrapper. Take another look at Example 6-18 and you should be able to figure out what it's going to do. The logging package is initialized using several options:

mode
> Either "file" or "syslog" or "both", to specify where log entries should be written.

name
> The filename to use (if writing to a file).

ident
> The identification string to use.

facility
> The facility to use (if writing to *syslog*).

We're not done using the configuration object, because `load_beep_profiles()` uses it as well. The configuration object first gets the "load_profiles" leaf element from the dataset. This element contains the names of zero or more elements found under the beep profiles container. For each element, it dynamically loads the corresponding library (libfile) and then runs the profile module entry point (initname) to get a PR. The return value for `load_beep_profiles()` is a linked list of the results. Finally, it's time to listen and accept incoming connections. The routine that does this for TCP in the threaded_os wrapper is called `tcp_bp_listen()`. It takes four parameters:

- The hostname or IP address to listen at, or the empty string that says to listen on all available interfaces
- The port number to listen on
- The list of profiles to register for each incoming connection
- The configuration object to use, as needed

Usually, this routine never returns—it just accepts connections, creates wrappers, manages traffic, and so on. However, if the process receives a termination signal, the routine will return, so we call `tcp_bp_library_shutdown()` to shutdown the library and exit.

The Initiating Driver

The driver for the initiator is a bit longer. Example 6-20 shows the beginning of the source file.

Example 6-20. beepng: The beginning

```
/*    includes */

#include <ctype.h>
#include <math.h>
```

Example 6-20. beepng: The beginning (continued)

```
#include <stdio.h>
#include <stdlib.h>
#include <string.h>
#include <syslog.h>
#ifdef  LINUX
#include <sys/time.h>
#endif
#include <unistd.h>

#include "../utility/bp_config.h"
#include "../utility/logutil.h"
#include "../wrapper/bp_wrapper.h"
#include "../transport/bp_tcp.h"
#include "../../profiles/null-profiles.h"
#include "../../profiles/sasl_anon_otp.h"
#include "../../profiles/tls-profiles.h"

#define DEFAULT_CONTENT_TYPE    "Content-Type: application/beep+xml\r\n\r\n"

/*    static variables */

static
char    *pgmname = "beepng";

static
char    *dataname = "default";

static
struct configobj *appconfig = NULL;
```

This code is nearly identical to the beginning of the listener shown in Example 6-16. In addition to including a few extra libc header files, it defines the MIME Content-Type that will be used for the data sent to the listener.

Example 6-21 shows the initialization phase of the initiator.

Example 6-21. beepng: Parsing arguments

```
/*    main */

int
main (int       argc,
      char      *argv[]) {
   int              i,
                    optchar;
   int              count,
                    debugP,
                    size;
   char             *ep,
                    buffer[BUFSIZ];
   char             certF[BUFSIZ],
                    *configF,
```

Example 6-21. beepng: Parsing arguments (continued)

```
                        *hostName,
                         keyF[BUFSIZ],
                         logF[BUFSIZ],
                        *mechanism,
                        *mode,
                         name1[BUFSIZ],
                         name2[BUFSIZ],
                         passPhrase[BUFSIZ],
                        *portNo;
DIAGNOSTIC              *d;
PROFILE_REGISTRATION
                        *pr,
                        *qr;
BP_CONNECTION           *w;

if (!(pgmname = strrchr (argv[0], '/')) || !(*++pgmname))
    pgmname = argv[0];

/* initialize tcp-based wrapper library */

tcp_bp_library_init ();

/* create a configuration object */

if (!(appconfig = config_new (NULL))) {
    fprintf (stderr, "config_new: failed\n");
    return 1;
}

configF = NULL, logF[0] = '\0';
mode = "echo", count = 10, size = 10240;
certF[0] = '\0', keyF[0] = '\0';
mechanism = "none", name1[0] = '\0', name2[0] = '\0', passPhrase[0] = '\0';
debugP = 0;
portNo = NULL;
while ((optchar = getopt (argc, argv, "a:c:df:k:l:M:m:P:p:s:T:t:U:"))
        != -1)
    switch (optchar) {
        case 'a':
            if (!(dataname = optarg))
                goto usage;
            break;

        case 'c':
            if (!optarg)
                goto usage;
            if (((count = strtol (optarg, &ep, 10)) == 0) || (*ep))
                goto usage;
            break;

        case 'd':
            debugP = 1;
```

Example 6-21. beepng: Parsing arguments (continued)

```
                break;

        case 'f':
            if (!optarg)
                goto usage;
            if (configF) {
                fprintf (stderr,
                            "specify \"-f configFile\" at most once\n");
                goto usage;
            }
            if ((i = config_parse_file (appconfig, configF = optarg))
                    != CONFIG_OK) {
                fprintf (stderr, "config_parse_file: failed %d\n", i);
                return 1;
            }
            break;

        case 'k':
            if (!optarg)
                goto usage;
            strcpy (keyF, optarg);
            if (!certF[0])
                strcpy (certF, optarg);
            break;

        case 'l':
            if (!optarg)
                goto usage;
            strcpy (logF, optarg);
            break;


        case 'M':
            if (!(mechanism = optarg)
                    || (strcmp (mechanism, "anonymous")
                            && strcmp (mechanism, "otp")
                            && strcmp (mechanism, "none")))
                goto usage;
            break;

        case 'm':
            if (!(mode = optarg)
                    || (strcmp (mode, "echo") && strcmp (mode, "sink")))
                goto usage;
            break;

        case 'P':
            if (!optarg)
                goto usage;
            strcpy (passPhrase, optarg);
            break;
```

Example 6-21. beepng: Parsing arguments (continued)

```
            case 'p':
                if ((!optarg) || (atoi (portNo = optarg) <= 0))
                    goto usage;
                break;

            case 's':
                if (!optarg)
                    goto usage;
                if (((size = strtol (optarg, &ep, 10)) < 0) || (*ep))
                    goto usage;
                break;


            case 'T':
                if (!optarg)
                    goto usage;
                strcpy (name2, optarg);
                break;

            case 't':
                if (!optarg)
                    goto usage;
                strcpy (certF, optarg);
                if (!keyF[0])
                    strcpy (keyF, optarg);
                break;

            case 'U':
                if (!optarg)
                    goto usage;
                strcpy (name1, optarg);
                break;

            default:
                goto usage;
        }

    if ((!strcmp (mechanism, "anonymous")) && (!name2[0]))
        goto usage;
    if ((!strcmp (mechanism, "otp")) && ((!name1[0]) || (!passPhrase[0])))
        goto usage;

    if (argc != optind + 1) {
usage: ;

        fprintf (stderr,
          "usage: %s [-a dataName]      [-f configFile] [-l logFile]\n\
    [-m \"echo\"|\"sink\"] [-c count]      [-s size]\n\
    [-t certFile]      [-k keyFile]\n\
    [-M \"none\"]\n\
    [-M \"anonymous\"      -T traceInfo]\n\
    [-M \"otp\"            -U userName     [-T targetName] -P passPhrase]\n\
```

Example 6-21. beepng: Parsing arguments (continued)

```
        [-d]
        [-p portNo]              hostName\n",
          pgmname);
        return 1;
    }
    hostName = argv[optind];

    if (!portNo) {
        sprintf (buffer, "beep %s application %s port_number",
                 pgmname, dataname);
        if (!(portNo = config_get (appconfig, buffer))) {
            fprintf (stderr, "specify \"-p portNo\"");
            if (configF)
                fprintf (stderr, " if \"-f %s\" doesn't define it", configF);
            else
                fprintf (stderr, " or use \"-f configFile\"");
            fprintf (stderr, "\n");
            goto usage;
        }
        if (atoi (portNo) <= 0) {
            fprintf (stderr, "invalid port_number in \"-f %s\": %s\n",
                     configF, portNo);
            goto usage;
        }
    }
}
```

Again, it's nearly identical to the listener's initialization phase shown in Example 6-17. The additional options are:

−m mode
> A flag indicating whether to use the echo or sink profile.

−c count
> The number of round-trips to make with the listener.

−s size
> The number of octets that should be sent in each transaction.

−M mechanism
> The SASL mechanism to use for tuning the session.
>
> none
>> Don't tune for authentication.
>
> anonymous
>> Provide trace information ("-T") instead of authenticating.
>
> otp
>> Tune using SASL/OTP using a username ("-U") and passphrase ("-P").

−t certFile
> The name of a file containing a public key certificate to use for tuning the session for privacy.

-k keyFile

The name of a file containing a secret key to use when tuning the session for privacy.

-d

Enables debug output.

The only other difference is that we require the user to specify a hostName to connect to. Example 6-22 shows what happens next.

Example 6-22. beepng: Doing work

```
/* configure logging package, initialize the log */

    if ((d = log_config (appconfig, pgmname, dataname, logF)) != NULL) {
        fprintf (stderr, "unable to configure logging: [%d] %s\n",
                d -> code, d -> message);
        bp_diagnostic_destroy (NULL, d);
        return 1;
    }

    /* initialize the profile we're going to use */

    switch (*mode) {
        case 'e':
            pr = null_echo_Init (appconfig);
            break;

        case 's':
            pr = null_sink_Init (appconfig);
            break;

        default:
            pr = NULL;
            break;
    }
    if (!(qr = pr)) {
        printf ("unable to load profile for \"-m %s\"\n", mode);
        return 1;
    }
    while (qr -> next)
        qr = qr -> next;

    /* get the TLS profile, if need be... */

    if (certF[0]) {
        config_set (appconfig, "beep profiles tls certfile", certF);
        config_set (appconfig, "beep profiles tls keyfile", keyF);

        if (!(qr -> next = tls_profile_Init (appconfig))) {
            printf ("unable to load TLS profile\n");
            return 1;
        }
```

Example 6-22. beepng: Doing work (continued)

```
        while (qr -> next)
            qr = qr -> next;
    }

    /* get the SASL profiles, if need be... */

    if (strcmp (mechanism, "none")) {
        config_set (appconfig, SASL_LOCAL_MECHANISM, mechanism);
        config_set (appconfig, SASL_LOCAL_TRACEINFO, name2);
        config_set (appconfig, SASL_LOCAL_USERNAME, name1);
        config_set (appconfig, SASL_LOCAL_TARGET, name2);
        config_set (appconfig, SASL_LOCAL_PASSPHRASE, passPhrase);
        if (debugP)
            config_set (appconfig, SASL_IDENTITY_DEBUG, "1");

        if (!(qr -> next = sasl_profiles_Init (appconfig))) {
            printf ("unable to load SASL profiles\n");
            return 1;
        }
        while (qr -> next)
            qr = qr -> next;
    }

    if (debugP)
        for (qr = pr; qr; qr = qr -> next)
            printf ("loaded profile for %s\n", qr -> uri);

    /* time for the real work */

    if ((d = tcp_bp_connect (hostName, atoi (portNo), pr, appconfig, &w))
            != NULL)
        printf ("[%d] %s\n", d -> code, d -> message);
    else if ((d = bp_wait_for_greeting (w)) != NULL)
        printf ("unable to establish session: [%d] %s\n", d -> code,
                d -> message);
    else {
        if (certF[0] && (d = tls_privatize (w, NULL)))
            printf ("unable to privatize session: [%d] %s\n", d -> code,
                    d -> message);
        else if (strcmp (mechanism, "none") && (d = sasl_login (w, NULL)))
            printf ("unable to authenticate: [%d] %s\n", d -> code,
                    d -> message);
        else
            (void) beepng (w, pr, *mode == 'e', count, size);

        tcp_bp_connection_close (w);
    }
    if (d)
        bp_diagnostic_destroy (w, d);

    /* finalize tcp-based wrapper library */
```

Example 6-22. beepng: Doing work (continued)

```
    tcp_bp_library_shutdown ( );

    /* de-allocate things we built that still remain... */

    log_destroy ( );
    bp_profile_registration_chain_destroy (NULL, pr);
    config_destroy (appconfig);

    return 0;
}
```

After making the usual call to `log_config( )` to initialize the logging package by using the configuration object, we call the entry point for the appropriate profile module, either `null_echo_Init( )` or `null_sink_Init( )`. If the user provided a certificate file, we call `tls_profile_Init( )` to initialize the TLS profile, and link the resulting PR into the chain. Similarly, if the user provided an authentication mechanism, we also call `sasl_profiles_Init( )` to initialize the TLS profile, and link the resulting PR into the chain. Note that it's possible for these initialization routines to return a PR chain of their own, so we take care to make sure everything gets linked in.

Next:

- We call `tcp_bp_connect( )` to make an outgoing connection. If we couldn't connect to the host, then a pointer to a DIAGNOSTIC structure is returned, which we print to the standard output.

- Otherwise, we call `bp_wait_for_greeting( )`, which does just what you'd think. If the peer transmits an error instead of a greeting, then a pointer to a DIAGNOSTIC structure is returned, which we print to the standard output.

- Otherwise, we look to see whether we should tune the session for privacy. If so, `tls_privatize( )` is called to do this. (If it returns a pointer to a DIAGNOSTIC structure, there was a problem.)

- Otherwise, we look to see whether we should tune the session for authentication. If so, `sasl_login( )` is called to do this. (If it returns a pointer to a DIAGNOSTIC structure, then there was a problem.)

- Otherwise, we call a routine of our own, `beepng( )`, that will perform the round-trips with the listener, followed by `tcp_bp_connection_close( )` which closes the connection.

Finally, before exiting, we:

- Destroy the PRO_LOCALDATA created for the PR we allocated.
- Close the logging package.
- Destroy the PR we allocated.
- Destroy the configuration object we built.

All that's left to discuss is the routine beepng( ). The real work in the initiating driver occurs here, as shown in Example 6-23.

Example 6-23. beepng: Round-tripping

```
static int
beepng (BP_CONNECTION         *w,
        PROFILE_REGISTRATION  *pr,
        int                   echoP,
        int                   count,
        int                   size) {
    int             cc,
                    cnt,
                    len,
                    nlP,
                    status;
    unsigned long   usecs[3],
                    *avg = &usecs[1],
                    *max = &usecs[2],
                    *min = &usecs[0];
    char            c,
                    prefix[BUFSIZ],
                    *b1,
                    *b2,
                    *cp,
                    *ep,
                    *sp;
    void            *v;

    if (!(v = null_start (w, pr, NULL)))
        return 1;

    if (!count)
        count = 1;
    if (size < 0)
        size = 0;

    len = size + (sizeof DEFAULT_CONTENT_TYPE - 1)
            + (sizeof "<data></data>" - 1) + 1;
    if (!(b1 = lib_malloc (len)) || !(b2 = lib_malloc (len))) {
        if (b1)
            lib_free (b1);
        printf ("unable to allocate buffers\n");
        return 1;
    }

    sprintf (sp = b1, "%s<data>", DEFAULT_CONTENT_TYPE);
    sp += strlen (sp);
    cp = sp, ep = b1 + len - sizeof "</data>";

    srandom (1L);
    while (cp < ep) {
        do {
```

Example 6-23. beepng: Round-tripping (continued)

```
        c = random () & 0x7f;
    } while (!isalnum (c) && (c != ' '));
    *cp++ = c;
}

strcpy (cp, "</data>");
len --;
cnt = 0;
*min = *avg = *max = 0L;
nlP = 0;
status = 0;
while ((count < 0)  || (cnt++ < count)) {
    unsigned long    clicks;
    struct timeval    tv1,
                      tv2;

    if (gettimeofday (&tv1, NULL) < 0) {
        perror ("gettimeofday");
        return 1;
    }

    if ((cc = null_trip (v, b1, len, b2, len)) < 0) {
        printf ("null_trip: failed %d\n", cc);
        status = 1;
        break;
    }

    if (gettimeofday (&tv2, NULL) < 0) {
        perror ("gettimeofday");
        return 1;
    }
    clicks = (tv2.tv_sec - tv1.tv_sec) * 1000000
                    + (tv2.tv_usec - tv1.tv_usec);
    if (*max <= 0)
        *min = *max = clicks;
    else {
        if (clicks < *min)
            *min = clicks;
        if (clicks > *max)
            *max = clicks;
    }
    *avg += clicks;

    if (echoP && ((cc != len) || memcmp (b1, b2, len))) {
        if (nlP)
            printf ("\n"), nlP = 0;
        printf ("%s mismatch\n", cc != len ? "length" : "data");
        fflush (stdout);
        status = 1;
        memcpy (b2, b1, len);
    } else
        printf (".");
```

Example 6-23. beepng: Round-tripping (continued)

```
        if (nlP++ >= 78) {
            printf ("\n");
            fflush (stdout);
            nlP = 0;
        }

        if (size > 1) {
            memcpy (sp + 1, b2 + (sp - b1), ep - (sp + 1));
            *sp = b2[(ep - b1) - 1];
        }
    }
    if (nlP)
        printf ("\n");

    lib_free (b1);
    lib_free (b2);

    sprintf (prefix, "%d round-trips: min/avg/max =", cnt);
    printf ("%s %lu %lu %lu (usecs)\n", prefix, *min, *avg = *avg/cnt, *max);
    if (size > 0) {
        unsigned long    *up,
                         *vp;

        len = strlen (prefix);
        printf ("%*.*s", len, len, "");

        for (vp = (up = usecs) + (sizeof usecs/sizeof usecs[0]);
                up < vp;
                up++)
            if (*up > 0) {
                int     speed = (int) ((size * 1000000.0) / *up) >> 10;
                len = log10 (*up) + 1;
                printf (" %*.*d", len, len, speed);
            } else
                printf ("   ");

        printf (" (KB/s)\n");
    }

    if ((cc != NULL_DONE) && (null_close (v) < 0)) {
        printf ("null_close: failed %d\n", cc);
        status = 1;
    }

    return status;
}
```

First, a call is made to null_start( ), which we saw back in Example 6-13. If it returns NULL, there was a problem (which it reported), so we just return. Otherwise, we make sure the count and size parmeters are normalized and allocate two character buffers.

Then, by using the pointer-arithmetic for which C is so despised by "programming progressives," we proceed to initialize the first buffer to look something like this:

```
Content-Type: application/beep+xml

<data>RaNdOm ChArAcTeRs</data>
```

without a trailing CR-LF.

Next, we enter a loop, possibly infinite:

- We get the current time.
- We call null_trip( ), which we saw back in Example 6-14, to make a round-trip transaction.
- We calculate how long this took, and update the min, max, and avg counters accordingly.
- If we're doing the echo profile, we make sure we got back what we sent out.
- Finally, we rotate the characters inside the "<data>...</data>".

If the loop does terminate, we print the round-trip statistics, and finally call null_close( ) (last seen in Example 6-15) to close the channel.

Let's Recap

We've just gone through 1,300 lines of C code. Although there's a lot of detail there, you should be able to pick out the key points. In particular, a profile module has three parts:

- A module entry point (e.g., null_echo_Init( )) that's used to build a PR used for the lifetime of the application
- Several callbacks that are used by the wrapper code as the protocol is executed
- Other entry points used by a driver (e.g., null_trip( ))

There are a couple of subtle aspects of this architecture to keep in mind.

First, a profile module is ultimately identified by the URI that it puts into the PR returned by its entry point. If your driver is interested exclusively in either the client side or the server side of using the profile module, you can implement "half a profile module" with only those parts that get used. However, if your driver wants to act both as a client and a server using that module, all the functionality has to be in that one profile module—the architecture doesn't let you have two "half-modules" advertising the same URI.

Second, the vast majority of a profile module is boilerplate. It won't change much from one application or profile module. In fact, I'll tell you a little secret: the hard work in writing a profile module for beepcore-c is deciding what the entry points for the driver are going to look like. Coding the callbacks for the wrapper/module interactions is a modest exercise in tedium.

To prove this point, we're now going to look at a second example, one whose behavior is fundamentally different than echo and sink, but whose implementation differs only in a few details.

Reliable Syslog

Let's see if we can implement reliable *syslog* in less than 1,200 lines of C. If you recall from "The Syslog Raw Profile" in Chapter 4, the *syslog* raw profile is an example of a server/client interaction:

1. The initiator establishes a connection to the listener and starts a channel for the profile.
2. The listener acts as a client by sending a MSG to the initiator.
3. The initiator acts as a server by sending zero or more syslog messages in response.
4. When the initiator is done, it closes the channel and the session.

Given what we just said about the hardest part of writing a profile module for beepcore-c, what about the entry points for the driver? For the initiator, they're going to look like this:

1. First, we call sr_Init( ), the initialization entry point for the module, which returns a PR.
2. Then, we call sr_initiator( ) on that PR to give it the address of a routine to call whenever something important happens.
3. At this point, we can establish a session. When this happens, the module will *automatically* start the channel for us and then use the callback to tell us what happened.
4. If the channel couldn't be started, the callback will tell us why, but for all intents and purposes, we're done.
5. Otherwise, the callback contains an opaque pointer that we'll use for the remainder of the session.
6. Then, whenever we want to send one or more syslog entries, we call sr_log( ) with the opaque pointer.
7. When we're done sending entries, we call sr_fin( ) and await the final callback.

It's even simpler for the listener:

1. First, we call sr_Init( ) followed by sr_listener( ) to register a callback.
2. Whenever we accept a connection, we register the PR returned by sr_Init( ) with the wrapper.
3. Whenever a channel is started for us, the module will *automatically* send the MSG to kick things off.

4. The listener just waits for the callback, which will indicate one of three things:

- We should get ready for some *syslog* entries.
- Here's a *syslog* entry.
- There's been a problem and no more *syslog* entries will be coming.

 We're going to discuss *new* things in the rest of this chapter. So, if you skipped over the earlier section "Echo and Sink," you really ought to read that thoroughly before proceeding.

The Header File

Example 6-24 shows the first part of the file *syslog-raw.h*.

Example 6-24. syslog-raw.h

```
/* includes */

#include "../threaded_os/utility/bp_config.h"
#include "../threaded_os/wrapper/bp_wrapper.h"

/* typedefs */

/* application callback */

typedef void (*sr_callback) (void *v, int code, char * message,
                             void *clientData);

/* configuration key */

#define SR_URI              "beep profiles syslog_raw uri"
#define SR_IMODES           "beep profiles syslog_raw initiator_modes"
#define SR_LMODES           "beep profiles syslog_raw listener_modes"
#define SR_WINDOWSIZE       "beep profiles syslog_raw window_size"
```

It begins by including the usual two header files from the threaded_os wrapper, then it defines a typedef for the callback used by the module to tell the driver what's going on. The parameters are:

- An opaque pointer
- An integer code and textual diagnostic
- Client data supplied by the driver to either sr_initiator( ) or sr_listener( )

Finally, we see the usual #defines used for accessing the configuration object. If you compare this header fragment to the one shown in Example 6-1, you'll see that outside of the obvious name changes (SR_) instead of (NULL_) it's practically identical. The one substantive change is the addition of a configuration key called SR_WINDOWSIZE used to tell the threaded_os wrapper how much buffer space to allocate for an incoming message.

Example 6-25 shows the remainder of the file *syslog-raw.h* by defining the entry points used by the driver.

Example 6-25. syslog-raw.h, part two

```
/* module entry points */

extern PROFILE_REGISTRATION *
sr_Init (struct configobj        *appconfig);

/* listener routines */

extern void
sr_listener (PROFILE_REGISTRATION    *pr,
             sr_callback              callback,
             void                    *clientData);

/* initiator routines */

extern void
sr_initiator (PROFILE_REGISTRATION    *pr,
              char                    *serverName,
              sr_callback              callback,
              void                    *clientData);

extern int
sr_log (void              *v,
        char              *entry);

extern int
sr_fin (void              *v);

#define SR_OK      0        /* no problema            */
#define SR_ERROR   (-1)     /* error performing task  */
#define SR_BUSY    (-2)     /* still doing sr_log     */
#define SR_DONE    (-3)     /* channel is closed      */
```

The first routine, sr_Init( ), creates a PR, and gets called by both initiating and listening drivers. After calling sr_Init( ), a listening driver will also call sr_listener( ) to register the routine to call whenever the initiator connects/disconnects, or when a *syslog* entry is received. For the initiating driver, there are three entry points provided:

sr_initiator( )
>   Allows the driver to register the routine to use for callbacks.

sr_log( )
>   Sends one or more *syslog* entries.

sr_fin( )
>   Makes sure all previous calls to sr_log were successful by closing the channel.

The first argument to sr_log( ) and sr_fin( ) is an opaque pointer given to the driver during a callback from the module.

The Source File

Now it's time to look at *syslog-raw.c*. Example 6-26 shows the beginning of the file.

Example 6-26. syslog-raw.c: The beginning

```
/*    includes */

#include "syslog-raw.h"
#include "../threaded_os/utility/logutil.h"

/*    defines and typedefs */

#define PRO_RAW_URI            "http://iana.org/beep/SYSLOG/RAW"

#define DEFAULT_CONTENT_TYPE   "\r\n"

typedef struct pro_localdata {
    int         pl_flags;              /* mode flags                  */
#define PRO_INITIATOR   (1<<0)         /* either initiator            */
#define PRO_LISTENER    (1<<1)         /*    or listener              */
#define PRO_ONCEONLY    (1<<2)         /* report only first problem   */
#define PRO_READY       (1<<3)         /* ready for sr_log/sr_fin     */
#define PRO_ABORTED     (1<<4)         /* the session is aborting     */

    long        pl_msgNo;              /* when answering a MSG        */
    long        pl_ansNo;              /*    ..                       */

    PROFILE_INSTANCE
                *pl_pi;                /* hook to wrappers            */

    char        *pl_serverName;        /* what you'd think            */

    sr_callback pl_callback;           /* application callback        */
    void        *pl_clientData;        /*    ..                       */
} PRO_LOCALDATA;
```

First, it includes the header file that we just defined. It then defines the default URI to identify the profile, along with the the MIME Content-Type that will be used for the data being sent. (Actually, it defines the lack of a MIME Content-Type, which in BEEP defaults to application/octet-stream.) Finally, we define a struct pro_localdata that is contains state information used by the module. Rather than spell out what each field of PRO_LOCALDATA does, we'll point this out as they are used.

Module Entry Points

Example 6-27 shows the entry points for the module.

Example 6-27. syslog-raw.c: Module entry points

```
PROFILE_REGISTRATION *
sr_Init (struct configobj  *appconfig) {
```

Example 6-27. syslog-raw.c: Module entry points (continued)

```
      PRO_LOCALDATA        *pl;
      PROFILE_REGISTRATION *pr;

      if (!(pr = (PROFILE_REGISTRATION *) lib_malloc (sizeof *pr +
                                            sizeof *pl))) {
          log_line (LOG_PROF, 6, "unable to allocate PR");
          return NULL;
      }
      memset (pr, 0, sizeof *pr);

      if (!(pr -> uri = config_get (appconfig, SR_URI)))
          pr -> uri = PRO_RAW_URI;

      if (!(pr -> initiator_modes = config_get (appconfig, SR_IMODES)))
          pr -> initiator_modes = "plaintext,encrypted";
      if (!(pr -> listener_modes = config_get (appconfig, SR_LMODES)))
          pr -> listener_modes = "plaintext,encrypted";

      pr -> full_messages = 1;

      pr -> proreg_connection_init = pro_connection_init;
      pr -> proreg_connection_fin = pro_connection_fin;
      pr -> proreg_session_init = pro_session_init;
      pr -> proreg_session_fin = pro_session_fin;
      pr -> proreg_greeting_indication = pro_greeting_indication;
      pr -> proreg_start_indication = pro_start_indication;
      pr -> proreg_start_confirmation = pro_start_confirmation;
      pr -> proreg_close_indication = pro_close_indication;
      pr -> proreg_close_confirmation = pro_close_confirmation;
      pr -> proreg_tuning_reset_indication = pro_tuning_reset_indication;
      pr -> proreg_tuning_reset_confirmation = pro_tuning_reset_confirmation;
      pr -> proreg_message_available = pro_message_available;
      pr -> proreg_window_full = pro_window_full;

      pr -> user_ptr = pl = (PRO_LOCALDATA *) (((char *) pr) + sizeof *pr);
      memset (pl, 0, sizeof *pl);

      return pr;
}

void
sr_listener (PROFILE_REGISTRATION      *pr,
             sr_callback               callback,
             void                      *clientData) {
    PRO_LOCALDATA       *pl = pr -> user_ptr;

    pl -> pl_flags = PRO_LISTENER;
    pl -> pl_callback = callback;
    pl -> pl_clientData = clientData;
}

void
```

Example 6-27. syslog-raw.c: Module entry points (continued)

```
sr_initiator (PROFILE_REGISTRATION     *pr,
              char                     *serverName,
              sr_callback               callback,
              void                     *clientData) {
    PRO_LOCALDATA       *pl = pr -> user_ptr;

    pl -> pl_flags = PRO_INITIATOR;
    pl -> pl_serverName = serverName;
    pl -> pl_callback = callback;
    pl -> pl_clientData = clientData;
}
```

sr_Init( ) looks a lot like pro_init( ) in Example 6-4. Observant readers will note that the only substantive differences are:

- The PR asks for the message-oriented interface, instead of the frame-based interface.
- A new callback, pro_greeting_indication( ), is included in the PR that's built.

In fact, the four "outer" callbacks (e.g., pro_connection_init( )) are identical to the ones shown earlier in the section "Outer callbacks." But what about the additional callback?

A New Callback

Example 6-28 shows the new callback, pro_greeting_indication( ).

Example 6-28. syslog-raw.c: pro_greeting_indication

```
static void
pro_greeting_indication (PROFILE_REGISTRATION *pr,
                         BP_CONNECTION        *w,
                         char                  status) {
    DIAGNOSTIC          *d;
    PRO_LOCALDATA       *pl = pr -> user_ptr,
                        *il;

    if (pl -> pl_flags & PRO_LISTENER)
        return;

    switch (status) {
        case PROFILE_PRESENT:
            break;

        case PROFILE_ABSENT:
            pro_upcall (pl, 500, "greeting: profile not present");
            return;

        case GREETING_ERROR:
            pro_upcall (pl, 500, "greeting: got error");
            return;
```

Example 6-28. syslog-raw.c: pro_greeting_indication (continued)

```
    }

    if (!(il = (PRO_LOCALDATA *) lib_malloc (sizeof *il))) {
        pro_upcall (pl, 500, "sr greeting: out of memory");
        return;
    }
    memcpy (il, pl, sizeof *il);

    if (d = pro_send_start (w, il)) {
        pro_upcall (pl, d -> code, d -> message);
        bp_diagnostic_destroy (w, d);
        lib_free (il);
    }
}
```

This routine is called whenever a greeting is received from the peer; i.e., when the session is first established and whenever a tuning reset occurs. We've already seen the first two parameters (for what seems like a thousand times). The third parameter is one of:

PROFILE_PRESENT
> The URI associated with this module was advertised in the peer's greeting.

PROFILE_ABSENT
> The URI wasn't advertised.

GREETING_ERROR
> Instead of receiving a greeting from the peer, an error was returned (e.g., the peer is congested).

The logic used by this routine is pretty simple:

1. If we're the listening peer, we do nothing—it's the initating peer's job to start the channel.

2. Otherwise, we make sure that the profile was advertised. If not, we call pro_ upcall( ) to deliver the bad news to the driver.

3. Otherwise, we clone the PRO_LOCALDATA structure that was built by sr_Init( ), and call pro_send_start( ) to start a channel for us.

Let's look at these two helper routines. The first, pro_upcall( ), is used to deliver bad news to the driver:

```
static void
pro_upcall (PRO_LOCALDATA     *il,
            int                code,
            char              *message) {
    if (!(il -> pl_flags & PRO_ONCEONLY)) {
        il -> pl_flags |= PRO_ONCEONLY;

        (*il -> pl_callback) (NULL, code, message, il -> pl_clientData);
    }
}
```

It uses the PRO_ONCEONLY flag to make sure that it makes the callback at most once.

The second helper routine, pro_send_start( ), starts a channel:

```
static DIAGNOSTIC *
pro_send_start (BP_CONNECTION    *w,
                PRO_LOCALDATA    *il) {
    PROFILE             ps,
                        *p = &ps;
    struct configobj *appconfig = bp_get_config (w);

    memset (p, 0, sizeof *p);
    if (!(p -> uri = config_get (appconfig, SR_URI)))
        p -> uri = PRO_RAW_URI;
    p -> piggyback_length = strlen (p -> piggyback = "");

    return bp_start_request (w, BLU_CHANO_CHANO_DEFAULT,
                             BLU_CHANO_MSGNO_DEFAULT, p, il -> pl_serverName,
                             pro_start_callback, (void *) il);
}
```

The design pattern is clearly based on null_start( ), which we saw earlier in Example 6-13. The key point is passing a pointer to the initiator's PRO_LOCALDATA structure as client data for pro_start_confirmation( ), which we'll look at next.

Finally, the pro_greeting_indication( ) is the one callback where you can call bp_start_request( ). (You might recall being warned earlier that calling this function inside a callback causes the current implementation of the threaded_os wrapper to wedge.)

Channel Start Callbacks

As you might expect, there are three callbacks used for events relating to starting a channel. Once again, as shown in Example 6-29, we see that all pro_start_confirmation( ) does is cross-link the PRO_LOCALDATA to the PI associated with the channel.

Example 6-29. syslog-raw.c: pro_start_confirmation

```
static void
pro_start_confirmation (void                    *clientData,
                        PROFILE_INSTANCE        *pi,
                        PROFILE                 *po) {
    PRO_LOCALDATA       *il = (PRO_LOCALDATA *) clientData;

    il -> pl_pi = pi, pi -> user_ptr1 = il;
}
```

As shown in Example 6-30, we see pro_start_callback( ) takes care of things if we can't start the channel, by reporting it to the driver using a callback (for the echo and sink profiles, we did a printf( ) instead in Example 6-7).

Example 6-30. syslog-raw.c: pro_start_callback

```
static void
pro_start_callback (void                    *clientData,
                    CHANNEL_INSTANCE        *ci,
                    DIAGNOSTIC              *error) {
    PRO_LOCALDATA       *il = (PRO_LOCALDATA *) clientData;

    if (error) {
        pro_upcall (il, error -> code, error -> message);
        lib_free (il);
    }
}
```

When the remote peer asks to start a channel, that's when pro_start_indication( )
(shown in Example 6-31) gets called.

Example 6-31. syslog-raw.c: pro_start_indication

```
static void
pro_start_indication (PROFILE_INSTANCE  *pi,
                      PROFILE           *po) {
    long            wsize;
    char            *buffer,
                    *cp;
    DIAGNOSTIC      ds,
                    *d = &ds;
    PRO_LOCALDATA   *pl = pi -> channel -> profile_registration
                                -> user_ptr,
                    *il;
    struct configobj *appconfig = bp_get_config (pi -> channel -> conn);

    memset (d, 0, sizeof *d);

    if (pl -> pl_flags & PRO_INITIATOR) {
        memset (d, 0, sizeof *d);
        d -> code = 521;
        d -> message = "not available";
        bpc_start_response (pi -> channel, po, d);
        return;
    }

    if (!(il = (PRO_LOCALDATA *) lib_malloc (sizeof *il))) {
        pro_upcall (pl, d -> code = 421, d -> message = "out of memory");
        bpc_start_response (pi -> channel, po, d);
        return;
    }
    memcpy (il, pl, sizeof *il);
    il -> pl_pi = pi, pi -> user_ptr1 = il;

    bpc_start_response (pi -> channel, po, NULL);

    if ((cp = config_get (appconfig, SR_WINDOWSIZE))
            && (wsize = (long) atol (cp)) > 4096)
```

Example 6-31. syslog-raw.c: pro_start_indication (continued)

```
      (void) bpc_set_channel_window (pi -> channel, wsize);

   if (!(buffer = bpc_buffer_allocate (pi -> channel,
                                      sizeof DEFAULT_CONTENT_TYPE - 1))) {
       pro_upcall (il, 500, "sr start: out of memory");
       return;
   }

   strcpy (buffer, DEFAULT_CONTENT_TYPE);
   bpc_send (pi -> channel, BLU_FRAME_TYPE_MSG, BLU_FRAME_MSGNO_DEFAULT,
             BLU_FRAME_IGNORE_ANSNO, BLU_FRAME_COMPLETE, buffer,
             strlen (buffer));

   (*il -> pl_callback) ((void *) il, 350, NULL, il -> pl_clientData);
}
```

Here's the logic we're using in this routine:

- First, we set pl to the PRO_LOCALDATA structure that was created by sr_Init( ). We do this by going from the PI we were passed to its dual CI, then to its PR, and then to its user-defined pointer.

- We see if we initiated the session. If so, we decline the request by calling bpc_start_response( ).

- Otherwise, we make a copy of the PRO_LOCALDATA structure.

- We call bpc_start_response( ) to accept the request to start the channel.

- We tell the threaded_os package how much buffer space to allocate. Unlike the echo and sink profile modules, we're using the message-based interface, so the wrapper is going to try to buffer frames until a complete message is received.

- Then, we allocate a buffer for the payload of the MSG. If you remember from "One Packet Trace" in Chapter 4, the contents of *syslog* raw's kick-off message is arbitrary. In our case, it's just going to be empty. Recall that bpc_buffer_allocate( ) always allocates an extra octet, so you can use strcpy( ) or sprintf( ) on the buffer it returns.

- Next, we call bpc_send( ) to send the message.

- Finally, a callback is made with code 350 (the reply code that means "ready to go") to tell the listening driver that we're about to get busy.

Channel Close Callbacks

And now, it's time for the callbacks relating to a channel being closed. Whenever it looks like the channel might be closing, pro_close_indication( ) (shown in Example 6-32) gets called by the wrapper.

Example 6-32. syslog-raw.c: pro_close_indication

```
static void
pro_close_indication (PROFILE_INSTANCE  *pi,
                      DIAGNOSTIC         *request,
                      char               origin,
                      char               scope) {
    PRO_LOCALDATA       *il = (PRO_LOCALDATA *) pi -> user_ptr1;

    switch (scope) {
        case PRO_ACTION_SESSION:
        case PRO_ACTION_CHANNEL:
            break;

        case PRO_ACTION_ABORT:
        default:
            il -> pl_flags |= PRO_ABORTED;
            break;
    }

    il -> pl_flags &= ~PRO_READY;
    bpc_close_response (pi -> channel, NULL);
}
```

The logic is pretty simple:

1. First, we note whether the entire session is closing (PRO_ACTION_SESSION) or not (PRO_ACTION_CHANNEL), or whether we have any choice in the matter (PRO_ACTION_ABORT).

2. Then, we disable future calls to sr_log( ).

3. Finally, we accept the request.

Again, regardless of whether we accept the request, a second callback gets made a little while later to indicate what actually happened.

When the wrapper finally decides whether or not the channel has actually closed, pro_close_confirmation( ) (shown in Example 6-33) gets called by the wrapper.

Example 6-33. syslog-raw.c: pro_close_confirmation

```
static void
pro_close_confirmation (PROFILE_INSTANCE      *pi,
                        char                   status,
                        DIAGNOSTIC             *error,
                        char                   origin,
                        char                   scope) {
    PRO_LOCALDATA       *il = (PRO_LOCALDATA *) pi -> user_ptr1;

    if (status != PRO_ACTION_SUCCESS) {
        if (il -> pl_flags & PRO_INITIATOR)
            il -> pl_flags |= PRO_READY;
        return;
    }
```

Example 6-33. syslog-raw.c: pro_close_confirmation (continued)

```
    pi -> user_ptr1 = NULL;

    if (il -> pl_flags & PRO_ABORTED)
        pro_upcall (il, 421, "session aborted");
    else
        pro_upcall (il, 220, NULL);

    lib_free (il);
}
```

The logic here is pretty simple, and similar to that show in Example 6-10:

- First, if the channel is staying open, then before returning, we undo the hold (if any) we put on calls to sr_log( ).

- Otherwise, we inform the driver that we're done, either due to the session being aborted (reply code 421), or because one of the peers is ready to go home (reply code 220).

- Finally, we free the PROLOCAL_DATA.

Example 6-34 shows pro_close_callback( ) that gets called after all the other callbacks are made, if any.

Example 6-34. syslog-raw.c: pro_close_callback

```
static void
pro_close_callback (CHANNEL_INSTANCE     *ci,
                    CLOSE_REQUEST        *request,
                    DIAGNOSTIC           *error,
                    void                 *clientData) {
    PRO_LOCALDATA     *il = (PRO_LOCALDATA *) clientData;

    if (error)
        pro_upcall (il, error -> code, error -> message);
}
```

As we'll see in a bit, there are two cases:

- For the listener, if we encounter a protocol error in pro_message_available( ), we'll ask to close the channel.

- For the initiator, when we ask to checkpoint the *syslog* entries previously sent out, we'll ask to close the channel.

Even though there are two reasons why this callback might be made, the actions are the same: if the channel can't be closed, call pro_upcall( ) to deliver the news to the driver.

Tuning Reset Callbacks

The two tuning reset callbacks are identical to the ones shown in the section "Tuning reset callbacks" in the "Echo and Sink" section of this chapter.

Data Exchange Callbacks

The message_available( ) callback is made whenever a complete message is available to be read. As always, the smartest thing to do is to first build a decision table:

Message received	Action taken by listener	Action taken by initiator
MSG	Send ERR	Tell the application we're ready for sr_log
ANS	Parse and pass up	N/A
NUL	Close channel	N/A
RPY	Abort channel	N/A
ERR	Abort channel	N/A

Since the *syslog* raw profile uses a one-to-many exchange, all the action revolves around what happens when we see an ANS. Example 6-35 shows the pro_message_available( ) call.

Example 6-35. syslog-raw.c: pro_message_available

```
static void
pro_message_available (PROFILE_INSTANCE *pi) {
    int                 code = 200,
                        size;
    char                *buffer;
    DIAGNOSTIC          *d;
    FRAME               *f;
    PRO_LOCALDATA       *il = (PRO_LOCALDATA *) pi -> user_ptr1;
    BP_CONNECTION       *w = pi -> channel -> conn;

    if (!(f = bpc_query_message (pi -> channel, BLU_QUERY_ANYTYPE,
                        BLU_QUERY_ANYMSG, BLU_QUERY_ANYANS)))
        return;

    switch (f -> msg_type) {
        case BLU_FRAME_TYPE_MSG:
            if (il -> pl_flags & PRO_INITIATOR) {
                il -> pl_msgNo = f -> message_number;
                il -> pl_ansNo = -1;

                il -> pl_flags |= PRO_READY;
                (*il -> pl_callback) ((void *) il, 350, NULL,
                                il -> pl_clientData);
            } else
                pro_send_error (pi, f -> message_number, 500, NULL,
                                "not expecting MSG");
```

Example 6-35. syslog-raw.c: pro_message_available (continued)

```
            break;

        case BLU_FRAME_TYPE_ANS:
            size = bpc_frame_aggregate (pi -> channel, f, &buffer);
            if (buffer) {
                pro_syslog (il, buffer, size);
                bpc_buffer_destroy (pi -> channel, buffer);
            } else
                bp_log (pi -> channel -> conn, LOG_PROF, 5,
                        "sr message: out of memory reading ANS");
            break;

        case BLU_FRAME_TYPE_RPY:
        case BLU_FRAME_TYPE_ERR:
            code = 500;
            il -> pl_flags |= PRO_ABORTED;
            /* and fall... */
        case BLU_FRAME_TYPE_NUL:
            if (d = bpc_close_request (pi -> channel, BLU_CHANO_MSGNO_DEFAULT,
                                       code, NULL,
                                       code == 500 ? "protocol error" : NULL,
                                       pro_close_callback,
                                       (void *) il)) {
                pro_upcall (il, d -> code, d -> message);
                bp_diagnostic_destroy (w, d);
            }
            break;

        default:
            break;
    }

    bpc_message_destroy (pi -> channel, f);
}
```

The first thing pro_message_available( ) does is call bpc_query_message( ) to return the first available message. The parameters are identical to the call to bpc_query_frame( ) we saw in Example 6-12. The logic of the routine is:

1. If we get a MSG then:

    a. If we're the initiator, this signals that the remote peer is ready to accept syslog entries. We remember the message number, set a flag to allow calls to sr_log( ), and make a code 350 callback to the initiating driver to let the games begin.

    b. If we're the listener, this is a protocol error. So call the helper routine pro_send_error( ), and we're done.

2. If we get an ANS then we're the listener (the wrapper knows what replies are outstanding). We call bpc_frame_aggregate( ) to get a copy of the message's payload. The reason is because even though we asked for the next available

message, bpc_query_message( ) always returns a FRAME structure. Sometimes the FRAME structure contains the entire message, but other times, the FRAME structure is the start of a linked list, each containing part of the message. We could traverse the list ourselves, but by calling bpc_frame_aggregate( ), we can have just one character buffer to hand over to the helper routine that breaks messages into one or more syslog entries. (We'll briefly look at that helper routine, pro_syslog( ), in a moment.)

3. If we get a RPY or an ERR, someone is implementing the wrong protocol; we mark the connection as irrecoverable, and fall into the code for NUL.

4. If we get a NUL, then the initiator is telling us that it's done sending *syslog* entries, so we, the listener, close the channel. We've already seen bpc_close_request( ) back in Example 6-15. The only tricky part is how code got initialized, either above the switch or because we got a RPY or ERR.

Finally, bpc_message_destroy( ) is called to destroy the message that starts with the FRAME structure returned by bpc_query_message( ).

 If you called bpc_query_message( ), be sure to call bpc_message_destroy( ) instead of bpc_frame_destroy( ).

Now let's look at a couple of helper routines that we haven't seen yet: pro_send_error( ) and pro_syslog( ).

pro_send_error( ) sends an ERR back in response to a MSG. The content of an ERR is usually an error element, e.g.:

```
Content-Type: application/beep+xml

<error code='500'>not expecting MSG</error>
```

pro_send_error( ) is just a couple of lines:

```
static void
pro_send_error (PROFILE_INSTANCE      *pi,
                long                  msgNo,
                int                   code,
                char                  *language,
                char                  *diagnostic) {
    char *buffer = bpc_error_allocate (pi -> channel, code, language,
                                       diagnostic);

    if (buffer)
        bpc_send (pi -> channel, BLU_FRAME_TYPE_ERR, msgNo,
                  BLU_FRAME_IGNORE_ANSNO, BLU_FRAME_COMPLETE, buffer,
                  strlen (buffer));
    else
        bp_log (pi -> channel -> conn, LOG_PROF, 5,
                "sr message: out of memory sending ERR");
}
```

You can probably guess about the parameters to this routine: the first is a pointer to the PI, the second is the message number we're responding to, and the remaining three are the numeric code, language and diagnostic strings that you'd find in a DIAGNOSTIC structure. As you can see, all of the real work is done by a library routine called bpc_error_allocate( ).

pro_syslog( ) takes a message and breaks it up into one or more syslog entries to be given to the listener via:

```
(*il -> pl_callback) ((void *) il, entry, len, il -> pl_clientData);
```

where entry and len are the address and size of a character string containing a single syslog entry.

There's nothing particularly interesting in pro_syslog( ) other than finding the end of the MIME headers: if the message starts with CR-LF, we've found the end; otherwise, we need to look for the first occurrence of CR-LF-CR-LF. We won't show the routine here. (You can download the source if you really, really care....)

Finally, one of the key differences between our null profiles module and this example is the use of the message-based interface. We're using the message-based interface because we'd have to be able to do a lot of reassembly and buffering of the answers coming from the initiator. Further, because one-to-many exchanges in BEEP allow for multiple answers to be simultaneously in-flight, we'd also have to be able to reassemble different answers at the same time. It's just code, but it doesn't add anything in the context of showing you how to use beepcore-c.

So, if the initiator sends a large message to the listener, the threaded_os wrapper may make a callback to pro_window_full( ) asking for help:

```
static void
pro_window_full (PROFILE_INSTANCE      *pi) {
    PRO_LOCALDATA      *il = (PRO_LOCALDATA *) pi -> user_ptr1;

    pro_upcall (il, 421, "session blocked, increase window size");
}
```

In this example, we call this a fatal error (pro_upcall( ) knows no other kind). In a more realistic example, we'd call bpc_set_channel_window( ), which we saw in Example 6-31, and ask to allocate a larger buffer in the wrapper for the PI.

Driver Entry Points

Here's some good news: two more routines and we're done with this example and the whole chapter! Let's start with sr_log( ), shown in Example 6-36.

Example 6-36. syslog-raw.c: sr_log

```
int
sr_log (void             *v,
        char             *entry) {
```

Example 6-36. syslog-raw.c: sr_log (continued)

```
int                 i;
char                *buffer,
                    *ep;
PRO_LOCALDATA       *il = (PRO_LOCALDATA *) v;
PROFILE_INSTANCE    *pi;

if (!(pi = il -> pl_pi)) {
    lib_free (il);
    return SR_DONE;
}
if (!(il -> pl_flags & PRO_READY))
    return SR_BUSY;

if ((i = strlen (ep = entry)) > 0) {
    ep += i - 1;
    if (*ep == '\n')
        ep--, i--;
    if ((i > 0) && (*ep == '\r'))
        i--;
}
if (i == 0)
    return SR_OK;

if (!(buffer = bpc_buffer_allocate (pi -> channel,
                            i
                            + (sizeof DEFAULT_CONTENT_TYPE - 1))))
    return SR_ERROR;
sprintf (buffer, "%s%*.*s", DEFAULT_CONTENT_TYPE, i, i, entry);

if (++il -> pl_ansNo > 2147483647)
    il -> pl_ansNo = 0;
bpc_send (pi -> channel, BLU_FRAME_TYPE_ANS, il -> pl_msgNo,
          il -> pl_ansNo, BLU_FRAME_COMPLETE, buffer, strlen (buffer));

return SR_OK;
}
```

When the module makes the first callback to the initiating driver, it's going to pass an opaque pointer or NULL. If the former, the driver can now start calling sr_log( ) to send syslog entries. The logic is:

- First, we look to see if something caused the PI to go away earlier, and if so, we free the PRO_LOCALDATA structure and return SR_DONE.

- Next, we make sure that this call is allowed (e.g., we're not in the middle of trying to checkpoint previously sent *syslog* entries).

- We then remove any CR-LF at the end of the entry/entries that we're given. (If you recall from the description of the *syslog* raw profile, if multiple entries are sent, they are separated by CR-LF, but the final entry doesn't have a CR-LF.)

- Next, we allocate a buffer to accommodate the MIME headers (actually, the lack thereof) and the entries being sent.
- A unique answer number is assigned, and bpc_send( ) called to send the message on its way.

When the initiating driver wants to close the channel, it calls sr_fin( ), shown in Example 6-37.

Example 6-37. syslog-raw.c: sr_fin

```
int
sr_fin (void                    *v) {
    char                *buffer;
    PRO_LOCALDATA       *il = (PRO_LOCALDATA *) v;
    PROFILE_INSTANCE    *pi;

    if (!(pi = il -> pl_pi)) {
        lib_free (il);
        return SR_DONE;
    }
    if (!(il -> pl_flags & PRO_READY))
        return SR_BUSY;

    if (!(buffer = bpc_buffer_allocate (pi -> channel, 0)))
        return SR_ERROR;

    il -> pl_flags &= ~PRO_READY;
    bpc_send (pi -> channel, BLU_FRAME_TYPE_NUL, il -> pl_msgNo,
            BLU_FRAME_IGNORE_ANSNO, BLU_FRAME_COMPLETE, buffer, 0);

    return SR_OK;
}
```

This, our last routine, is to the point:

- We make the usual "already closed" and "busy" checks.
- If all is well, we set a flag to indicate that we're checkpointing, we set another flag to indicate we're busy, we allocate a zero-length buffer, and then we send a NUL to the listener.

## CHAPTER 7

BEEP in Tcl

Unlike the other two beepcore implementations, beepcore-tcl is intended primarily for prototyping—it's optimized for flexibility, not speed. The Tcl version of beepcore is the oldest; in fact, it predates BEEP itself! It started as an implementation of BEEP's predecessor, BXXP. Fortunately, there hasn't been a lot of "feature creep" with this version—once an idea proves useful, older code implementing the same functionality is usually removed.

In this chapter, we're going to look at how to modify the Tcl SOAP package to use BEEP in addition to HTTP. There are three reasons for this:

- It provides an illustrative example of how to retarget an HTTP-based application to one that uses BEEP.

- It provides a concrete follow-up to "Client/Server" in Chapter 4 that shows how BEEP supports client/server exchanges.

- It's a cool demonstration of the superiority of the Tcl programming language.

As with all the versions of beepcore, go to *http://beepcore.org/* to find out where to download the current release of beepcore-tcl. Inside that release, in the *docs/* directory, you'll find the most current documentation for the API, including the definitions of each call.

Introduction to Tcl SOAP

The Tcl SOAP project page is at *http://sourceforge.net/projects/tclsoap*. The author of Tcl SOAP is Pat Thoyts. Version 1.6 of Tcl SOAP is used in these examples, and it's a pretty good late-stage beta. From the protocol perspective, there are only two significant limitations of this version:

- There isn't any support for one-way or 1-request/N-response exchanges (only single request-response exchanges are allowed).

- There isn't any support for SOAP packages (the envelopes exchanged must contain only XML information).

Both of these "extras" were discussed back in "SOAP Extras" in Chapter 4.

Client Functions

It's easy to write a Tcl client that uses SOAP. There are only three steps:

1. Load the Tcl SOAP package (package require SOAP is all it takes).
2. Create a binding to each remote method you want to invoke.
3. Execute the bindings as often as you like.

Bindings are created using [SOAP::create], e.g.:

```
% SOAP::create getTemp                        \
        -uri    urn:xmethods-Temperature \
        -params { zipcode string }            \
        -proxy  http://services.xmethods.net/soap/servlet/rpcrouter
```

This says to:

- Execute [SOAP::create] to define a new procedure named [getTemp].
- [getTemp] invokes a remote method named [getTemp] defined in the urn: xmethods-Temperature namespace.
- The method [getTemp] takes one parameter, a string named zipcode.
- The procedure [getTemp] is located using HTTP talking to the resource /soap/ servlet/rpcrouter on the host services.xmethod.net.

If we execute getTemp 95865, then the envelope that gets generated is:

```
<SOAP-ENV:Envelope
  xmlns:SOAP-ENV='http://schemas.xmlsoap.org/soap/envelope/'
  SOAP-ENV:encodingStyle='http://schemas.xmlsoap.org/soap/encoding/'
  xmlns:xsi='http://www.w3.org/1999/XMLSchema-instance'
  xmlns:xsd='http://www.w3.org/1999/XMLSchema'>
    <SOAP-ENV:Body>
        <ns:getTemp xmlns:ns='urn:xmethods-Temperature'>
            <zipcode xsi:type='xsd:string'>95865</zipcode>
        </ns:getTemp>
    </SOAP-ENV:Body>
</SOAP-ENV:Envelope>
```

We've seen most of this before—the remote procedure call is sandwiched in the <SOAP-ENV:Body>.

Of course, the whole point of SOAP is that the programmer doesn't see any of this. Here's what you see:

```
% getTemp 95865
42.0
```

which says that the temperature in Zip Code 95865 is 42 degrees Fahrenheit.

This is SOAP at its simplest, and it's pretty good. Unfortunately, there are a couple of complications.

First, you may need to worry about the administrative configuration of the network. For example, you may need to tell the package to go through an HTTP proxy. So, there's a procedure named [SOAP::configure] that lets you do that, e.g.:

```
% SOAP::configure -transport http \
        -proxy proxyhost:8080          \
        -headers { Proxy-Authorization
                   "Basic dXNlcm5hbWU6oiBwYXNzd29yZA==" }
```

which, for the HTTP transport, tells the Tcl SOAP package the name and port number to use for an HTTP proxy, along with a special header to use when talking to the proxy.

The other complication is a matter of programming convention: while in Tcl, everything's a string, in SOAP, each parameter is named (e.g., zipcode) and datatyped (e.g., string). SOAP datatypes are either scalars, structures, or arrays—check out *Programming Web Services with SOAP* for the grisly details.

The Tcl SOAP package provides a set of routines to manage the mappings. For example:

```
package require rpcvar

rpcvar::typedef -namespace http://soapinterop.org/xsd {
    varString string
    varInt    int
    varFloat  float
} SOAPStruct

SOAP::create echoStruct ... \
    -params { inputStruct SOAPStruct }

echoStruct { varString "Hello, world." varInt 42 varFloat 69.0 }
```

The important part is that it's up to you to tell the Tcl SOAP package how many parameters the method takes, and the name and datatype for each parameter. For example, earlier if we had said:

```
% SOAP::create getTemp ...
    -params { zipcode string elevation int }
```

the Tcl SOAP package wouldn't have complained. It's not until we execute the [getTemp] procedure that we hear something's wrong—the SOAP server will return an error because it wasn't expecting a parameter named elevation. (Of course, it's anyone's guess as to why the zipcode parameter isn't an int...)

Server Functions

It's also pretty easy to implement a SOAP service using Tcl. Before you define a service, you need to tell your HTTP server about the Tcl SOAP package. The package integrates as a CGI script. After installing the script but before you enable it in your server, you create a directory in your HTTP server area that contains two things:

- A mapping file (usually named *soapmap.dat*) that gives the CGI script hints as to which Tcl files to source.
- The method files themselves.

You edit the first few lines of the CGI script to indicate the location of the mapping file and method file directory.

The layout of the mapping file is pretty simple:

```
#
# hint                    file(s)                    interpreter
#
  urn:xmethods-Temperature temperature.tcl           safeInterp
  urn:soapinterop          soapinterop.tcl
  urn:example              { file1.tcl file2.tcl }
```

The only tricky part is if there's a third element on a line. This determines which interpreter is used when the method is invoked—if no such element is present, the main interpreter is used; otherwise, the element names a safe interpreter that is created, executes the method, and is then destroyed.

Although each "hint" looks like a namespace, it's simply an arbitrary string. The CGI script looks for a header named SOAPAction: in the HTTP request. If it's present and the value is non-empty, that value must be listed as a hint in the mapping file. If it's either not present or the value is empty, the CGI script sources all the files in the directory containing the method files.

Regardless, the layout of a method file is also pretty simple:

```
package require SOAP

namespace eval urn:xmethods-Temperature {
    SOAP::export getTemp

    proc getTemp {zipcode} {
# ... the real work gets done here ...

        return $tempF
    }
}
```

The key thing to note here is the execution of [SOAP::export] to bind the namespace to the method. After the CGI script has parsed the envelope, it looks at the datastructures built by [SOAP::export] to make sure that the appropriate method has been defined by one of the files that got sourced.

Here's another example, this time using structs:

```
package require SOAP
package require rpcvar
```

```
namespace import -force rpcvar::*

namespace eval http://soapinterop.org {
    SOAP::export echoStruct

    rpcvar::typedef -namespace http://soapinterop.org/xsd {
        varString  string
        varInt     int
        varFloat   float
    } SOAPStruct

    proc echoStruct {inputStruct} {
        return [rpcvar SOAPStruct $inputStruct]
    }
}
```

Adding BEEP Support to the Client

One of Tcl's great strengths is ease of integration. There are three things we need to do:

- Modify [SOAP::create] to know about BEEP URLs.
- Modify [SOAP::configure] to know about configuration options for beepcore-tcl.
- Add an invocation driver to do the actual client/server exchange.

Creation

Let's start with the first example that we saw at the beginning of the section "Client Functions":

```
% SOAP::create getTemp                         \
        -uri     urn:xmethods-Temperature \
        -params  { zipcode string }       \
        -proxy   http://services.xmethods.net/soap/servlet/rpcrouter
```

At first glance, all we really need to do is modify the part of [SOAP::create] that looks at the argument to -proxy.

For example, if we execute something like:

```
% SOAP::create getTemp                         \
        -uri     urn:xmethods-Temperature \
        -params  { zipcode string }       \
        -proxy   soap.beep://example.com/xmethods-Temperature
```

then the "right thing" should "just happen."

To make this happen transparently, we modify the routine used by [SOAP::create] that looks at the argument to -proxy. It parses the argument as a URL, and if the scheme is either soap.beep or soap.beeps, then it executes a procedure named [SOAP::create_beep] to do the heavy lifting, starting with what's shown in Example 7-1. (Recall that we discussed these two URL schemes back in "BEEP URIs" in Chapter 4.)

Example 7-1. SOAP::create_beep

```
proc SOAP::create_beep {procVarName scheme host port resource} {
# load necessary packages

    package require log
    package require mixer


# create a global expected by those packages

    global debugP
    if { ![info exists debugP] } {
        set debugP 0
    }


# create a "log" token

    set logT [set [subst $procVarName](logT) \
                 [::log::init $Transport::beep::options(-logfile) \
                     $Transport::beep::options(-logident)]]
```

This procedure is shown in three more examples, running through Example 7-4. The procedure has five parameters:

procVarName
> The name of a state array containing information on the binding.

scheme
> Either soap.beep or soap.beeps.

host
> The hostname portion of the URL.

port
> The port number portion of the URL (possibly empty).

resource
> The resource portion of the URL (possibly empty).

For example, given *soap.beep://example.com/xmethods-Temperature*, we'd have:

scheme
> soap.beep

host
> example.com

port
> the empty string

resource
> /xmethods-Temperature

The procedure starts off by loading two packages: log::, a general purpose logging facility, and mixer::, the client-side BEEP routines. The choice of the name mixer:: is historical—the original application developed for BEEP's predecessor used the term "mixer" to describe its clients. The other bit of detritus is the fact that both packages look at a global variable named debugP to control a lot of their logging behavior (yuk)!

Both of these packages allow you to have multiple instances of logfiles or BEEP sessions. Each instance is referenced using a *token* and, as we'll see, a token gets created by executing a package's [::init] method, then gets passed as a parameter to the other methods in that package. So, after making sure that the global variable exists, [log::init] is executed to create a log token. (Later on, we'll see where the parameters to this procedure come from.)

As shown in Example 7-2, the next step is to start a new BEEP session.

Example 7-2. Starting a session

```
# initialize the options array for use with mixer::init

# TBD: when the RFC issues, update the default port number...
    if { $port == {} } {
        set port 10288
    }
    if { $resource == {} } {
        set resource /
    }
    switch -- $scheme {
        soap.beep {
            set privacy none
        }

        soap.beeps {
            set privacy strong
        }
    }
    array set options [array get Transport::beep::options]
    unset options(-logfile) \
         options(-logident)
    array set options [list -port       $port    \
                            -privacy    $privacy \
                            -servername $host]

# initialize the BEEP client library

    switch -- [catch { eval [list ::mixer::init $logT $host] \
                        [array get options] } mixerT] {
        0 {
# normal return, return value is a "mixer" token

            set [subst $procVarName](mixerT) $mixerT
        }

        7 {
```

Example 7-2. Starting a session (continued)

```
# exceptional return, return value is a reply array

            array set parse $mixerT
            ::log::entry $logT user \
                         "mixer::init $parse(code): $parse(diagnostic)"

            error $parse(diagnostic)
        }

        default {
# error return, return value is a string

            ::log::entry $logT error mixer::init $mixerT

            error $mixerT
        }
    }
}
```

The work that's done before executing [mixer::init] is all about initializing the options array. Here are the possibilities.

Options relating to authentication:

-mechanism
> Indicates which SASL profile to use for tuning the session. Current choices are: none (the default), anonymous, or otp. (As of this writing, beepcore-tcl supports only these two SASL profiles—in the future, support for digest-md5 is likely.)

-trace
> Must be present for -mechanism anonymous. The value is a string, typically an email address.

-username
> Must be present for -mechanism otp, along with either -passphrase or -passback. The value is a string.

-passphrase
> A string that is used as part of the -mechanism otp input to generate the response to a cryptographic challenge.

-passback
> A procedure that is executed by -mechanism otp to generate the response to a cryptograhic challenge. Example 7-10 shows an example of a procedure that prompts the user for a passphrase and then performs the calculation. Of course, in order to get a passphrase, this procedure could just as easily have put up a dialog box, or query a configuration file, or talk to a database, etc.

Options relating to privacy:

-privacy
> Indicates whether the session should be tuned for privacy. Current choices are: none (the default), weak, or strong. At present, [mixer::init] makes a cursory

glance as to key length to decide which of the available encryption algorithms are considered weak or strong.

Miscellaneous options:

-port
> Indicates the TCP port number to use. The default is 10288.

-servername
> Indicates the serverName attribute to use for channel creation, if any. Consult "Virtual hosting" in Chapter 3 for the details.

-debug
> Enables additional debugging in the mixer:: package. The default is false.

After the options array is initialized, it's time to execute [mixer::init] to start a new BEEP session. This procedure has both a return code and a return value:

- If it makes a normal return (code 0), the return value is a token for the BEEP session that gets used for subsequent calls to the mixer:: package.
- If it makes an exceptional return (code 7), the return value is a "reply array."
- If it makes an error return (any other return code), the return value is an error string generated by the Tcl interpreter.

On a normal return, we save the mixer token (mixerT) in the state array (procVarName). Otherwise, we log the exception or error and return an error ourselves. So, the only real work is in deciphering the contents of the reply array, which gets used a lot in the mixer:: package.

A reply array has three members (code, diagnostic, and language) that correspond to the localized error diagnostics described back in "Localization (L10N)" in Chapter 3, e.g.:

```
<error code='500'
       xml:lang='en-US'>none of the profiles are supported</error>
```

If the remote BEEP peer sends back an error, it gets converted to a reply array by the mixer:: package. Similarly, if the package detects an error on its own, it will also use a reply array to convey this information.

As shown in Example 7-3, the next step is to create the channel for the SOAP profile. As a part of this code, we're going to piggyback the bootmsg initialization message.

Example 7-3. Creating the channel

```
# URI for SOAP profile

    set profile http://clipcode.org/beep/soap

# create a "<bootmsg resource='...' />"

    set doc [dom::DOMImplementation create]
```

Example 7-3. Creating the channel (continued)

```
    set bootmsg [dom::document createElement $doc bootmsg]
    dom::element setAttribute $bootmsg resource $resource
    set data [dom::DOMImplementation serialize $doc]

# strip off XML declarations

    if { [set x [string first [set y "<!DOCTYPE bootmsg>\n"] $data]] >= 0 } {
        set data [string range $data [expr $x+[string length $y]] end]
    }
    dom::DOMImplementation destroy $doc

# mixer::init has automatically tuned the session
# now open a channel for SOAP

    switch -- [set code [catch { ::mixer::create $mixerT $profile $data } \
                            channelT]] {
        0 {
# normal return, return value is a "channel" token

            set [subst $procVarName](channelT) $channelT
        }


        7 {
# error return, return value is a reply array

            array set parse $channelT
            ::log::entry $logT user \
                    "mixer::create $parse(code): $parse(diagnostic)"

            destroy_beep $procVarName
            error $parse(diagnostic)
        }


        default {
# error return, return value is a reply array

            ::log::entry $logT error mixer::create $channelT

            destroy_beep $procVarName
            error $channelT
        }
    }
```

We first use the dom:: package to create a bootmsg object and then serialize it into a string. The string returned by the serialization process looks something like this:

```
<?xml version='1.0'?>
<!DOCTYPE bootmsg>
<bootmsg resource='/xmethods-Temperature'/>
```

One of the rules for using the SOAP profile is that you don't send XML declarations, so these are stripped off.

It's time to execute [mixer::create] to create a channel on the BEEP session. As with [mixer::init], this procedure has both a return code and a return value. The only difference is that, on success, the return value is a channel token (channelT).

As shown in Example 7-4, the final step is to parse the response that got returned with the piggyback.

Example 7-4. Parsing the response

```
# retrieve piggybacked data

    if { [catch { ::peer::getprop $channelT datum } data] } {
        ::log::entry $logT error peer::getprop $data

        destroy_beep $procVarName
        error $data
    }


# parse it into "doc"
    if { [catch { dom::DOMImplementation parse $data } doc] } {
        ::log::entry $logT error dom::parse $doc

        destroy_beep $procVarName
        error "bootrpy is invalid xml: $doc"
    }

    if { [set node [selectNode $doc /bootrpy]] != {} } {
# it's "<bootrpy ...", so get the "features" attribute

        catch { set [subst $procVarName](features) \
                    [set [dom::node cget $node -attributes](features)] }

        dom::DOMImplementation destroy $doc

    } elseif { [set node [selectNode $doc /error]] != {} } {
# it's "<error ...", so get the "code" attribute and contents

        if { [catch { set code [set [dom::node cget $node -attributes](code)]
                    set diagnostic [getElementValue $node] }] } {
            set code 500
            set diagnostic "unable to parse boot reply"
        }

        ::log::entry $logT user "$code: $diagnostic"

        dom::DOMImplementation destroy $doc

        destroy_beep $procVarName
        error "$code: $diagnostic"
```

Example 7-4. Parsing the response (continued)

```
    } else {
# what is it?

        dom::DOMImplementation destroy $doc

        destroy_beep $procVarName
        error "invalid protocol: the boot reply is invalid"
    }

# set handlers for future use

    set [subst $procVarName](transport) \
        [namespace current]::Transport::beep::xfer
    set [subst $procVarName](wait) \
        [namespace current]::Transport::beep::wait
    set [subst $procVarName](destroy) \
        [namespace current]::destroy_beep
}
```

We first execute [peer::getprop] to retrieve the piggybacked data. (The peer:: package is the layer below the mixer:: package—it contains a lot of utility routines such as this one.) Next, the dom:: package is used to parse the data:

- If the top-level element is a bootrpy, we save the features attribute.
- Otherwise, if the top-level element is an error, we extract the code and textual contents and throw an error.
- Otherwise, we give up and throw an error.

At last, we set three more variables in the state array:

transport
    Points to a procedure that will perform a client/server exchange.

wait
    Points to a procedure that will wait for asynchronous invocations to complete (if needed).

destroy
    Points to a procedure that is executed when the binding is deleted.

So, what does [SOAP::destroy_beep] do? It's pretty simple:

```
proc SOAP::destroy_beep {procVarName} {
# extract mixer and log tokens

    set mixerT [set [subst $procVarName](mixerT)]
    set logT [set [subst $procVarName](logT)]

    if { [catch { ::mixer::fin $mixerT } result] } {
        ::log::entry $logT error mixer::fin $result
    }
```

```
    # make this once-only

        set [subst $procVarName](mixerT) {}
    }
```

It simply executes [`mixer::fin`], which releases the BEEP session and invalidates the mixer token.

Configuration

It turns out that the modifications to [`SOAP::configure`] are trivial. Our goal is to support something like:

```
% SOAP::configure -transport beep \
        -mechanism otp            \
        -username fred            \
        -passback do_passback
```

So, we define some defaults for an array of BEEP-specific options, and add an additional case to a `switch` statement. Here's how the defaults get set:

```
namespace eval SOAP::Transport::beep {
    variable options

    array set options [list -logfile  /dev/null \
                            -logident soap]
}
```

Here's the additional code that gets executed:

```
beep {
        if { $args != {} } {
            array set Transport::beep::options $args
        } else {
            return [array get Transport::beep::options]
        }
    }
```

If arguments are provided, then the `options` array is updated; otherwise, it returns the current settings in the array.

Invocation

Four more procedures to describe and we're done! Example 7-5 shows [`SOAP::Transport::beep::xfer`]. This procedure has three parameters:

procVarName
    The name of a state array containing information on the binding.

url
    The argument that was given to -proxy earlier.

request
    A string containing the SOAP envelope to be sent.

Example 7-5. SOAP::Transport::beep::xfer

```
proc SOAP::Transport::beep::xfer {procVarName url request} {
# did user supply a callback for asynchronous invocations?

    if {[set [subst $procVarName](command)] != {}} {
        set rpyV "[namespace current]::asynchronous $procVarName"
    } else {
        set rpyV {}
    }

# extract mixer, channel, and log tokens

    set mixerT [set [subst $procVarName](mixerT)]
    set channelT [set [subst $procVarName](channelT)]
    set logT [set [subst $procVarName](logT)]

# strip off XML declarations

    if {[set x [string first [set y "?>\n"] $request]] >= 0 } {
        set request [string range $request [expr $x+[string length $y]] end]
    }

# turn request string into MIME object

    set reqT [::mime::initialize -canonical application/xml -string $request]

    switch -- [set code [catch { ::peer::message $channelT $reqT \
                                 -replyCallback $rpyV } rspT]] {
        0 {
# normal return

            ::mime::finalize $reqT

# asynchronous invocation? if so, we're done
            if { $rpyV != {} } {
                return
            }

# otherwise, get Content-Type: and contents of reply

            set content [::mime::getproperty $rspT content]
            set response [::mime::getbody $rspT]

            ::mime::finalize $rspT

# make sure there aren't any attachments, Tcl SOAP doesn't support them

            if {[string compare $content application/xml]} {
                error "not application/xml reply, not $content"
            }

# return response as a string
```

Example 7-5. SOAP::Transport::beep::xfer (continued)

```
            return $response
        }

        7 {
# exceptional return, return value should be an "<error ..."

            array set parse [::mixer::errscan $mixerT $rspT]
            ::log::entry $logT user "$parse(code): $parse(diagnostic)"

            ::mime::finalize $reqT
            ::mime::finalize $rspT
            error "$parse(code): $parse(diagnostic)"
        }

        default {
# error return, return value is a string
            ::log::entry $logT error peer::message $rspT

            ::mime::finalize $reqT
            error $rspT
        }
    }
}
```

We start by seeing whether the remote method is to be invoked asynchronously; if so, rpyV is set to the name of a routine that is executed when a reply is received. Regardless, we extract the mixer, channel, and log tokens from the state array. Next, we strip off the XML declaration. We then use the mime:: package to create a MIME object from the string, and then [peer::message] is executed to send the request and optionally wait for a response. (If blocking wasn't an issue, we'd then execute [mixer::exch], which sends a message containing a MIME object, waits for a response, and then returns the corresponding MIME object.)

The [peer::message] procedure has both a return code and a return value:

- If it makes a normal return (code 0), the return value is either a MIME token for the response (for synchronous exchanges), or a unique integer (for asynchronous exchanges).

- If it makes an exceptional return (code 7), the return value is also a MIME object.

- If it makes an error return (any other return code), the return value is an error string generated by the Tcl interpreter.

On a normal return, the first thing we do is release the MIME object we created for the request. Then, for an asynchronous exchange, we simply return. Otherwise, for a synchronous exchange, we extract the Content-Type: and contents of the response, and release the corresponding MIME object. We then make sure that the MIME object is an application/xml (remember that Tcl SOAP doesn't support attachments), and return the contents.

On an exceptional return, we're expecting an error element, so [mixer::errscan] is executed to create a reply array, and the information is logged. We release the MIME objects corresponding to the request and the response, and return an error. Otherwise, on an error return, the MIME object corresponding to the request is released and we return an error.

Example 7-6 shows the procedure that gets executed when a reply is received for an asynchronous exchange, [SOAP::Transport::beep::async].

Example 7-6. SOAP::Transport::beep::async

```
proc SOAP::Transport::beep::async {procVarName channelT args} {
# invoke auxiliary routine to do the work

    if { [catch { eval [list async2 $procVarName] $args } result] } {
# caught an error, did the user supply an error handler?

        if { [set [subst $procVarName](errorCommand)] != {} } {
# yes, so invoke it

            set errorCommand [set [subst $procVarName](errorCommand)]
            if { ![catch { eval $errorCommand [list $result] } result] } {
                return
            }

# user's error handler threw an error!
        }

# user-supply code didn't handle the error, use the procedure of last resort

        bgerror $result
    }
}
```

This procedure has three parameters:

channelT
> A channel token identical to the one that was given to [peer::message].

procVarName
> The name of a state array containing information on the binding.

args
> A variable-length list of parameter/value pairs. The parameters in args are:

> msgNo
>> The integer that was the return value of [peer::message].

> status
>> Either positive or negative.

> mimeT
>> A MIME object containing the reply.

This procedure doesn't do much; it's just a wrapper to catch any errors that might occur in [SOAP::Transport::beep::async2], shown in Example 7-7.

Example 7-7. SOAP::Transport::beep::async2

```
proc SOAP::Transport::beep::async2 {procVarName args} {
# convert variable argument list into a handy array

    array set argv $args

    switch -- $argv(status) {
        positive {
# positive reply, given to us as a MIME object

# get the Content-Type: and the contents

            set content [::mime::getproperty $argv(mimeT) content]
            set reply [::mime::getbody $argv(mimeT)]
            ::mime::finalize $argv(mimeT)

# make sure there aren't any attachments

            if {[string compare $content application/xml]} {
                error "not application/xml reply, not $content"
            }

# parse the SOAP envelope and invoke the user-supplied code

            set reply [SOAP::invoke2 $procVarName $reply]
            set command [set [subst $procVarName](command)]
            return [eval $command [list $reply]]
        }

        negative {
# negative reply, should contain an "<error ..."

            set mixerT [set [subst $procVarName](mixerT)]
            set logT [set [subst $procVarName](logT)]

            array set parse [::mixer::errscan $mixerT $argv(mimeT)]
            ::log::entry $logT "$parse(code): $parse(diagnostic)"

            ::mime::finalize $argv(mimeT)
            error "$parse(code): $parse(diagnostic)"
        }

        default {
# what is it? it's a reply in a one-to-many exchange

            ::mime::finalize $argv(mimeT)

            error "not expecting $argv(status) reply"
        }
    }
}
```

[`SOAP::Transport::beep::async2`] has two parameters:

procVarName
> The name of a state array containing information on the binding.

args
> A variable-length list of parameter/value pairs.

After initializing the `argv` array from the args parameter, we look at `argv(status)` and act accordingly:

- If positive, we then extract the `Content-Type:` and contents of the response, and release the corresponding MIME object. We then make sure that the MIME object is an `application/xml`, and execute [`SOAP::invoke2`] to convert the SOAP envelope into a reply. Finally, the user's command handler is executed.

- If negative, we're expecting an `error` element, so [`mixer::errscan`] is executed to create a reply array and the information is logged. The corresponding MIME object is released, and an error is returned.

- Otherwise, we release the MIME object and throw an error. (This possibility arises if the server starts a one-to-many response.)

As shown in Example 7-8, [`SOAP::Transport::beep::wait`] has one parameter, procVarName, the name of the state array containing information on the binding. This procedure simply executes [`mixer::wait`], which waits for any outstanding responses to be delivered. That's it!

Example 7-8. SOAP::Transport::beep::wait

```
proc SOAP::Transport::beep::wait {procVarName} {
    set mixerT [set [subst $procVarName](mixerT)]

    ::mixer::wait $mixerT
}
```

Example 7-9 shows the code used to cache BEEP sessions.

Example 7-9. Caching BEEP sessions

```
variable sessions

# see if a session is already cached...

set signature ""
foreach option [lsort [array names options]] {
    append signature $option $options($option)
}
foreach mixerT [array name sessions] {
    catch { unset props }
    array set props $sessions($mixerT)

    if { ($props(host) != $host) \
```

Example 7-9. Caching BEEP sessions (continued)

```
            || ($props(resource) != $resource) \
            || ($props(signature) != $signature) } {
        continue
    }

# yes, use it...
    incr props(refcnt)
    set sessions($mixerT) [array get props]

    return $mixerT
}

# otherwise, create new session...

# add a new session to the cache...

set props(host) $host
set props(resource) $resource
set props(signature) ""
foreach option [lsort [array names options]] {
    append props(signature) $option $options($option)
}
set props(refcnt) 1
set sessions($mixerT) [array get props]

return $mixerT
```

In truth, there is one optimization that we should make in this code. Specifically, in [SOAP::create_beep], we should keep track of the BEEP sessions we've created and reuse them when creating new bindings to the same resource. This example shows some code that manages a package variable named sessions for that purpose. The key is to use a deterministic algorithm when creating props(signature) to avoid false negatives.

An interesting follow-up question is what to do when asked to create a binding to a different resource on the same host—should we create a new channel on the existing session?

More Packet Traces

Here are some more packet traces. Let's start by configuring for strong authentication:

```
% SOAP::configure -transport beep \
        -mechanism otp          \
        -username fred           \
        -passback do_passback    \
        -logfile soap.log
```

This command doesn't emit any packets, it just sets some options for later use. Now let's define a binding to a remote method:

```
% SOAP::create echoInteger           \
        -uri    http://soapinterop.org/ \
        -params { inputInteger int }    \
        -proxy  soap.beep://example.com/soapinterop
```

This results in [SOAP::create] ultimately executing [mixer::init] like this:

```
# TBD: when the RFC issues, update the default port number...

mixer::init $logT example.com \
        { -mechanism otp    -username fred -passback do_passback
          -port        10288 -privacy none -servername example.com }
```

[mixer::init] establishes a TCP connection to the specified port on example.com and sends an empty greeting (i.e., <greeting />).

Of course, as soon as the TCP connection was established, the peer sent a greeting of its own:

```
<greeting>
    <profile uri='http://clipcode.org/beep/soap' />
    <profile uri='http://iana.org/beep/SASL/ANONYMOUS' />
    <profile uri='http://iana.org/beep/TLS' />
    <profile uri='http://xml.resource.org/profiles/NULL/ECHO' />
    <profile uri='http://xml.resource.org/profiles/NULL/SINK' />
    <profile uri='http://iana.org/beep/SASL/OTP' />
</greeting>
```

Next, [mixer::init] tunes the session for authentication using SASL's OTP. It asks to start a channel for the corresponding profile and piggybacks the user identity:

```
<start number='1' serverName='qawoor.dbc.mtview.ca.us'>
    <profile uri='http://iana.org/beep/SASL/OTP'>&lt;blob>AGZyZWQ=
&lt;/blob></profile>
</start>
```

(For the detail-oriented, because SASL exchanges are arbitrary octets, the piggy-backed data is encoded inside a blob element using base64—the string you see here represents a NUL followed by the four characters fred.)

The peer creates the channel and piggybacks a challenge:

```
<profile uri='http://iana.org/beep/SASL/OTP'>
&lt;blob>b3RwLXNoYTEgOTk5OCBjbXR2aWV3Y2F1czE0OTM4IGV4dA==
&lt;/blob></profile>
```

There are four components to the challenge: an algorithm (sha1), a sequence number (998), a seed (cmtviewcaus14938), and the string "ext". Now, [mixer::init] executes the user-supplied callback, [do_passback] (shown in Example 7-10), to generate the response. The user enters the passphrase, and [do_passback] returns the cryptographic response.

Example 7-10. Example callback for -passback

```
proc do_passback {serverD name algorithm seqno seed} {
# get the user's input

    puts -nonewline \
        "enter secret password for $name@$serverD\n$seqno $seed: "
    if {[gets stdin passphrase] <= 0} {
        return ""
    }


# run the OTP response algorithm

    incr seqno 1
    set key $seed$passphrase
    while {[incr seqno -1] >= 0} {
        set key [otp_$algorithm -- $key]
    }


# return the response as hexidecimal

    return hex:[hex -mode encode -- $key]
}
```

The response is sent to the peer on the newly created channel:

```
<blob>aGV4OjU1RDIxOTYwMONCMjZDRDA=</blob>
```

The peer decides that it's acceptable and says so by replying with:

```
<blob status='complete' />
```

on the newly created channel.

Having successfully tuned the session, [mixer::init] sends a message to close the channel. (Closing the channel is optional, and [mixer::init] won't even bother waiting for the reply.) When it receives the response from the peer, control is returned back to [SOAP::create], which constructs a bootmsg and executes [mixer::create].

[mixer::create] sends a message asking to start a channel for the SOAP profile and piggybacks the bootmsg:

```
<start number='3'>
    <profile uri='http://clipcode.org/beep/soap'>
&lt;bootmsg resource='/soapinterop' /></profile>
</start>
```

The peer creates the channel and piggybacks the bootrpy:

```
<profile uri='http://clipcode.org/beep/soap'>
&lt;bootrpy features='' /></profile>
```

At this point, [mixer::create] returns control back to SOAP::create, which parses the piggybacked data, and we're done.

If you're keeping score, that's half a round-trip for the exchange of greetings, two round-trips for the SASL OTP authentication, and one round-trip to start and initialize the channel for SOAP. (We're not counting the round-trip to close the SASL OTP channel, because [`mixer::init`] didn't have to wait for it.) Let's execute `echoInteger` 10 and see what happens.

[`echoInteger`] ultimately executes [`SOAP::Transport::beep::xfer`], which executes [`peer::message`] to send an envelope that looks like this:

```
<SOAP-ENV:Envelope
  xmlns:xsi='http://www.w3.org/1999/XMLSchema-instance'
  xmlns:SOAP-ENV='http://schemas.xmlsoap.org/soap/envelope/'
  SOAP-ENV:encodingStyle='http://schemas.xmlsoap.org/soap/encoding/'
  xmlns:xsd='http://www.w3.org/1999/XMLSchema'>
    <SOAP-ENV:Body>
        <ns:echoInteger xmlns:ns='http://soapinterop.org/'>
            <inputInteger xsi:type='xsd:int'>10</inputInteger>
        </ns:echoInteger>
    </SOAP-ENV:Body>
</SOAP-ENV:Envelope>
```

and waits for a reply. The peer replies with this envelope:

```
<SOAP-ENV:Envelope
  xmlns:xsi='http://www.w3.org/1999/XMLSchema-instance'
  xmlns:SOAP-ENV='http://schemas.xmlsoap.org/soap/envelope/'
  xmlns:SOAP-ENC='http://schemas.xmlsoap.org/soap/encoding/'
  xmlns:xsd='http://www.w3.org/1999/XMLSchema'>
    <SOAP-ENV:Body>
        <ns:echoIntegerResponse
          xmlns:ns='::http://soapinterop.org/'
          SOAP-ENV:encodingStyle='http://schemas.xmlsoap.org/soap/encoding/'>
            <return xsi:type='xsd:int'>10</return>
        </ns:echoIntegerResponse>
    </SOAP-ENV:Body>
</SOAP-ENV:Envelope>
```

At this point, [`peer::message`] returns control back to [`SOAP::Transport::beep::xfer`], which returns the envelope to its caller; the caller strips out the response and ultimately has a return value of 10.

Adding BEEP Support to the Server

Using the `beepcore-tcl` server, we can implement the SOAP profile for BEEP in less than 230 lines.

We're going to do this by reusing many of the routines from the CGI script that implements the server-side of Tcl SOAP. The `beepcore-tcl` server isn't very sophisticated—it runs under `inetd` and doesn't have any management capabilities. It does, however, have a pretty simple API—the Profile API—for someone who wants to write a Tcl module that implements a profile.

We start by creating a profile module in a file named *scripts/profile-sudsy.tcl*. The file starts off simply enough:

```
package provide sudsy  1.0

package require log
package require sasl
package require util
```

The package defined on the first line is very important—it must match the part of the file's name after `profile-`. The other lines bring in the packages that we'll need.

Because there can be more than one SOAP channel running on the same BEEP session, the profile module has to keep track of which instance it's talking about. It does this by using a package-specific variable:

```
namespace eval sudsy {
    variable sudsy
    array set sudsy { uid 0 }

    namespace export info boot init fin exch2
}
```

The last line identifies the five methods that the profile module exports for use with the Profile API. Let's look at each in turn.

The Info and Boot Methods

The [info] method, shown in Example 7-11, is used by the server configuration program, *etc/beepd-init.tcl*, to tell the server what profiles may be available. The reason this is a "may be" instead of an "are," is because the profile module might require access to additional libraries or packages before it can operate.

Example 7-11. The info method
```
proc sudsy::info {logT} {
    return [list 0 \
                [list http://clipcode.org/beep/soap] \
                [list bootV  sudsy::boot  \
                    initV  sudsy::init  \
                    exch2V sudsy::exch2 \
                    finV   sudsy::fin]]
}
```

The [info] method takes a logging token as its sole parameter and returns a list with three elements:

- The first indicates whether the profile implemented by this profile module performs transport security (1) or not (0).

- The second is a list of URIs that identify profiles implemented by this profile module (if more than one URI is present, this is typically used for transitional purposes).

- The third is a list of method/procedure pairs used by the server to communicate with the profile module.

Later on, in the section "Configuring the Server," we'll look at how the server configuration program is used.

The [boot] method, shown in Example 7-12, is invoked by the server before issuing a greeting. Once again, the sole parameter is a logging token.

Example 7-12. The boot method

```
proc sudsy::boot {logT} {
# the beepcore-tcl server already initialized this

    global debugP

# we'll use this to keep track of SOAP channels

    variable sudsy

# load the packages we need

    foreach package [list dom SOAP SOAP::CGI SOAP::Utils] {
        if {[catch { package require $package } result]} {
# missing a package, so don't advertise this profile

            return -code 7 [list code 451 diagnostic $result]
        }
    }

# initialize the SOAP CGI package

    set SOAP::CGI::soapdir     soap/method-scripts
    set SOAP::CGI::soapmapfile soap/soapmap.dat
    set SOAP::CGI::logfile     logs/soap.log
    if {$debugP} {
        set SOAP::CGI::debugging 1
    } else {
        set SOAP::CGI::debugging 0
    }
}
```

The job of the [boot] method is two-fold:

- It loads whatever libraries or packages are needed for operation.
- It performs whatever global initializations are needed for those resources.

If, for some reason, a resource is unavailable, an exceptional return (code 7) containing a reply array is made to tell the server that the URIs associated with this profile module shouldn't be advertised in the greeting.

For the SOAP profile, we load some packages, and then initialize the configuration variables for the SOAP:CGI:: package.

The Init and Fin Methods

The [init] method, shown in Example 7-13, is invoked by the server when the remote peer asks to create a channel bound to a profile implemented by this module.

Example 7-13. The init method

```
proc sudsy::init {logT serverD clientA upcallV uri} {
    variable sudsy

# assign a new token for this new SOAP channel

    set token [namespace current]::[incr sudsy(uid)]

# create an array to keep track of the channel's state information

    variable $token
    upvar 0 $token state

    array set state [list logT $logT resource "" features {}]

    return $token
}
```

The parameters are:

logT
> A logging token.

server
> The value of the serverName attribute used to start the channel.

clientA
> A serialized array of unauthenticated information from the transport service.

upcallV
> A callback method used by the profile module to initiate an exchange.

uri
> The identity of the profile to be started.

It turns out that the SOAP profile doesn't use the callback method, so we can ignore upcallV. As far as clientA goes, it contains things like the remote IP address and TCP port.

The job of the [init] method is pretty simple: it creates a new state array, initializes it with information that's specific to this instance of the SOAP channel (array set state ...), and returns a profile token. This token is used by the server when it invokes other methods in this profile module.

For the SOAP profile, there are only two state variables used by the profile module:

resource
> The resource attribute from the bootmsg used to initialize the channel.

features

A list identifying the SOAP "features" negotiated for use on this channel.

The [fin] method, shown in Example 7-14, is invoked by the server when the channel is being closed. The first parameter is the profile token, and the second parameter, status, says whether the close is graceful (+) or abortive (–). (Why the plus/minus characters instead of keywords? Just a bit of detritus.)

Example 7-14. The fin method

```
proc sudsy::fin {token status} {
    variable $token
    upvar 0 $token state

# unset each element of the array and then the token itself

    foreach name [array names state] {
        unset state($name)
    }
    unset $token
}
```

For the SOAP profile, there's nothing to do: we simply unset the state array and the profile token.

The Exch2 Method

The [exch2] method is shown in two examples, starting with Example 7-15.

Example 7-15. The exch2 method

```
proc sudsy::exch2 {peerT token mimeT} {
    global env

    variable $token
    upvar 0 $token state

# get the Content-Type: and the contents of the message

    set content [mime::getproperty $mimeT content]
    set data [mime::getbody $mimeT]
    mime::finalize $mimeT

# have we processed a "bootmsg" yet?

    if {$$state(resource) == {}} {
# no, parse it into 'doc"

        if {[catch { dom::DOMImplementation parse $data } doc]} {
# parse error, so don't start this channel

            return -code 7 [peer::errfmt $peerT 500 \
```

Example 7-15. The exch2 method (continued)

```
                              "bootmsg is invalid xml: $data"]
        }

        if {[set node [SOAP::Utils::selectNode $doc /bootmsg]] != {}} {
# it's "<bootmsg ...", so get the the "resource" and "features" attributes

            if {[catch {
                set state(resource) \
                    [set [dom::node cget $node -attributes](resource)]

                if {$state(resource) == {}} {
                    set state(resource) /
                }
            }]} {
                set reason "bootmsg missing resource attribute"
            }

            catch {
                set features \
                    [set [dom::node cget $node -attributes](features)]

                if {$features != {}} {
                    log::entry $state(logT) info requested $features
                }
            }
        } else {
            set reason "expecting bootmsg"
        }

        dom::DOMImplementation destroy $doc

        if {$state(resource) == {}} {
# some kind of error ocurred, so don't start this channel

            return -code 7 [peer::errfmt $peerT 500 $reason]
        }

        switch -- $state(resource) {
            / {
            }

            default {
# turn the resource into a "hint" for the SOAP CGI package

                if {[string first / $state(resource)] == 0} {
                    set state(resource) \
                        urn:[string range $state(resource) 1 end]
                }

# ask the SOAP CGI package to validate the "hint"

                if {[catch { SOAP::CGI::soap_implementation \
```

Example 7-15. The exch2 method (continued)

```
                                    $state(resource) }]} {
                    return -code 7 [peer::errfmt $peerT 500 \
                                      "resource unavailable"]


                }
            }
        }

        log::entry $state(logT) info resource $state(resource)

# ask the server if access is authorized

        if {[catch { sasl::allowP $state(logT) \
                        invoke soap:$state(resource) } replyA]} {
# no, so take a reply array and turn it into an "<error ..."

            return -code 7 [peer::errfmt3 $peerT $replyA]
        }

# create a "<bootrpy features='...' />"

        set doc [dom::DOMImplementation create]
        set bootrpy [dom::document createElement $doc bootrpy]
        dom::element setAttribute $bootrpy features $state(features)
        set data [dom::DOMImplementation serialize $doc]
        if {[set x [string first [set y "<!DOCTYPE bootrpy>\n"] $data]] \
                >= 0 } {
            set data [string range $data [expr $x+[string length $y]] end]
        }
        dom::DOMImplementation destroy $doc

# convert "bootrpy" into a MIME object and return it

        return [mime::initialize -canonical application/xml -string $data]
    }
}
```

The procedure has three parameters:

peerT

    A peer token.

token

    A profile token.

mimeT

    A MIME token containing the message sent by the remote peer.

The peer token is used by the server to keep track of the session. The reason that it's passed to the profile module is to allow access to several support routines (e.g., [peer::errfmt], which we'll see in a moment).

The first thing we do is extract the Content-Type: and contents of the message, and release the corresponding MIME object. We then check to see if we've assigned something to the resource state variable. If not, we should be looking at a bootmsg object, so we use the dom:: package to parse it. By now, you should be able to guess what happens on an error: we execute [peer::errfmt] to generate a MIME object containing an error element, and we do an exceptional return of that.

Otherwise, if the top-level element in the message is bootmsg, we try to extract the resource and features attributes. (If the resource attribute is present, but empty, we default the value to /.) If we couldn't find a resource attribute, [peer::errfmt] is exceptionally returned.

Now we have to do a "hack." I think it's a good idea to let folks use the same mapping file for both the SOAP profile module and the SOAP CGI script. We therefore need to make the resource attribute resemble the kind of hints used by the CGI script. The hack is to change resources that look like /soapinterop into resources that look like urn:soapinterop. Regardless, unless the resource is the default value, we execute [SOAP::CGI::soap_implementation]. This procedure looks for the resource in the mapping file and errors if it isn't found. (We don't use the procedure on the default value, because the mapping file won't be used in the default case.)

Next, we log the resource request and ask the server if the user associated with this session has permission to invoke the resource. The procedure that does this is named [sasl::allowP] and takes three parameters:

logT
   A logging token.

action
   The desired permission, which in this case is invoke.

scope
   A naming scope.

What [sasl::allowP] does is look at how the session was tuned for authentication, look at the server's authorization database, look at the action being requested, and then make an exceptional return (containing a reply array) if it's not happy with the request. In that case, we execute [peer::errfmt3], which takes a reply array, builds an error element, and returns the corresponding MIME object.

So, who defines the actions and the naming scopes? The answer is the writer of the profile module. The way you avoid naming collisions is to pick a unique prefix for the naming scope; in this case, we're using soap:. This particular profile module has only one action, invoke, but other profile modules can have as many actions as necessary (e.g., read, create, update, delete, rename, and so on).

Finally, we use the dom:: package to create a bootrpy object, serialize it into a string, strip off the XML declarations, and then return the corresponding MIME object to the server.

As shown in Example 7-16, if we have already assigned something to the resource state variable, we should be looking at a SOAP-ENV:Envelope object.

Example 7-16. The exch2 method, part two

```
# we've already processed a "bootmsg", so this is an Envelope

# make sure there aren't any attachments

    if {[string compare $content application/xml]} {
        return -code 7 \
                [peer::errfmt $peerT 500 \
                    "expecting application/xml in request, not $content"]
    }

# initialize the SOAP CGI package's debug facility

    set SOAP::CGI::debuginfo {}

    set doc {}

    set code [catch {
        switch -- $state(resource) {
            / {
                set env(HTTP_SOAPACTION) {}
            }

            default {
                set env(HTTP_SOAPACTION) $state(resource)
            }
        }

# let the SOAP CGI package do the parse, dispatch, and bundle...

        SOAP::CGI::soap_invocation \
            [set doc [dom::DOMImplementation parse $data]]
    } result]

# sometimes it's already been free'd, go figure...

    catch { dom::DOMImplementation destroy $doc }

# log any debug info collected by the SOAP CGI package

    foreach item $SOAP::CGI::debuginfo {
        log::entry $state(logT) debug SOAP::CGI $item
    }

# on an error return, make sure the return value isn't XML

    if {$code && ([string first "<?xml " $result] != 0)} {
        return -code 7 [peer::errfmt $peerT 500 $result]
    }
```

Example 7-16. The exch2 method, part two (continued)

```
# strip off XML declarations

    if {[set x [string first [set y "?>\n"] $result]] >= 0 } {
        set result [string range $result [expr $x+[string length $y]] end]
    }

# convert the Envelope into a MIME object and return it

    return [mime::initialize -canonical application/xml -string $result]
}
```

We check to make sure that the Content-Type: is an application/xml. We then execute [SOAP::CGI::soap_invocation] which does all the real work. Prior to doing this, we have to set the HTTP_SOAPACTION environment variable, because this procedure uses that value as the hint for the mapping file. If the SOAP::CGI:: package saved any debugging information, we log that.

The tricky part is looking at the return code and value from the catch that contained the execution of SOAP::CGI::soap_invocation. If the return value is a SOAP envelope, regardless of the return code, we return the corresponding MIME object; otherwise, [peer::errfmt] is executed and an exceptional return is made.

That's it! Just 225 lines of glue.

In truth, though, we could optimize this code a fair bit by shifting more functionality from the SOAP::CGI:: package to the profile module. For example, if multiple instances of the SOAP profile were started on a session, we could cache the mapping file. Similarly, if multiple exchanges occur on the same channel and a safe interpreter is used, we could keep the interpreter around between exchanges. For our purposes, however, optimizations such as these would distract from the main lessons.

Configuring the Server

After we've put the profile module in the *bxxd/scripts/* directory, the beepcore-tcl server should be configured.

There are three things we need to do:

1. Create a *bxxd/soap/* directory, and put the *soapmap.dat* file and *method-scripts/* directory there.
2. Run *etc/beepd-boot.tcl* to tell the server about the new profile.
3. For each user we want to authorize to use the profile, run *etc/otp-init.tcl*.

(Notice the use of bxxd here instead of beepd? It's just a little more dust left over from the early days.)

The first step is pretty easy, because the SOAP profile uses the same formats and conventions as the CGI script. For the second step, most folks run etc/beepd-boot. tcl like this:

```
$ etc/beepd-boot.tcl . no no yes
```

which basically says that privacy isn't required to start a data exchange profile (the first no), that authentication isn't required to start a data exchange profile (the second no), and that anonymous logins are allowed (yes).

You need to rerun *etc/beepd-boot.tcl* whenever you update the profile modules in the *bxxd/scripts/* directory, so you should use whatever parameters you used the first time. The configuration program looks at all the profile modules and generates some configuration files for the beepcore-tcl server telling it what profiles it can advertise. (*etc/beepd-boot.tcl* looks at all the files named *profile-*.tcl* in the *bxxd/scripts/* directory, and invokes the [info] method in each of them to figure out things.)

Finally, for each authorized user, you need to run etc/otp-init.tcl, e.g.:

```
$ etc/otp-init.tcl . logs/otp-init.log fred \
                   "soap:urn:tclsoap*" soap:urn:soapinterop
```

Obviously fred is the user being authorized.

The parameters that follow the username are the authorization "scopes." The string to the left of the first colon (e.g., soap) is usually unique to each profile, and the string to the right of the first colon is specific to that profile. In the case of the SOAP profile, you need to authorize whatever resources are necessary. So, in this example, fred is authorized to access any resource starting with tclsoap, and also the soapinterop resource.

I'll confess that the authorization database used by the beepcore-tcl server is very primitive—each user is stored in its own text file, and the configuration editor is whatever text editor you're comfortable with. In defense, I'll merely note that beepcore-tcl was written for prototyping, not production use.

## CHAPTER 8

Futures

So, where are we now and what's next?

Experiences

There have been eight projects and three BEEP API implementations in six months.

Within the first six months of BEEP's publication, eight different BEEP-based standards efforts were started. Some of them we've already looked at in brief (e.g., reliable *syslog*). Based on questions sent to some of the mailing lists, there appear to be quite a few private BEEP-based projects underway as well.

In terms of BEEP API implementations, the three open source beepcore libraries appear to be the only well-known implementations. This is both a strength and a weakness. It's a strength in the sense that there are a lot of tricky things you have to get right in an API, so having a small number of well-debugged, widely used implementations is a good thing. It's also a weakness because few other engineers are motivated to gain that knowledge. Further, since there's a lot of overlap between the folks doing the work on the different implementations, a bug in one may not get caught during interoperability testing with the other two.

Why did BEEP API implementation knowledge get concentrated like this? There are a couple of reasons, but perhaps the greatest influence is "the Lear compact" from the BEEP working group. During earlier discussions, there was concern that application implementors would each try to write their own "mini BEEP" layer, each deficient is some way. Presumably, by having open source implementations for different languages, there's a lot less pressure to "roll your own." It's a mixed bag.

Fortunately, the situation is improving—different groups are looking at doing BEEP implementations for Python and Ruby! I'm looking forward to seeing some determined testing among all five implementations in the months ahead.

Stability and Evolution

Planned evolution is the key to stability.

The *Simple Network Management Protocol* (SNMP, RFC 1157) teaches a lot of lessons with respect to this. In SNMP, the core mechanisms (i.e., the protocol and data model) were cast in stone—easier to elect a libertarian to national office than to add an opcode. Regardless, SNMP extensions were the focus of over 30 successful working groups for several years. How can this be?

The answer is that SNMP allowed anyone—working groups, corporations, and individuals—to define new kinds of data to manage. So, the fiber-heads got to define SNMP modules that dealt with fiber optics, the asset management guys got to define SNMP modules that dealt with that, and so on. Most importantly, the rules for defining these extensions, termed MIB modules, were designed in such a way as to make sure that these guys couldn't interfere with each other. Everyone could rely on a stable platform, and anyone could plug in their own specific modules.

BEEP tries to follow the same philosophy: the BEEP core specification is largely immutable, and, thanks to the use of URIs, no coordination is required when different groups define their own profiles. Another benefit of this approach is that the folks who implement APIs for BEEP (or SNMP) implementations can publish their specifications for third-parties to develop these add-ons.

Even so, unlike SNMP, BEEP does provide a way to change its core behavior, through the use of "feature negotiation" when greetings are exchanged. Recall from "The Greeting" in Chapter 3 that as soon as a session is started, both peers send a greeting. In addition to supported profiles and preferred languages for diagnostics, the greeting may contain a list of optional features. The intersection of the features supported by each peer is what's allowed to be used on the session.

For example, consider these two greetings:

```
<greeting features='a b c'>
    ...
</greeting>

<greeting features='a c x'>
    ...
</greeting>
```

The features a and c may be used on the session.

Although there's been talk about different possible features, none has been standardized yet. It's unlikely that features will do things like change the framing protocol. More likely, each feature will define one or more additions to the channel management profile (see "Channel Management" in Chapter 3).

For example, it turns out that one of the more interesting impacts on server scalability has to do with who tries to close a TCP connection first. In "The TIME-WAIT

State in TCP and Its Effect on Busy Servers," Faber, Touch, and Yue present considerable insight as to how this issue affects servers. In BEEP, as with most protocols, there is no explicit token that gets exchanged as to who should close first. Of course, it's a simple matter to define a BEEP feature that allows the two sides to negotiate this.

Tunneling

One more tuning profile is on the horizon.

The SASL family of profiles and the TLS profile cover the major bases in terms of security tuning. However, there's a new profile being defined for handling a different kind of tuning—application proxying.

Some of the folks working in the security area of the IETF had an interesting requirement: end-to-end transport security through multiple application entities. (How's that for an opaque requirement?) What this means is that, although a network may be administratively configured so that traffic has to pass through one or more application proxies, the traffic from the originator to the (ultimate) recipient should be safe from the intermediaries. This is illustrated in Figure 8-1.

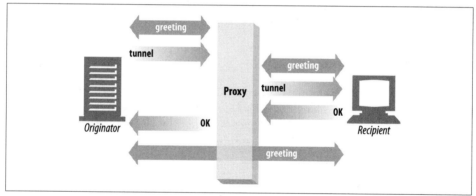

Figure 8-1. The tunneling precept

To try and make this clear, let's look at what happens when an originator has to go through one proxy to get to the recipient:

1. The originator establishes a BEEP session to the proxy, and tunes the session for authentication, but not privacy.

2. The originator starts the tunneling profile, and sends an operation on that channel that specifies the recipient's address.

3. The proxy decides if the originator is authorized to tunnel. If so, the proxy establishes a BEEP session to the recipient, and tunes the session.

4. The proxy starts the tunneling profile, and sends an operation on that channel that tells the recipient that it's the ultimate destination.

5. The recipient decides whether it's willing to tunnel, and if so, sends back an acknowledgement to the proxy, and then performs a tuning reset.

6. The proxy reports the outcome to the originator and, if successful, starts acting as a transparent pipe—it's no longer doing BEEP on either of the two connections.

7. The originator, on a successful outcome, performs a tuning reset, and both the originator and recipient exchange greetings.

One of the clever things about the tunneling profile specification, *The Tunnel Profile*, is that it easily supports multiple proxies in a row, such as several layers of firewalls, without any additional work.

The key thing to appreciate is that unlike approaches that do "stealth tunneling," BEEP's tunneling profile provides administrators with a well-defined mechanism for authenticating and authorizing application traffic through firewalls.

Transport Mappings

Beyond one or two features, a new tuning profile, and a lot of exchange profiles, the only other thing on the horizon is whether additional transport mappings will be defined for BEEP. Right now, there's just one mapping—a BEEP session maps onto a single TCP connection. However, there's talk about defining two other mappings:

- A mapping onto multiple TCP sessions.
- A mapping onto the *Stream Control Transmission Protocol* (SCTP, RFC 2960).

The advantage of the first mapping is that it makes it a lot easier for BEEP to manage simultaneous channels on a single session—TCP does all the work! The second mapping has a similar advantage (each SCTP association supports multiple streams), and also takes advantage of some of SCTP's features such as multihoming.

It turns out that because of BEEP's design, using a new transport mapping won't have any impact on any BEEP profiles. Though the underlying implementation may behave more efficiently or perform better, the functionality remains the same. In fact, the only noticeable change will be if a URI is used to identify a service running over BEEP.

Recall from "BEEP URIs" in Chapter 4 that there isn't a "generic" URL scheme for BEEP. Instead, each BEEP-based service may have its own URL scheme (e.g., *soap. beep://example.com/StockQuote*). Since the URL scheme is designed to identify things like transport issues, it's just a matter of defining a new (similarly named) scheme for the service when it uses a new mapping, e.g., *soap.beep.sctp://*.

Finally

How can you keep informed as to what's going on with BEEP? Get the latest at the BEEP community web site, *http://beepcore.org*.

Thanks for reading, and I hope you enjoyed the book!

On the Design of Application Protocols

This is a reprint of the design document for BXXP, BEEP's predecessor, written by Carl Malamud and myself in early 2000. BXXP was the input to the IETF working group that produced BEEP. (At the very end of the design document, the interesting differences between BXXP and BEEP are listed.)

Some readers may be interested in an analysis on the design principles of application protocols, but that level of design detail probably isn't appropriate for the depth of this book—that's why it has been placed in this appendix.

A Problem 19 Years in the Making

SMTP (RFC 821) is close to being the perfect application protocol: it solves a large, important problem in a minimalist way. It's simple enough for an entry-level implementation to fit on one or two screens of code, and flexible enough to form the basis of very powerful product offerings in a robust and competitive market. Modulo a few oddities (e.g., SAML), the design is well-conceived and the resulting specification is well-written and largely self-contained. There is very little about good application protocol design that you can't learn by reading the SMTP specification.

Unfortunately, there's one little problem: SMTP was originally published in 1981, and since that time a lot of application protocols have been designed for the Internet but there hasn't been a lot of reuse going on. You might expect this if the application protocols were all radically different, but this isn't the case: most are surprisingly similar in their functional behavior, even though the actual details vary considerably.

In late 1998, as Carl Malamud and I were sitting down to review the Blocks architecture, we realized that we needed to have a protocol for exchanging Blocks. The conventional wisdom is that when you need an application protocol, there are four ways to proceed:

1. Find an existing exchange protocol that (more or less) does what you want.

2. Define an exchange model on top of the World Wide Web infrastructure that (more or less) does what you want.

3. Define an exchange model on top of the electronic mail infrastructure that (more or less) does what you want.

4. Define a new protocol from scratch that does exactly what you want.

An engineer can make reasoned arguments about the merits of each of the these approaches. Here's the process we followed....

The most appealing option is to find an existing protocol and use that. (In other words, we'd rather "buy" than "make.") So, we did a survey of many existing application protocols and found that none of them were a good match for the semantics of the protocol we needed.

For example, most application protocols are oriented toward client/server behavior, and emphasize the client pulling data from the server; in contrast with Blocks, a client usually pulls data from the server, but it also may request the server to asynchronously push (new) data to it. Clearly, we could mutate a protocol such as FTP (RFC 0959) or SMTP into what we wanted, but by the time we did all that, the base protocol and our protocol would have more differences than similarities. In other words, the cost of modifying an off-the-shelf implementation becomes comparable with starting from scratch.

Another approach is to use HTTP (RFC 1945) as the exchange protocol and define the rules for data exchange over that. For example, IPP (RFC 256, the Internet Printing Protocol) uses this approach. The basic idea is that HTTP defines the rules for exchanging data and then you define the data's syntax and semantics. Because you inherit the entire HTTP infrastructure (e.g., HTTP's authentication mechanisms, caching proxies, and so on), there's less for you to have to invent (and code!). Or, conversely, you might view the HTTP infrastructure as too helpful. As an added bonus, if you decide that your protocol runs over port 80, you may be able to sneak your traffic past older firewalls, at the cost of port 80 saturation.

HTTP has many strengths: it's ubiquitous, it's familiar, and there are a lot of tools available for developing HTTP-based systems. Another good thing about HTTP is that it uses MIME (RFC 2045) for encoding data.

Unfortunately for us, even with HTTP 1.1 (RFC 2616) there still wasn't a good fit. As a consequence of the highly desirable goal of maintaining compatibility with the original HTTP, HTTP's framing mechanism isn't flexible enough to support server-side asynchronous behavior and its authentication model isn't similar to other Internet applications.

Mapping IPP onto HTTP 1.1 illustrates the former issue. For example, the IPP server is supposed to signal its client when a job completes. Since the HTTP client must originate all requests and since the decision to close a persistent connection in HTTP is unilateral, the best that the IPP specification can do is specify this functionality in a non-deterministic fashion.

Further, the IPP mapping onto HTTP shows that even subtle shifts in behavior have unintended consequences. For example, requests in IPP are typically much larger than those seen by many HTTP server implementations—resulting in oddities in many HTTP servers (e.g., requests are sometimes silently truncated). The lesson is that HTTP's framing mechanism is very rigid with respect to its view of the request/response model.

Lastly, given our belief that the port field of the TCP header isn't a constant 80, we were immune to the seductive allure of wanting to sneak our traffic past unwary site administrators.

The third choice, layering the protocol on top of email, was attractive. Unfortunately, the nature of our application includes a lot of interactivity with relatively small response times. So, this left us the final alternative: defining a protocol from scratch.

To begin, we figured that our requirements, while a little more stringent than most, could fit inside a framework suitable for a large number of future application protocols. The trick is to avoid the kitchen-sink approach. (Dave Clark has a saying: "One of the roles of architecture is to tell you what you can't do.")

You Can Solve Any Problem...

...if you're willing to make the problem small enough.

Our most important step is to limit the problem to application protocols that exhibit certain features:

- They are connection-oriented.
- They use requests and responses to exchange messages.
- They allow for asynchronous message exchange.

Let's look at each, in turn.

First, we're only going to consider connection-oriented application protocols (e.g., those that work on top of TCP (RFC 0793)). Another branch in the taxonomy, connectionless, consists of those that don't want the delay or overhead of establishing and maintaining a reliable stream. For example, most DNS (RFC 1034) traffic is characterized by a single request and response, both of which fit within a single IP datagram. In this case, it makes sense to implement a basic reliability service above the transport layer in the application protocol itself.

Second, we're only going to consider message-oriented application protocols. A "message"—in our lexicon—is simply structured data exchanged between loosely coupled systems. Another branch in the taxonomy, tightly coupled systems, uses remote procedure calls as the exchange paradigm. Unlike the connection-oriented/connectionless dichotomy, the issue of loosely or tightly coupled systems is similar to a continuous spectrum. Fortunately, the edges are fairly sharp.

For example, NFS (RFC 1094) is a tightly coupled system using RPCs. When running in a properly configured LAN, a remote disk accessible via NFS is virtually indistinguishable from a local disk. To achieve this, tightly coupled systems are highly concerned with issues of latency. Hence, most (but not all) tightly coupled systems use connection less RPC mechanisms; further, most tend to be implemented as operating system functions rather than user-level programs. (In some environments, the tightly coupled systems are implemented as single-purpose servers on hardware specifically optimized for that one function.)

Finally, we're going to consider the needs of application protocols that exchange messages asynchronously. The classic client/server model is that the client sends a request and the server sends a response. If you think of requests as "questions" and responses as "answers," then the server answers only those questions that it's asked, and it never asks any questions of its own. We'll need to support a more general model, peer-to-peer. In this model, for a given transaction one peer might be the "client" and the other the "server," but for the next transaction, the two peers might switch roles.

It turns out that the client/server model is a proper subset of the peer-to-peer model: it's acceptable for a particular application protocol to dictate that the peer that establishes the connection always acts as the client (initiates requests), and that the peer that listens for incoming connections always acts as the server (issuing responses to requests).

There are quite a few existing application domains that don't fit our requirements, e.g., nameservice (via the DNS), fileservice (via NFS), multicast-enabled applications such as distributed video conferencing, and so on. However, there are a lot of application domains that do fit these requirements, e.g., electronic mail, file transfer, remote shell, and the World Wide Web. So, the bet we are placing in going forward is that there will continue to be reasons for defining protocols that fit within our framework.

Protocol Mechanisms

The next step is to look at the tasks that an application protocol must perform and how it goes about performing them. Although an exhaustive exposition might identify a dozen (or so) areas, the ones we're interested in are:

Framing
    Tells how the beginning and ending of each message is delimited.

Encoding
> Tells how a message is represented when exchanged.

Reporting
> Tells how errors are described.

Asynchrony
> Tells how independent exchanges are handled.

Authentication
> Tells how the peers at each end of the connection are identified and verified.

Privacy
> Tells how the exchanges are protected against third-party interception or modification.

A notable absence in this list is naming—we'll explain why later on.

Framing

There are three commonly used approaches to delimiting messages: octet-stuffing, octet-counting, and connection-blasting.

An example of a protocol that uses octet-stuffing is SMTP. Commands in SMTP are line-oriented (each command ends in a CR-LF pair). When an SMTP peer sends a message, it first transmits the DATA command, then it transmits the message, then it transmits a . (dot) followed by a CR-LF. If the message contains any lines that begin with a dot, the sending SMTP peer sends two dots; similarly, when the other SMTP peer receives a line that begins with a dot, it discards the dot, and, if the line is empty, it knows it's received the entire message. Octet-stuffing has the property that you don't need the entire message in front of you before you start sending it. Unfortunately, it's slow because both the sender and receiver must scan each line of the message to see if they need to transform it.

An example of a protocol that uses octet-counting is HTTP. Commands in HTTP consist of a request line followed by headers and a body. The headers contain an octet count indicating how large the body is. The properties of octet-counting are the inverse of octet-stuffing: before you can start sending a message you need to know the length of the whole message, but you don't need to look at the content of the message once you start sending or receiving.

An example of a protocol that uses connection-blasting is FTP. Commands in FTP are line-oriented, and when it's time to exchange a message, a new TCP connection is established to transmit the message. Both octet-counting and connection-blasting have the property that the messages can be arbitrary binary data; however, the drawback of the connection-blasting approach is that the peers need to communicate IP addresses and TCP port numbers, which may be "transparently" altered by NATs (RFC 2663) and network bugs. In addition, if the messages being exchanged are small (say less than 32k), then the overhead of establishing a connection for each message contributes significant latency during data exchange.

Encoding

There are many schemes used for encoding data (and many more encoding schemes have been proposed than are actually in use). Fortunately, only a few are burning brightly on the radar.

The messages exchanged using SMTP are encoded using the 822 style (RFC 822). The 822 style divides a message into textual headers and an unstructured body. Each header consists of a name and a value and is terminated with a CR-LF pair. An additional CR-LF separates the headers from the body.

It is this structure that HTTP uses to indicate the length of the body for framing purposes. More formally, HTTP uses MIME, an application of the 822 style, to encode both the data itself (the body) and information about the data (the headers). That is, although HTTP is commonly viewed as a retrieval mechanism for HTML (RFC 1866), it is really a retrieval mechanism for objects encoded using MIME, most of which are either HTML pages or referenced objects such as GIFs.

Reporting

An application protocol needs a mechanism for conveying error information between peers. The first formal method for doing this was defined by SMTP's "theory of reply codes." The basic idea is that an error is identified by a three-digit string, with each position having a different significance:

The first digit
    Indicates success or failure, either permanent or transient.

The second digit
    Indicates the part of the system reporting the situation (e.g., the syntax analyzer).

The third digit
    Identifies the actual situation.

Operational experience with SMTP suggests that the range of error conditions is larger than can be comfortably encoded using a three-digit string (i.e., you can report on only 10 different things going wrong for any given part of the system). RFC 2034 provides a convenient mechanism for extending the number of values that can occur in the second and third positions.

Virtually all of the application protocols we've discussed thus far use the three-digit reply codes, although there is less coordination between the designers of different application protocols than most would care to admit. (A variation on the theory of reply codes is employed by IMAP (RFC 1731), which provides the same information using a different syntax.)

In addition to conveying a reply code, most application protocols also send a textual diagnostic suitable for human, not machine, consumption. (More accurately, the textual diagnostic is suitable for people who can read a widely used variant of the English language.) Since reply codes reflect both positive and negative outcomes, there have been some innovative uses made for the text accompanying positive responses, e.g., prayer wheels. Regardless, some of the more modern application protocols include a language localization parameter for the diagnostic text.

Finally, since the introduction of reply codes in 1981, two unresolved criticisms have been raised:

- A reply code is used both to signal the outcome of an operation and a change in the application protocol's state.

- A reply code doesn't specify whether the associated textual diagnostic is destined for the end-user, administrator, or programmer.

Asynchrony

Few application protocols today allow independent exchanges over the same connection. In fact, the more widely implemented approach is to allow pipelining, e.g., command pipelining (RFC 2197) in SMTP or persistent connections in HTTP 1.1. Pipelining allows a client to make multiple requests of a server, but requires the requests to be processed serially. (Note that a protocol needs to explicitly provide support for pipelining, since—without explicit guidance—many implementors produce systems that don't handle pipelining properly; typically, an error in a request causes subsequent requests in the pipeline to be discarded.)

Pipelining is a powerful method for reducing network latency. For example, without persistent connections, HTTP's framing mechanism is really closer to connection-blasting than octet-counting, and it enjoys the same latency and efficiency problems.

In addition to reducing network latency (the pipelining effect), asynchrony also reduces server latency by allowing multiple requests to be processed by multithreaded implementations. Note that if you allow any form of asynchronous exchange, then support for parallelism is also required, because exchanges aren't necessarily occurring under the synchronous direction of a single peer.

Unfortunately, when you allow parallelism, you also need a flow control mechanism to avoid starvation and deadlock. Otherwise, a single set of exchanges can monopolize the bandwidth provided by the transport layer. Further, if a peer is resource-starved, it may not have enough buffers to receive a message, and deadlock results.

Flow control is typically implemented at the transport layer. For example, TCP uses sequence numbers and a sliding window: each receiver manages a sliding window that indicates the number of data octets that may be transmitted before receiving further permission. However, it's now time for the second shoe to drop: segmentation.

If you do flow control then you also need a segmentation mechanism to fragment messages into smaller pieces before sending, and then reassemble them as they're received.

Both flow control and segmentation have an impact on how the protocol does framing. Before we defined framing as "how to tell the beginning and end of each message"—in addition, we need to be able to identify independent messages, send messages only when flow control allows us to, and segment them if they're larger than the available window (or too large for comfort).

Segmentation impacts framing in another way: it relaxes the octet-counting requirement that you need to know the length of the whole message before sending it. With segmentation, you can start sending segments before the whole message is available. In HTTP 1.1, you can "chunk" (segment) data to get this advantage.

Authentication

Perhaps for historical (or hysterical) reasons, most application protocols don't do authentication. That is, they don't authenticate the identity of the peers on the connection or the authenticity of the messages being exchanged. If authentication is done, it is often domain-specific for each protocol. For example, FTP and HTTP use entirely different models and mechanisms for authenticating the initiator of a connection. (Independent of mainstream HTTP, there is a little-used variant (RFC 2660) that authenticates the messages it exchanges.)

A large part of the problem is that different security mechanisms optimize for strength, scalability, or ease of deployment. So, a few years ago, SASL (RFC 2222, the Simple Authentication and Security Layer) was developed to provide a framework for authenticating protocol peers. SASL lets you describe how an authentication mechanism works, e.g., an OTP (RFC 2444, One-Time Password) exchange. It's then up to each protocol designer to specify how SASL exchanges are generically conveyed by the protocol. For example, RFC 2554 explains how SASL works with SMTP.

A notable exception to the SASL bandwagon is HTTP, which defines its own authentication mechanisms (RFC 2617). There is little reason why SASL couldn't be introduced to HTTP, although to avoid certain race conditions, the persistent connection mechanism of HTTP 1.1 must be used.

SASL has an interesting feature in that in addition to explicit protocol exchanges to authenticate identity, it can also use implicit information provided from the layer below. For example, if the connection is running over IPSec (RFC 2401), then the credentials of each peer are known and verified when the TCP connection is established.

Finally, as its name implies, SASL can do more than authentication—depending on which SASL mechanism is in use, message integrity or privacy services may also be provided.

Privacy

HTTP is the first widely used protocol to make use of a transport security protocol to encrypt the data sent on the connection. The current version of this mechanism, TLS (RFC 2246), is available to all application protocols, e.g., SMTP and ACAP (RFC 2244, the Application Configuration Access Protocol).

The key difference between the original mechanism and TLS is one of provisioning, not technology. In the original approach to provisioning, a World Wide Web server listens on two ports (one for plaintext traffic and the other for secured traffic); in contrast, by today's conventions, a server implementing an application protocol that is specified as TLS-enabled (e.g., RFC 2487 and RFC 2595) listens on a single port for plaintext traffic, and, once a connection is established, the use of TLS on that connection is negotiable.

Finally, note that both SASL and TLS are about "transport security," not "object security." What this means is that they focus on providing security properties for the actual communication; they don't provide any security properties for the data exchanged independent of the communication.

Let's Recap

Let's briefly compare the properties of the three main connection-oriented application protocols in use today:

Mechanism	ESMTP	FTP	HTTP 1.1
Framing	Stuffing	Blasting	Counting
Encoding	822-style	Binary	MIME
Reporting	3-digit	3-digit	3-digit
Asynchrony	Pipelining	None	Pipelining and chunking
Authentication	SASL	User/pass	User/pass
Privacy	SASL or TLS	None	TLS (nee SSL)

Note that the username/password mechanisms used by FTP and HTTP are entirely different with one exception: both can be termed a "username/password" mechanism.

These three choices are broadly representative: as more protocols are considered, the patterns are reinforced. For example, POP (RFC 1939) uses octet-stuffing, but IMAP uses octet-counting, and so on.

Protocol Properties

When we design an application protocol, there are a few properties that we should keep an eye on.

Scalability

A well-designed protocol is scalable.

Because few application protocols support asynchrony, a common trick is for a program to open multiple simultaneous connections to a single destination. The theory is that this reduces latency and increases throughput. The reality is that both the transport layer and the server view each connection as an independent instance of the application protocol, and this causes problems.

In terms of the transport layer, TCP uses adaptive algorithms to efficiently transmit data as networks conditions change. But what TCP learns is limited to each connection. So, if you have multiple TCP connections, you have to go through the same learning process multiple times—even if you're going to the same host. Not only does this introduce unnecessary traffic spikes into the network, but because TCP uses a slow-start algorithm when establishing a connection, the program still sees additional latency. To deal with the fact that a lack of asynchrony in application protocols causes implementors to make sloppy use of the transport layer, network protocols are now provisioned with increasing sophistication, e.g., RED (RFC 2309). Further, suggestions are also being considered for modification of TCP implementations to reduce concurrent learning, e.g., RFC 2140.

In terms of the server, each incoming connection must be dispatched and (probably) authenticated against the same resources. Consequently, server overhead increases based on the number of connections established, rather than the number of remote users. The same issues of fairness arise: it's much harder for servers to allocate resources on a per-user basis, when a user can cause an arbitrary number of connections to pound on the server.

Another important aspect of scalability to consider is the relative numbers of clients and servers. (This is true even in the peer-to-peer model, where a peer can act both in the client and server role.) Typically, there are many more client peers than server peers. In this case, functional requirements should be shifted from the servers onto the clients. The reason is that a server is likely to be interacting with multiple clients and this functional shift makes it easier to scale.

Efficiency

A well-designed protocol is efficient.

For example, although a compelling argument can be made that octet-stuffing leads to more elegant implementations than octet-counting, experience shows that octet-counting consumes far fewer cycles.

Regrettably, we sometimes have to compromise efficiency in order to satisfy other properties. For example, 822 (and MIME) use textual headers. We could certainly define a more efficient representation for the headers if we were willing to limit the header names and values that could be used. In this case, extensibility is viewed as more important than efficiency. Of course, if we were designing a network protocol instead of an application protocol, then we'd make the trade-offs using a razor with a different edge.

Simplicity

A well-designed protocol is simple.

Here's a good rule of thumb: a poorly designed application protocol is one in which it is equally as "challenging" to do something basic as it is to do something complex. Easy things should be easy to do and hard things should be harder to do. The reason is simple: the pain should be proportional to the gain.

Another rule of thumb is that if an application protocol has two ways of doing the exact same thing, then there's a problem somewhere in the architecture underlying the design of the application protocol.

Hopefully, simple doesn't mean simple-minded: something that's well-designed accommodates everything in the problem domain, even the troublesome things at the edges. What makes the design simple is that it does this in a consistent fashion. Typically, this leads to an elegant design.

Extensibility

A well-designed protocol is extensible.

As clever as application protocol designers are, there are likely to be unforeseen problems that the application protocol will be asked to solve. So, it's important to provide the hooks that can be used to add functionality or customize behavior. This means that the protocol is evolutionary, and there must be a way for implementations reflecting different steps in the evolutionary path to negotiate which extensions will be used.

It's important to avoid falling into the extensibility trap: the hooks provided should not be targeted at half-baked future requirements. Above all, the hooks should be simple.

Of course, good design goes a long way towards minimizing the need for extensibility. For example, although SMTP initially didn't have an extension framework, it was only after ten years of experience that its excellent design was altered. In contrast, a poorly designed protocol such as Telnet (RFC 0854) can't function without being built around the notion of extensions.

Robustness

A well-designed protocol is robust.

Robustness and efficiency are often at odds. For example, although defaults are useful to reduce packet sizes and processing time, they tend to encourage implementation errors.

Counterintuitively, Postel's robustness principle ("Be conservative in what you send, liberal in what you accept") often leads to deployment problems. Why? When a new implementation is initially fielded, it is likely that it will encounter only a subset of existing implementations. If those implementations follow the robustness principle, then errors in the new implementation will likely go undetected. The new implementation then sees some, but not widespread deployment. This process repeats for several new implementations. Eventually, the not-quite-correct implementations run into other implementations that are less liberal than the initial set of implementations. The reader should be able to figure out what happens next.

Accordingly, explicit consistency checks in a protocol are very useful, even if they impose implementation overhead.

The BXXP Framework

Finally, we get to the money shot: here's what we did.

We defined an application protocol framework called BXXP (the Blocks eXtensible eXchange Protocol). The reason it's a "framework" instead of an application protocol is that we provide all the mechanisms discussed earlier without actually specifying the kind of messages that get exchanged. So, when someone else needs an application protocol that requires connection-oriented, asynchronous interactions, they can start with BXXP. It's then their responsibility to define the last 10% of the application protocol, the part that does, as we say, "the useful work."

So, what does BXXP look like?

Mechanism	BXXP
Framing	Counting, with a trailer
Encoding	MIME, defaulting to text/xml
Reporting	3-digit and localized textual diagnostic
Asynchrony	Channels
Authentication	SASL
Privacy	SASL or TLS

Framing and Encoding

Framing in BXXP looks a lot like SMTP or HTTP: there's a command line that identifies the beginning of the frame, then there's a MIME object (headers and body).

Unlike SMTP, BXXP uses octet-counting, but unlike HTTP, the command line is where you find the size of the payload. Finally, there's a trailer after the MIME object to aid in detecting framing errors.

Actually, the command line for BXXP has a lot of information; it tells you:

- What kind of message is in this frame.
- Whether there's more to the message than just what's in this frame (a continuation flag).
- How to distinguish the message contained in this frame from other messages (a message number).
- Where the payload occurs in the sliding window (a sequence number) along with how many octets are in the payload of this frame.
- Which part of the application should get the message (a channel number).

(The command line is textual and ends in a CR-LF pair, and the arguments are separated by a space.)

Since you need to know all this stuff to process a frame, we put it all in one easy-to-parse location. You could probably devise a more efficient encoding, but the command line is a very small part of the frame, so you wouldn't get much bounce from optimizing it. Further, because framing is at the heart of BXXP, the frame format has several consistency checks that catch the majority of programming errors. (The combination of a sequence number, an octet count, and a trailer allows for very robust error detection.)

Another trick is in the headers: because the command line contains all the framing information, the headers may contain minimal MIME information (such as Content-Type). Usually, however, the headers are empty. That's because the BXXP default payload is XML. (Actually, it's a Content-Type: text/xml with binary transfer encoding.)

We chose XML as the default because it provides a simple mechanism for nested, textual representations. (Alas, the 822-style encoding doesn't easily support nesting.) By design, XML's nature isn't optimized for compact representations. That's okay because we're focusing on loosely coupled systems, and besides, there are efficient XML parsers available. Further, there's a fair amount of anecdotal experience—and we'll stress the word "anecdotal"—that if you have any kind of compression (either at the link-layer or during encryption), then XML encodings squeeze down nicely.

Even so, use of XML is probably the most controversial part of BXXP. After all, there are more efficient representations around. We agree, but the real issue isn't efficiency, it's ease of use: there are a lot of people who grok the XML thing and there are a lot of XML tools out there. The pain of recreating this social infrastructure far outweighs any benefits of devising a new representation. If the "make" option is too expensive, is there something else we can "buy" besides XML? Well, there's ASN.1/BER (just kidding).

In the early days of the SNMP (RFC 1157), which does use ASN.1, the same issues arose. In the end, the working group agreed that the use of ASN.1 for SNMP was axiomatic, but not because anyone thought that ASN.1 was the most efficient, or the easiest to explain, or even well liked. ASN.1 was given axiomatic status because the working group decided it was not going to spend the next three years explaining an alternative encoding scheme to the developer community.

So—and we apologize for appealing to dogma—use of XML as the favored encoding scheme in BXXP is axiomatic.

Reporting

We use 3-digit error codes, with a localized textual diagnostic. (Each peer specifies a preferred ordering of languages.)

In addition, the reply to a message is flagged as either positive or negative. This makes it easy to signal success or failure and allow the receiving peer some freedom in the amount of parsing it wants to do on failure.

Asynchrony

Despite the lessons of SMTP and HTTP, there isn't a lot of field experience to rely on when designing the asynchrony features of BXXP. (Actually, there were several efforts in 1998 related to application layer framing, e.g., *SMUX Protocol Specification*, but none appear to have achieved orbit.)

Here's what we did: frames are exchanged in the context of a "channel." Each channel has an associated "profile" that defines the syntax and semantics of the messages exchanged over a channel.

Channels provide both an extensibility mechanism for BXXP and the basis for parallelism. Remember the last parameter in the command line of a BXXP frame? The "part of the application" that gets the message is identified by a channel number.

A profile is defined according to a "Profile Registration" template. The template defines how the profile is identified using a URI (RFC 2396), and what kind of messages get exchanged, along with the syntax and semantics of those messages. When you create a channel, you identify a profile and maybe piggyback your first message. If the channel is successfully created, you get back a positive response; otherwise, you get back a negative response explaining why.

Perhaps the easiest way to see how channels provide an extensibility mechanism is to consider what happens when a session is established. Each BXXP peer immediately sends a greeting on channel zero identifying the profiles that each support. (Channel zero is used for channel management—it's automatically created when a session is opened.) If you want transport security, the very first thing you do is to create a channel that negotiates transport security, and, once the channel is created, you tell it to do its thing. Next, if you want to authenticate, you create a channel that performs user authentication, and, once the channel is created, you tell it to get busy. At this point, you create one or more channels for data exchange. This process is called "tuning"; once you've tuned the session, you start using the data exchange channels to do "the useful work."

The first channel that's successfully started has a trick associated with it: when you ask to start the channel, you're allowed to specify a "service name" that goes with it. This allows a server with multiple configurations to select one based on the client's suggestion. (A useful analogy is HTTP 1.1's Host: header.) If the server accepts the "service name," then this configuration is used for the rest of the session.

To allow parallelism, BXXP allows you to use multiple channels simultaneously. Each channel processes messages serially, but there are no constraints on the processing order for different channels. So, in a multithreaded implementation, each channel maps to its own thread.

This is the most general case, of course. For one reason or another, an implementor may not be able to support this. BXXP allows for both positive and negative replies when a message is sent, so, if you want the classic client/server model, the client program should simply reject any new message sent by the server. This effectively throttles any asynchronous messages from the server.

Of course, we now need to provide mechanisms for segmentation and flow control. For the former, we just put a "continuation" or "more to come" flag in the command line for the frame. For the latter, we introduced the notion of a "transport mapping."

What this means is that BXXP doesn't directly define how it sits of top of TCP. Instead, it lists a bunch of requirements for how a transport service needs to support a BXXP session. Then, in a separate document, we defined how you can use TCP to meet these requirements.

This second document pretty much says "use TCP directly," except that it introduces a flow control mechanism for multiplexing channels over a single TCP connection. The mechanism we use is the same one used by TCP (sequence numbers and a sliding window). It's proven, and can be trivially implemented by a minimal implementation of BXXP.

The introduction of flow control is a burden from an implementation perspective—although TCP's mechanism is conceptually simple, an implementor must take great care. For example, issues such as priorities, queue management, and the like should be addressed. Regardless, we feel that the benefits of allowing parallelism for intra-application streams is worth it. (Besides, our belief is that few application implementors will actually code the BXXP framework directly—rather, we expect them to use third-party packages that implement BXXP.)

Authentication

We use SASL. If you successfully authenticate using a channel, then there is a single user identity for each peer on that session (i.e., authentication is per-session, not per-channel). This design decision mandates that each session correspond to a single user regardless of how many channels are open on that session. One reason why this is important is that it allows service provisioning, such as quality of service (e.g., as in RFC 2549) to be done on a per-user granularity.

Privacy

We use SASL and TLS. If you successfully complete a transport security negotiation using a channel, then all traffic on that session is secured (i.e., confidentiality is per-session, not per-channel, just like authentication).

We defined a BXXP profile that's used to start the TLS engine.

Things We Left Out

We purposefully excluded two things that are common to most application protocols: naming and authorization.

Naming was excluded from the framework because, outside of URIs, there isn't a commonly accepted framework for naming things. To our view, this remains a domain-specific problem for each application protocol. Maybe URIs are appropriate in the context of a particular problem domain, maybe not. So, when an application protocol designer defines their own profile to do "the useful work," they'll have to deal with naming issues themselves. BXXP provides a mechanism for identifying profiles and binding them to channels. It's up to you to define the profile and use the channel.

Similarly, authorization was explicitly excluded from the framework. Every approach to authorization we've seen uses names to identify principals (i.e., targets and subjects), so if a framework doesn't include naming, it can't very well include authorization.

Of course, application protocols do have to deal with naming and authorization—those are two of the issues addressed by the applications protocol designer when defining a profile for use with BXXP.

From Framework to Protocol

So, how do you go about using BXXP? To begin, call it "BEEP," not "BXXP" (we'll explain why in a moment).

First, get the BEEP core specification (RFC 3080) and read it. Next, define your own profile. Finally, get one of the open source SDKs (in C, Java, or Tcl) and start coding.

The BEEP specification defines several profiles itself: a channel management profile, a family of profiles for SASL, and a transport security profile. In addition, there's a second specification (RFC 3081) that explains how a BEEP session maps onto a single TCP connection.

For a complete example of an application protocol defined using BEEP, look at reliable syslog (RFC 3195). Figure A-1 exemplifies the formula.

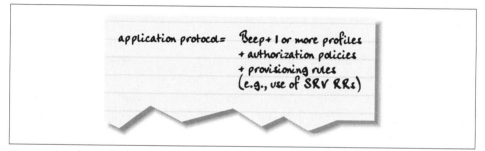

Figure A-1. Relationship between an application protocol and BEEP

BXXP Is Now BEEP

We started work on BXXP in the Fall of 1998. The IETF formed a working group on BXXP in the Summer of 2000. Although the working group made some enhancements to BXXP, three are the most notable:

- The payload default is `application/octet-stream`. This is primarily for wire-efficiency—if you care about wire-efficiency, then you probably wouldn't be using `text/xml`.
- One-to-many exchanges are supported (the client sends one message and the server sends back many replies).
- BXXP is now called BEEP (more comic possibilities).

References

Barton, John, Satish Thatte, and Henrik Frystyk Nielsen. "SOAP Messages with Attachments." December 2000. *www.w3.org/TR/SOAP-attachments*

Box, Don, David Ehnebuske, Gopal Kakivaya, Andrew Layman, Noah Mendelsohn, Henrik Frystyk Nielsen, Satish Thatte, and Dave Winer. "Simple Object Access Protocol (SOAP) 1.1." May 2000. *www.w3.org/TR/SOAP*

Gettys, Jim and Henrik Frystyk Nielsen. "SMUX Protocol Specification," Working Draft WD-mux-19980710. July 1998. *www.w3.org/TR/WD-mus*

Hall, Eric. *Internet Core Protocols: The Definitive Guide.* O'Reilly & Associates, Inc., 2000.

Harold, Elliotte Rusty, and W. Scott Means. *XML in a Nutshell: A Desktop Quick Reference.* O'Reilly & Associates, Inc., 2001.

New, Darren. "The Tunnel Profile," draft-ietf-idwg-beep-tunnel (work in progress). August 2001.

O'Tuathail, Eamon, and Marshall Rose. "Using SOAP in BEEP," draft-etal-beep-soap (work in progress). January 2002.

Rescorla, Eric. *SSL and TLS.* Addison-Wesley, 2000.

Sloan, Joseph. *Network Troubleshooting Tools.* O'Reilly & Associates, Inc., 2001.

Snell, James, Doug Tidwell, and Pavel Kulchenko. *Programming Web Services with SOAP.* O'Reilly & Associates, Inc., 2001.

St. Laurent, Simon, Joe Johnston, and Edd Dumbill. *Programming Web Services with XML-RPC.* O'Reilly & Associates, Inc., 2001.

Wong, Clinton. *HTTP Pocket Reference.* O'Reilly & Associates, Inc., 2000.

Wood, David. *Programming Internet Email.* O'Reilly & Associates, Inc., 1999.

World Wide Web Consortium. "Extensible Markup Language (XML) 1.0," W3C XML. February 1998.

Index

A

AbortChannelException, 75
addStartChannelListener( ) method, 59, 69
adviseProfile( ) method, 60, 63
ANONYMOUS SASL mechanism, 29
application/beep+xml content type, 18
asynchronous exchange, Tcl SOAP, 158
asynchrony, 183
    BXXP, 192
    pipelining and, 185
attributes, XML, 17
authentication, 183
    application protocol design, 186
    BXXP, 194
    SASL, 28–31
    Tcl SOAP, 150, 161
    tuning and, 31
    users, session tuning and, 20
availableSegment( ) method, 74

B

BEEP URIs, 37
beep.core classes, 65
beepcore-c, 78
    architecture, 78
    driver entry points, 125
    portability, 78
    wrappers, 79
beepcore-java, 48
    ByteOutputDataStream class, 52
    Channel.close( ), 48
    Channel.sendMSG( ), 48
    classes, 65–77

core.SessionTuningProperties, 56
data streams, 73–75
echo initiation, 47
echo profile, listener peer, 54–65
exceptions, 75
getNextReply( ) method, 53
import statements, 49
InputStream.read( ), 48
logging, 76
main( ) method, 49, 54
OutputDataStream class, 52
profile Collections, 51
Profile interface, 59
profile.Profile, 56
profile.ProfileConfiguration, 56
Reply.getNextReply( ), 48
ReplyListener interface, 53
requirements, 47
Session.close( ), 48
Session.startChannel( ), 48
startChannel ( ) method, 51
StringOutputDataStream class, 52
TCPSessionCreator class, 50
TCPSessionCreator.initiate( ), 48
TLSProfile.getDefaultInstance( ), 51
TLSProfile.startTLS( ), 48
util.Log, 56
beepcore.org web site, 9
Beepd( ) method, 54
Beepd class implementation, 54
beepd elements constructor methods, 57
Beepd objects Collection, 62
BEEPError, 51

We'd like to hear your suggestions for improving our indexes. Send email to *index@oreilly.com*.

About the Author

Marshall T. Rose is the prime mover of the BEEP Protocol. Marshall formerly held the position of the Internet Engineering Task Force (IETF) area director for network management, one of a dozen individuals who oversaw the Internet's standardization process. He is responsible for the design, specification, and implementation of several Internet-standard technologies and is the author of over 60 of the Internet's requests for comment (RFCs) and several professional texts. Rose received a Ph.D. in information and computer science from the University of California, Irvine, in 1984.

Colophon

Our look is the result of reader comments, our own experimentation, and feedback from distribution channels. Distinctive covers complement our distinctive approach to technical topics, breathing personality and life into potentially dry subjects.

The animal on the cover of *BEEP: The Definitive Guide* is a coyote, a name derived from the Aztec *coyotl*. Its Latin name, *Canis latrans*, means "barking dog"—a tribute to its reputation as one of the most vocal mammals in North America. The coyote howls and yips to communicate with family members and to signal its presence to other coyotes. The coyote is the most widely distributed large predator in North America. Its amazing adaptability has led to the coyote's being one of the few mammals whose range is increasing in spite of human encroachment. Although a native of the American desert and plains, the coyote's range now includes Alaska's North Slope, the Guatemalan highlands, and the forests of New England. Extermination of the wolf in central and northern America significantly aided the coyote's spread.

The coyote's eating habits are as versatile as its habitats. Primarily carnivorous (90% of their diet), coyotes consume large amounts of carrion if fresh meat isn't available. They also eat birds, snakes, leaves, seeds, fruits, vegetables, and garbage.

Coyotes are intelligent and wily hunters. They sometimes form "hunting partnerships" with the badger—the coyote locating rodents with its keen sense of smell and the badger digging them up with its powerful claws. The partners then share the catch.

The coyote continues to threaten livestock herds, as well as family pets. On the other hand, with pelts valued at about $17 each, coyotes face even greater threats from hunters.

Jane Ellin was the production editor and proofreader for *BEEP: The Definitive Guide*. David Futato was the copyeditor. Colleen Gorman provided quality control. Phil Dangler, Sue Willing, Darren Kelly, and Sheryl Avruch provided production support. Johnna VanHoose Dinse wrote the index.

Ellie Volckhausen designed the cover of this book, based on a series design by Edie Freedman. The cover image is from *Animal Creations*, Volume I. Emma Colby produced the cover layout with QuarkXPress 4.1 using Adobe's ITC Garamond font.

David Futato designed the interior layout. Neil Walls converted the files from XML to FrameMaker 5.5.6 using tools created by Mike Sierra, as well as tools written in Perl by Erik Ray, Jason McIntosh, and Neil Walls. The text font is Linotype Birka; the heading font is Adobe Myriad Condensed; and the code font is LucasFont's TheSans Mono Condensed. The illustrations that appear in the book were produced by Robert Romano and Jessamyn Read using Macromedia FreeHand 9 and Adobe Photoshop 6. The tip and warning icons were drawn by Christopher Bing. This colophon was written by Sheryl Avruch.

3336

How to stay in touch with O'Reilly

1. Visit Our Award-Winning Web Site

http://www.oreilly.com/

★ "Top 100 Sites on the Web" —PC Magazine
★ CIO Magazine's Web Business 50 Awards

Our web site contains a library of comprehensive product information (including book excerpts and tables of contents), downloadable software, background articles, interviews with technology leaders, links to relevant sites, book cover art, and more. File us in your bookmarks or favorites!

2. Join Our Email Mailing Lists

Sign up to get email announcements of new books and conferences, special offers, and O'Reilly Network technology newsletters at:
elists.oreilly.com.
It's easy to customize your free elists subscription so you'll get exactly the O'Reilly news you want.

3. Get Examples from Our Books

To find example files for a book, go to:
http://www.oreilly.com/catalog
select the book, and follow the "Examples" link.

4. Contact Us via Email

order@oreilly.com
For answers to problems regarding your order or our products. To place a book order online visit:
http://www.oreilly.com/order_new/

catalog@oreilly.com
To request a copy of our latest catalog.

booktech@oreilly.com
For book content technical questions or corrections.

proposals@oreilly.com
To submit new book proposals to our editors and product managers.

international@oreilly.com
For information about our international distributors or translation queries. For a list of our distributors outside of North America check out:
http://international.oreilly.com/distributors.html

5. Work with Us

Check out our web site for current employment opportunites:
http://jobs.oreilly.com/

6. Register your book

Register your book at:
http://register.oreilly.com

O'Reilly & Associates, Inc.
1005 Gravenstein Hwy North
Sebastopol, CA 95472 USA
TEL   707-827-7000 or 800-998-9938
        (6am to 5pm PST)
FAX   707-829-0104

International Distributors

http://international.oreilly.com/distributors.html • international@oreilly.com

UK, EUROPE, MIDDLE EAST, AND AFRICA (EXCEPT FRANCE, GERMANY, AUSTRIA, SWITZERLAND, LUXEMBOURG, AND LIECHTENSTEIN)

INQUIRIES
O'Reilly UK Limited
4 Castle Street
Farnham
Surrey, GU9 7HS
United Kingdom
Telephone: 44-1252-711776
Fax: 44-1252-734211
Email: information@oreilly.co.uk

ORDERS
Wiley Distribution Services Ltd.
1 Oldlands Way
Bognor Regis
West Sussex PO22 9SA
United Kingdom
Telephone: 44-1243-843294
UK Freephone: 0800-243207
Fax: 44-1243-843302 (Europe/EU orders)
or 44-1243-843274 (Middle East/Africa)
Email: cs-books@wiley.co.uk

FRANCE
INQUIRIES & ORDERS
Éditions O'Reilly
18 rue Séguier
75006 Paris, France
Tel: 33-1-40-51-71-89
Fax: 33-1-40-51-72-26
Email: france@oreilly.fr

GERMANY, SWITZERLAND, AUSTRIA, LUXEMBOURG, AND LIECHTENSTEIN
INQUIRIES & ORDERS
O'Reilly Verlag
Balthasarstr. 81
D-50670 Köln, Germany
Telephone: 49-221-973160-91
Fax: 49-221-973160-8
Email: anfragen@oreilly.de (inquiries)
Email: order@oreilly.de (orders)

CANADA
(FRENCH LANGUAGE BOOKS)
Les Éditions Flammarion ltée
375, Avenue Laurier Ouest
Montréal, QC H2V 2K3 Canada
Tel: 1-514-277-8807
Fax: 1-514-278-2085
Email: info@flammarion.qc.ca

HONG KONG
City Discount Subscription Service, Ltd.
Unit A, 6th Floor, Yan's Tower
27 Wong Chuk Hang Road
Aberdeen, Hong Kong
Tel: 852-2580-3539
Fax: 852-2580-6463
Email: citydis@ppn.com.hk

KOREA
Hanbit Media, Inc.
Chungmu Bldg. 210
Yonnam-dong 568-33
Mapo-gu
Seoul, Korea
Tel: 822-325-0397
Fax: 822-325-9697
Email: hant93@chollian.dacom.co.kr

PHILIPPINES
Global Publishing
G/F Benavides Garden
1186 Benavides Street
Manila, Philippines
Tel: 632-254-8949/632-252-2582
Fax: 632-734-5060/632-252-2733
Email: globalp@pacific.net.ph

TAIWAN
O'Reilly Taiwan
1st Floor, No. 21, Lane 295
Section 1, Fu-Shing South Road
Taipei, 106 Taiwan
Tel: 886-2-27099669
Fax: 886-2-27038802
Email: mori@oreilly.com

INDIA
Shroff Publishers & Distributors PVT. LTD.
C-103, MIDC, TTC Pawane
Navi Mumbai 400 701
India
Tel: (91-22) 763 4290, 763 4293
Fax: (91-22) 768 3337
Email: spdorders@shroffpublishers.com

CHINA
O'Reilly Beijing
SIGMA Building, Suite B809
No. 49 Zhichun Road
Haidian District
Beijing, China PR 100080
Tel: 86-10-8809-7475
Fax: 86-10-8809-7463
Email: beijing@oreilly.com

JAPAN
O'Reilly Japan, Inc.
Yotsuya Y's Building
7 Banch 6, Honshio-cho
Shinjuku-ku
Tokyo 160-0003 Japan
Tel: 81-3-3356-5227
Fax: 81-3-3356-5261
Email: japan@oreilly.com

SINGAPORE, INDONESIA, MALAYSIA, AND THAILAND
TransQuest Publishers Pte Ltd
30 Old Toh Tuck Road #05-02
Sembawang Kimtrans Logistics Centre
Singapore 597654
Tel: 65-4623112
Fax: 65-4625761
Email: wendiw@transquest.com.sg

AUSTRALIA
Woodslane Pty., Ltd.
7/5 Vuko Place
Warriewood NSW 2102
Australia
Tel: 61-2-9970-5111
Fax: 61-2-9970-5002
Email: info@woodslane.com.au

NEW ZEALAND
Woodslane New Zealand, Ltd.
21 Cooks Street (P.O. Box 575)
Waganui, New Zealand
Tel: 64-6-347-6543
Fax: 64-6-345-4840
Email: info@woodslane.com.au

ARGENTINA
Distribuidora Cuspide
Suipacha 764
1008 Buenos Aires
Argentina
Phone: 54-11-4322-8868
Fax: 54-11-4322-3456
Email: libros@cuspide.com

ALL OTHER COUNTRIES
O'Reilly & Associates, Inc.
1005 Gravenstein Hwy North
Sebastopol, CA 95472 USA
Tel: 707-827-7000
Fax: 707-829-0104
Email: order@oreilly.com

O'REILLY®

TO ORDER: **800-998-9938** • **order@oreilly.com** • **www.oreilly.com**
ONLINE EDITIONS OF MOST O'REILLY TITLES ARE AVAILABLE BY SUBSCRIPTION AT **safari.oreilly.com**
ALSO AVAILABLE AT MOST RETAIL AND ONLINE BOOKSTORES